TAMING INDIAN INFLATION

Editors
RAHUL ANAND
PAUL CASHIN

INTERNATIONAL MONETARY FUND

RAWAT PUBLICATIONS
Jaipur • New Delhi • Bangalore • Guwahati • Kolkata

ISBN 978-81-316-0912-5

Indian Reprint, 2017

This edition is published in India by Rawat Publications.

First published in 2016 by
International Monetary Fund, Publication Services
P.O. Box 92780, Washington, DC 20090, U.S.A.
Tel.: (202) 623-7430 Fax: (202) 623-7201
E-mail: publications@imf.org
Internet: www.elibrary.imf.org
www.imfbookstore.org

Published by
Prem Rawat for **Rawat Publications**
Satyam Apts., Sector 3, Jawahar Nagar, Jaipur - 302 004 (India)
Phone: 0141 265 1748 / 7006 Fax: 0141 265 1748
E-mail : info@rawatbooks.com
Website: rawatbooks.com

New Delhi Office
4858/24, Ansari Road, Daryaganj, New Delhi 110 002
Phone: 011-23263290

Also at *Bangalore, Guwahati* and *Kolkata*

Printed in India.

Table of Contents

Foreword

This book is a timely look at an important Indian macroeconomic issue—inflation. High and persistent inflation has been a serious macroeconomic challenge for India, particularly in the past decade. India's high rates of inflation have been underpinned chiefly by high and persistent rates of food price inflation, which cascade quickly into rural and urban wages and into nonfood inflation. Well-entrenched inflation expectations have also been a key driver of India's high inflation rates.

Over the past decade India has increasingly opened itself to the global economy and has become one of the world's fastest-growing economies. As it seeks to sustain rapid growth and improve the welfare of its large and fast-growing population, India also needs to aim for greater price stability.

This book documents and analyzes India's long-ongoing quest to bring inflation down. It grew out of the IMF staff's ongoing policy dialogue with the Indian authorities, in particular at the Reserve Bank of India and the Ministry of Finance. The focus of several of the chapters evolved from the exchange of views with officials from these agencies, and with the many Indian academics interested in these issues.

The IMF is contributing to the advancement of the Indian economy through our ongoing policy dialogue, analytical work, and capacity building. I am sure this book will help in this effort and give due recognition to the authorities' efforts directed at taming inflation to reduce poverty, raise domestic consumption and growth, and improve the welfare of over 1.2 billion Indian citizens.

Christine Lagarde
Managing Director
International Monetary Fund

Preface

High and persistent inflation has presented a serious macroeconomic challenge in India in recent years, increasing the country's domestic and external vulnerabilities. For example, high inflation contributed to an historic widening of the current account deficit, exposing India to global financial market turbulence and slowing growth. As Reserve Bank of India Governor Raghuram Rajan pointed out at the 8th R. N. Kao Memorial Lecture in 2014, "inflation is a destructive disease ... we can't push inflation under the carpet as a central banker. We have to deal with it."

A number of factors underpin India's high rates of inflation, including food inflation feeding quickly into wages and core inflation; entrenched inflation expectations; cost-push shocks from binding sector-specific supply constraints (particularly in agriculture, energy, and transportation); pass-through from a weaker rupee; and ongoing energy price increases. This book analyzes various facets of Indian inflation and their implications for the conduct of monetary policy. Indeed, several chapters are devoted to analyzing and managing food inflation, given the very important role of food inflation in driving overall inflation dynamics in India. Building on this analysis of inflation dynamics, several chapters discuss the role of monetary policy in taming inflation, which is important for the country given the economic and social costs of its high and persistent inflation.

Using the Phillips curve framework, Roberto Guimarães and Laura Papi, in Chapter 1, find that inflation in India can be reasonably well modeled with standard Phillips curves, augmented with a measure of relative international commodity prices. They show that India's inflation dynamics are explained by both backward- and forward-looking inflation components, and that the output gap, though empirically relevant, is not robust across model specifications. Evidence suggests that the effect of the output gap on inflation is larger at higher levels of inflation, but that inflation becomes more inertial at higher levels.

Because food inflation has played a key role in shaping the dynamics of inflation in India, and made monetary management more difficult, the next few chapters delve deeper into analyzing food inflation. It is widely believed that fluctuations in food and energy prices represent supply shocks, and as such are transitory, volatile, and nonmonetary in nature. For these reasons, food prices are generally excluded from the measures of inflation most closely watched by policymakers in advanced economies.

James Walsh, in Chapter 2, focuses on the role of food inflation in lower-income countries and emerging markets, and finds that food price inflation is not only more volatile in these economies, but also higher than nonfood inflation on average. Walsh shows that food inflation is in many cases more persistent than nonfood inflation, and that food price shocks in many countries propagate strongly into nonfood inflation. Under these conditions, a policy focus on measures of core inflation that exclude food prices can misspecify inflation, leading to higher inflationary expectations, a downward bias to forecasts of future inflation, and lags in policy responses. In constructing measures of core inflation, policymakers should therefore not assume that excluding food price inflation will provide a clearer picture of underlying inflation trends than headline inflation.

Chapter 3, by Prachi Mishra and Devesh Roy, examines food inflation in India using a high-frequency, commodity-level data set spanning the past two decades. Documenting stylized facts about the behavior of food inflation, the authors explicitly quantify the contribution of specific commodities to food inflation in India. Their analysis suggests that animal source foods (milk, fish), processed food (sugar, edible oils), fruits and vegetables (for example, onions), and cereals (rice and wheat) have been the primary drivers of food price inflation. Insights from this analysis of overall food inflation, as well as individual case studies, are used to make specific policy recommendations for curbing inflation.

In Chapter 4, Rahul Anand, Naresh Kumar, and Volodymyr Tulin investigate the demand and supply factors behind the contribution of relative food inflation to general inflation. They find that India's food inflation developments over the past decade appear to have largely reflected demand pressures (driven by strong private consumption growth), which have often outpaced supply of key food commodities. Their analysis suggests that in the absence of a stronger food supply growth response, food inflation may exceed nonfood inflation by 2½–3 percentage points per year. Given this, the sustainability of a long-term inflation target of 4 percent under India's recently adopted flexible inflation-targeting framework will depend on enhancing food supply, agricultural market-based pricing, and reducing price distortions. A well-designed cereal buffer stock liquidation policy could also help mitigate food inflation volatility.

The next few chapters explore the costs of inflation in India—on both growth and inclusiveness—and document the spillovers of Indian inflation to the neighboring countries of Nepal and Bhutan. In Chapter 5, Kamiar Mohaddes and Mehdi Raissi examine the long-term relationship between the consumer price index for industrial workers (CPI-IW) inflation and GDP growth in India. Using a sample of 14 Indian states over 1989–2013, the chapter's findings suggest that, on average, there is a negative long-term relationship between inflation and economic growth. The authors find there is a statistically significant inflation-growth threshold effect in states with persistently elevated consumer price index inflation rates of over 5½ percent. These findings suggest that the Reserve Bank of India needs to balance the short-term growth-inflation trade-off, in light of the long-term negative effects on growth of persistently high inflation.

In Chapter 6, James Walsh and Jiangyan Yu analyze the effects of inflation on income inequality, and find these can be differentiated by the type of inflation. Higher nonfood inflation is strongly associated with greater income inequality, but food inflation has more mixed effects. Across a sample of Indian states, nonfood inflation is associated with worsening income inequality in both urban and rural areas. On the other hand, higher food inflation has an ambiguous relationship with income inequality in urban areas, but is strongly associated with lower income inequality in rural areas.

Sonali Das, Adil Mohammad, and Yasuhisa Ojima, in Chapter 7, explore the spillovers of Indian inflation—particularly food inflation—on Nepal and Bhutan. Inflation dynamics in both countries are closely linked to those in India, given their exchange rate pegs to the Indian rupee. The authors suggest that food inflation in Nepal, a key driver of the country's headline inflation, is highly correlated with food price changes in India. Similarly, headline inflation in Bhutan over the past three decades shows a tendency to comove with India's headline CPI inflation rate. Given their exchange rate regimes and close trade ties with India, it is unlikely that inflation will be delinked from India in the near term.

Against a backdrop of the high cost of inflation and spillovers to neighboring countries, Chapters 8 and 9 discuss the role of monetary policy in taming India's high and persistent inflation. Sonali Das, in Chapter 8, evaluates the effectiveness of the credit channel of monetary policy transmission. Using stepwise estimation of vector error correction models, she finds significant, albeit slow, pass-through of policy rate changes to bank interest rates, and evidence of asymmetric adjustment to monetary policy. Here, bank lending rates adjust more quickly to monetary tightening than to loosening. Moreover, the speed of adjustment of bank deposit and lending rates to changes in the policy rate has increased in recent years.

In Chapter 9, Rahul Anand and Volodymyr Tulin discuss the role of monetary policy in combating food inflation in India, as this has presented challenges for monetary management. It is a widely held view that central banks should only respond to changes in underlying core inflation and to any second-round effects on core inflation of commodity price shocks. This chapter estimates the size of these second-round effects and finds particularly large effects in India. The results also indicate that India's inflation is highly inertial and persistent. The authors' analysis suggests that to durably reduce India's relatively high rates of inflation, the monetary policy stance needs to remain tight for a considerable length of time.

Paul Cashin and Agustín Roitman, in Chapter 10, examine the role of optimal monetary policy in the presence of large and persistent supply shocks. They show that responding to headline inflation is welfare superior to responding to core inflation, and that this often proves to be a more effective response in containing overall inflation, as well as in mitigating consumption and output fluctuations. Moreover, having a clear, easy-to-understand, and transparent rule can help with the formation of accurate and realistic inflation expectations, and serve as an effective nominal anchor in the face of international commodity price fluctuations. Implementing such a rule is also useful to build and enhance the credibility of the monetary authority, and thereby increase the effectiveness of monetary policy in seeking to achieve and maintain price stability.

PART I

Causes of Inflation

CHAPTER 1

Inflation Dynamics in India: What Can We Learn from Phillips Curves?

ROBERTO F. GUIMARÃES AND LAURA PAPI

Inflation in India trended higher from the mid-2000s after being low for decades and below levels in other emerging markets. It reached 10–11 percent by 2008 and remained elevated for several years. Even though inflation fell substantially in 2014, it has started to rise again, and inflation expectations have stayed above the Reserve Bank of India's target, raising the question of whether the reduction will be sustained.

India's persistently elevated inflation has sparked an intense debate about its causes, centered on the contribution of various shocks and their propagation mechanisms. The fact that the sharp increase of 2007–08 coincided with the run-up in international commodity prices has induced some to emphasize these explanations (Patra and others 2013). Others (Chand 2010; Gokarn 2011; Mohanty 2013) have pointed to excess demand. Several authors have studied the role of food prices in India's inflation, directly and via the expectation channel (Anand, Ding, and Tulin 2014; Mishra and Roy 2011; Walsh 2011). Shah (2011) stated that India is in a "trap of high inflation expectations." Of course, these explanations can coexist, as highlighted in Basu (2011) and in various issues of the IMF's Article IV Consultation country reports during 2010–15.

This chapter studies the dynamics of inflation in India, including the role of fuel and food prices. It uses the prism of the New Keynesian Phillips curve and sheds light on the relative importance of various factors, including the output gap, inflation expectations, and food and fuel prices. Given the changes in India's inflation and substantial evidence that the pernicious effects of inflation on output may materialize when inflation reaches certain levels, the chapter also uses quantile regressions to investigate whether the output-inflation trade-off has evolved over time. The analysis is carried out for various measures of inflation.

We find that the New Keynesian Phillips curve framework augmented with a measure of imported inflation captures India's inflation dynamics fairly well. Both forward-looking and backward-looking inflation are important determinants of inflation, with the weights close to half. The latter finding points to significant inertia in line with other studies (for example, Patra and Kapur 2010; Anand, Ding, and Tulin 2014).The output gap is significant in most regressions. International commodity prices also exert an effect on inflation. We find evidence that the inflation-output trade-off changes with inflation: at higher inflation levels, inertia rises and the coefficient on the output gap becomes larger. Although these two effects go in opposite directions, the size of the estimated coefficients suggests that the inertia effect dominates, pointing to a higher sacrifice ratio at higher levels of inflation.

The chapter begins with a description of stylized facts, and a study of structural breaks and inflation thresholds. This is followed by an analysis of the role of commodity prices and an initial exploration of the output gap. We then present the results of the estimations of several Phillips curves, including the New Keynesian version and the quantile regression estimates of accelerationist Phillips curves.

STYLIZED FACTS

India's inflation compared favorably to other emerging markets during the 1990s and early 2000s (Figure 1.1). Annual consumer price index (CPI) inflation—which throughout the chapter refers to the All-India CPI from its 2010 inception and to CPI-Industrial Workers before that—was 7.5 percent during 1990–2005 versus 45 percent for emerging markets. And it was only one percentage point above other Asian countries, a region known for stable prices. Similarly, wholesale price index (WPI) inflation, which was India's headline inflation measure until 2013, averaged 7 percent during 1990–2005. Inflation volatility was also low in this period (Figure 1.1, panels 7 and 8).

However, all measures of inflation began to increase in 2005–06, and rose sharply in 2007–08, with both the CPI and WPI reaching about 11 percent in late 2008. Even though WPI inflation dropped substantially with the onset of the global financial crisis, it quickly returned to 8–10 percent, and CPI did not fall below 9 percent until 2014. Inflation volatility also picked up considerably as inflation rose.

The increase in India's inflation coincided with rapidly rising food and commodity prices. Food prices rose sharply starting from 2008 and by the end of 2013 had nearly doubled compared to the end of 2007. While the reasons for this are multifaceted and covered elsewhere in this book, fast-rising food prices had an important direct impact on overall consumer prices, given a weight of close to half in the CPI, and also a considerable indirect impact owing to second-round effects on other prices (Anand, Ding, and Tulin 2014; Walsh 2011) and via inflation expectations (Tulin 2015). International commodity prices, especially oil prices, have had a sizable impact on the WPI, where commodities account for about a quarter of the index. Indeed, the salient turning points in WPI inflation since 2007 have been immediately preceded by sharp changes in oil prices.

Core inflation also rose substantially from 2006–07, pointing to a generalized process. CPI core inflation, which averaged 6½ percent in the decade to 2005, rose to about 8 percent in 2006–13. WPI core inflation displayed greater volatility, but nevertheless increased from 4 percent in the decade to 2005 to about

Figure 1.1 Inflation Dynamics, 1995–2015

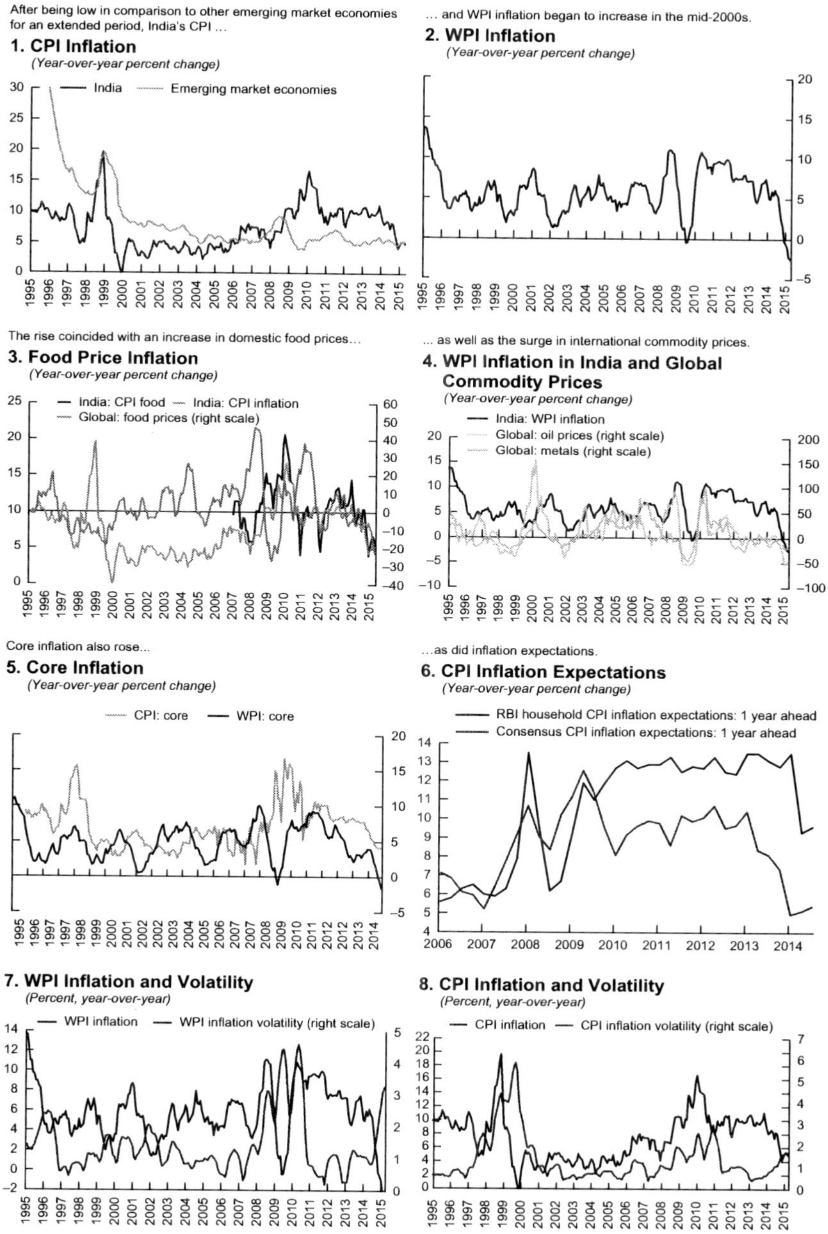

Sources: Consensus Economics, *Consensus Forecasts*; Haver Analytics; Reserve Bank of India; and authors' calculations.
Note: CPI = consumer price index; WPI = wholesale price index.

6 percent in 2006–13, peaking at over 7 percent in 2010–12. The contribution of core inflation reached just over half for CPI inflation and nearly two-thirds for WPI inflation in 2010–12.

Inflation expectations have also generally increased since the mid-2000s. Household inflation expectations from the Reserve Bank of India survey picked up later than Consensus Economics' *Consensus Forecasts* and showed a higher degree of persistence. Also, while *Consensus Forecasts* expectations display a high degree of correlation (0.53) with core inflation, the inflation expectations of households are loosely correlated only with food inflation. The correlation between the two measures of inflation expectations is negative, though once *Consensus Forecasts* expectations are lagged they become positively correlated.

Starting in late 2013, inflation declined substantially, reflecting slack in the economy and lower oil prices, but it has already turned and is projected to rise further. WPI inflation fell to –2½ percent in mid-2015 and even CPI inflation dropped to about 5 percent. In the past, changes related to commodity prices have tended to be short-lived, and the expected pick-up in growth points in the same direction. Indeed, momentum measures of inflation have started to increase and CPI inflation is projected to rise to 6.5 percent in 2015–16. Furthermore, although households' inflation expectations also eased, they are still in the 8–9 percent range compared to the Reserve Bank of India's targets of 6 percent for January 2016 and 4 percent for 2018. In sum, it is still worth trying to analyze what is behind India's inflation, which can also help answer the question of whether the most recent decline is likely to be sustained. This is covered in the next section.

EXPLORATORY DATA ANALYSIS, STRUCTURAL BREAKS, AND INFLATION THRESHOLDS

India's CPI inflation can be characterized as a *stationary* autoregressive process.[1] For instance, standard augmented Dickey-Fuller tests easily reject the unit root null hypothesis (the *t*-statistic is –6.12, significant at less than one percent). The autocorrelations of CPI inflation are also relatively low at 0.32 at lag one and 0.12 at lag two, compared with those of the United States for example, where inflation behaves much more like an I(1) process, as shown in Stock and Watson (2007). The variance ratio statistic (Figure 1.2), which measures the degree of persistence of the series (Lo and MacKinlay 1988), shows that shocks die out, but the process exhibits some degree of persistence. The variance ratio statistic is still about 0.15–0.20 after 10 quarters (with zero indicating no persistence and 1 being a random walk).[2]

The evidence of structural breaks in headline CPI inflation for India is on the whole mixed, but there is some evidence of a break in 2008. Despite the rise in

[1] This is based on annualized quarterly changes of the log of the seasonally adjusted series. The results are qualitatively robust to seasonally adjusting the series with X12 or quarterly dummies.

[2] The variance ratio statistic allows for heteroscedasticity and is computed with demeaned data (allows for a drift in inflation). The conclusions are robust to these two assumptions.

Figure 1.2 Variance Ratio Statistic for Inflation (with robust two standard deviation bands)

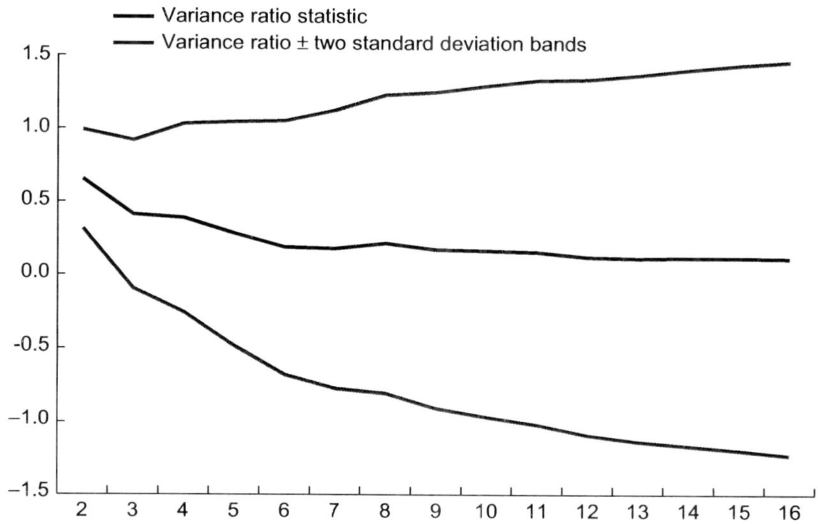

Source: Authors' calculations.

inflation since the mid-2000s and its stickiness, which has led to conjectures of inflation hovering in a new plateau, more formal tests of structural breaks show a mixed picture (Table 1.1). For CPI, applying the Quandt-Andrews tests to autoregressive (AR) models AR(1) and AR(4) yields no evidence of a structural

TABLE 1.1

Structural Break: Quandt-Andrews and Bai-Perron Tests for AR(1) Model

	F-statistic
CPI (constant and slope shift)	
Maximum LR *F*-statistic	3.73
Exponential LR *F*-statistic	0.97
Average LR *F*-statistic	1.77
Bai-Perron *F*-statistic (no breaks)	16.54**
Bai-Perron *F*-statistic (one break)	8.12
CPI (constant shifts only)	
Maximum LR *F*-statistic	7.43*
Exponential LR *F*-statistic	1.89*
Average LR *F*-statistic	2.52*
Bai-Perron *F*-statistic (no breaks)	9.52**
Bai-Perron *F*-statistic (one break)	5.61

Source: IMF staff calculations.
Note: CPI = consumer price index; LR = likelihood ratio.
* denotes significance at the 10 percent level; ** significance at the 5 percent level.

Figure 1.3. Quandt-Andrews Breakpoint Test

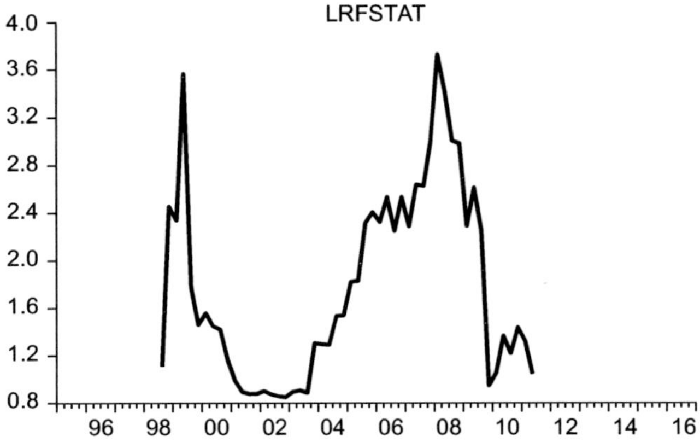

Source: Authors' calculations.
Note: AR(1) model, sequential average likelihood ratio F-statistic (LRFSTAT).

break at the 5 percent significance level.[3] For instance, the average likelihood ratio (LR) *F*-statistics spike in the first quarter of 1999 and the first quarter of 2008, but remain below significance levels (see Figure 1.3). When only the constant is subject to a break in the AR(4) model, some evidence of a structural break (higher inflation average) is found at the 10 percent significance level. Allowing for multiple breaks in the CPI (and again based on a simple AR(1) specification) points to the existence of one structural break in the CPI. Using the Bai-Perron multiple and sequential breakpoint test points to one structural break in the first quarter of 2008 consistent with a level-shift in CPI inflation.

In the case of the WPI, the evidence for a structural break is even weaker. Neither set of tests identifies any breaks at the 5 percent or even 10 percent significance levels. Reasons behind the inconclusive evidence include the relatively short sample (1996–2014), the higher volatility of the WPI, and the occurrence of a potential break in the last part of the sample (after 2008). Mishra and Roy (2011) find evidence of multiple breaks applying Bai-Perron tests, but they use a much longer sample going back to the late 1980s. Pattanaik and Nadhanael (2011) do not find any evidence of a break in the relationship between growth and inflation using the Quandt-Andrews tests.

---

[3] The sample is trimmed at 15 percent. Both AR(1) and AR(4) models are estimated. Six test statistics are computed for each model (maximum, exponential, and average of *F*- and Wald statistics over the trimmed sample). And in each model two sets of breaks are analyzed; the first one involves only the constant, and the second involves all the coefficients in the regression. The latter case comprises the constant and the first autocorrelation of the series (given by the AR coefficient) in the AR(1) model. The AR(1) model is selected over the AR(4) based on both the Akaike and Bayesian lag selection criteria.

The vector autoregression results are also broadly in line with those of the single equation estimations. The estimated threshold is 5½–7 percent (but is not robust to the vector autoregression specification). In addition, the results of the impulse response function confirm that although inflation shocks have a positive impact on growth, for levels above the threshold, incremental inflation has a negative and lasting cumulative impact on GDP. The evidence is only suggestive, though, because the inflation vector autoregression shock is likely to reflect a combination of supply and demand structural shocks.

COMMODITY PRICES AND THE OUTPUT GAP

International commodity prices exert an important influence on India's inflation, despite the existence of administered prices in key components of the WPI and CPI, as well as other relative price policies, as is the case in most other emerging markets. India's WPI inflation is significantly correlated with international commodity prices, albeit with a lag: the average 12-month rolling correlation is 0.4 in 1996–2014. The energy (fuel) component of the WPI comoves strongly with international oil prices. The comovements are stronger when international oil prices are lagged. The domestic energy component of the WPI is also correlated with domestic core inflation, suggesting that movements in domestic underlying inflation have occurred in tandem with shocks to international oil prices. CPI inflation is less correlated with international oil prices with a correlation of 0.1 over the sample period. However, this correlation appears to have increased in recent years, and may rise further following the deregulation of retail fuel prices in 2013. And while international food prices have an effect on India's inflation, food prices on the whole are more affected by domestic factors.

India's inflation is also correlated with different measures of the output gap. The correlations are statistically significant and range from 0.29 for CPI inflation to 0.21 in the case of core inflation (CPI excluding food and energy), both measured in sequential terms (annualized quarterly changes).[4] While the relationship between headline CPI inflation and the output gap has been subject to a number of shifts, the overall correlation is positive. The correlation of the WPI with the output gap is also relatively high and statistically significant at 0.25.

Different measures of the output gap show that the global financial crisis had a significant impact on the estimated slack in the domestic economy. While in 2007–08 GDP was advancing faster than its potential growth rate, in early 2009 there was substantial slack in the economy. With the swift rebound in growth, the output gap is estimated to have closed. Our preferred measure of the gap—based on the Christiano-Fitzgerald asymmetric trend assuming that real log GDP is integrated of order one with a time trend—shows a small negative gap of

[4] These correlations are for the linear-quadratic detrended GDP. The Hodrick-Prescott-based output gap is close to zero and not statistically significant. Interestingly, the correlation between these two output gap measures is high at 0.69.

Figure 1.4 Output Gap
(Percent of potential)

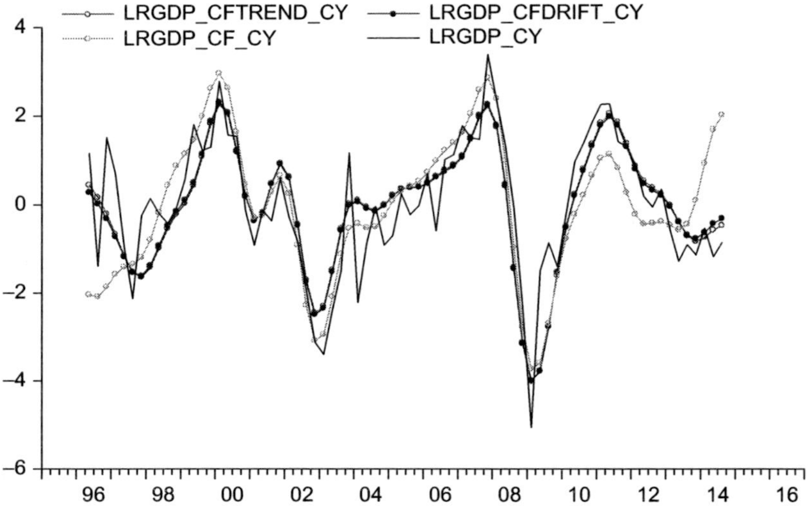

Source: Authors' calculations.
Note: LRGDP_CY = output gap computed with HP filter (log-real GDP);
LRGDP_CF_CY = output gap computed with CF filter (log-real GDP);
LRGDP_CFTREND_CY = output gap computed with CF filter (trend adjusted log-real GDP);
LRGDP_CFDRIFT_CY = output gap computed with CF filter (drift adjusted log-real GDP).

–0.1 percent at the end of 2014 (Christiano and Fitzgerald 2003). This is also consistent with a measure of the output gap that excludes agriculture, which is used later in the estimations.

It is worth noting that calculating a measure of the output gap for India is challenging for several reasons. For one thing, there are no reliable data on capacity utilization or employment. The economy has also been undergoing major structural changes, including the secular decline in the share of agriculture in GDP, rapid urbanization, increased trade, and financial openness, all of which may have contributed to the acceleration of economic growth since 2003. A new series for national accounts data at market prices was recently released, which may also have complicated the picture. With these caveats in mind, standard statistical procedures are used to generate a trend level of GDP, which is taken as a proxy for potential GDP and used in the calculations of the output gap (Figure 1.4).[5]

[5] This may not be fully satisfactory, but it is hardly controversial. Also, several filters are used for robustness and the results are broadly consistent in qualitative terms with a simple unobserved component model-based estimation and log-linear detrending.

PHILLIPS CURVE AND NEW KEYNESIAN PHILLIPS CURVE ESTIMATES

The New Keynesian Phillips curve combines the traditional Phillips curve with optimizing behavior by price setters and rational expectations. In its augmented form, it also allows for some inflation inertia, either in the form of indexation to past inflation or backward-looking inflation expectations. The New Keynesian Phillips curve identifies expected inflation, past inflation, and a cyclical measure of economic activity as determinants of inflation. According to the New Keynesian Phillips curve, inflation is given by:

$$\pi_t = \lambda mc_t + \beta E_t\{\pi_{t+1}\}$$

where $\pi_t = 400(\ln CPI_t - \ln CPI_{t-1})$ and $\lambda = (1-\theta)(1-\beta\theta)/\theta$, where θ is the probability that prices remain unchanged in a given period, and mc is a measure of marginal cost. In the case of the augmented New Keynesian Phillips curve, a lagged inflation term is added to account for backward-looking price setting or expectations:

$$\pi_t = \lambda mc_t + \gamma_f E_t\{\pi_{t+1}\} + \gamma_b \pi_{t-1}$$

Empirically, the model may require a proxy for the marginal cost term and additional assumptions about inflation expectations and other supply shifters. Gali and Gertler (2000) use the labor share of income and the GDP-based output gap.[6] For the output gap, several measures can be used but, typically in single equation estimations, the Hodrick-Prescott or band-pass filters (such as the Christiano-Fitzgerald filter) are commonly used. As in the seminal Gali and Gertler (2000, 2005) papers, a measure of the output gap based on linear-quadratic detrended log real GDP is also used in the estimations.

To account for the openness of an economy to international trade, further modifications to the standard New Keynesian Phillips curve are introduced. In an open economy, marginal costs faced by firms are directly affected by imported inputs, and the New Keynesian Phillips curve is augmented with a measure of relative import prices or international commodity prices.[7] Three measures are considered, but the estimated coefficients are robust to different measures used in the estimations: (1) an index of oil prices in domestic currency, (2) an index of fuel and nonfuel commodity prices in domestic currency, and (3) the same index as in (1) relative to domestic CPI (which proxies

---

[6] Some assumptions are needed for the output gap to be a reasonable proxy for real marginal costs. The use of the output gap in the estimations presented here is solely dictated by data availability.

[7] Because the impact of the imported input on marginal costs depends on its degree of substitutability with the domestic input (labor), it is assumed here that the import price (expressed in domestic currency) enters the New Keynesian Phillips curve separately. The coefficient on this variable will depend on the lambda and on the degree of substitutability between domestic and foreign inputs.

for wage costs). The baseline estimation results that follow are based on the third measure, namely:

$$\pi_t = constant + \gamma_f E_t\{\pi_{t+1}\} + \gamma_b \pi_{t-1} + \lambda(y_t - y_t^*) + \psi \Delta \ln(ePoil / CPI)_{t-1} + \varepsilon_t$$

where the output gap term is given by $(y_t - y_t^*)$ and y is the log of real GDP and the relative price of oil in domestic currency is given by *ePoil/CPI*. The coefficient on the output gap depends on the degree of nominal price rigidity in the economy. More specifically, a small coefficient on the output gap, implies a high degree of price rigidity.[8]

For expected inflation, survey-based data could be used or the equation can be estimated by the generalized method of moments (GMM), which instruments expected inflation with past inflation and other exogenous variables (generally lagged regressors). In India's case, while household survey data are available, the sample size for econometric estimations would be relatively short, because such data are available only from 2006. Instead, *Consensus Forecasts* data are used, which are available from 2003. The equation is also estimated by the GMM. In the latter case, four lags of the output gap, the real relative price of oil, and inflation (starting at $t - 2$) are used as instruments. The *J*-test of overidentifying restrictions is computed for all the GMM estimations.

Given the relatively short sample and to assess the robustness of the results, backward-looking versions of the Phillips curve or specifications where survey data are used for forward-looking inflation are also estimated. In particular, the Phillips curve estimated contains lags of inflation, the output gap, the real relative price of oil (the supply shifter), and a moving average of core inflation, which is also used sometimes as a proxy for expected inflation (see Ball 2015). The moving average of core inflation is highly correlated with the *Consensus Forecasts* measure of expected inflation, with a correlation coefficient of 0.49, and is available from 1996. The empirical specification is given by:

$$\pi_t = constant + A(L)\pi_{t-1} + \beta\pi_{t-1}^C + \lambda(y_t - y_t^*) + \psi\Delta \ln(eP / CPI)_{t-1} + \varepsilon_t,$$

where $\pi_{t-1}^C = (1/4)(\pi_{t-1} + \pi_{t-2} + \pi_{t-3} + \pi_{t-4})$ and $A(L)$ is a lag polynomial. In the case of specifications with survey data, the *Consensus Forecasts* measure is used, and the rest of the equation remains unchanged.

The New Keynesian Phillips curve is fitted to headline and core CPI inflation (CPI excluding food and energy).[9] Different measures of the output gap are used

---

[8] For example, assuming the discount factor of firms is equal to one, $\lambda = 0.05$ is consistent with $\theta = 0.8$, which in turn implies that prices remain fixed on average for five quarters since the average duration of "price contracts" is given by $1/(1 - \theta)$. A coefficient on the output gap of 0.5, on the other hand, implies a much lower degree of price rigidity ($\theta = 0.5$), or an average duration of two quarters. In the following results, the estimates of the slope of the Phillips curve imply an average duration of price rigidity between two and five quarters.

[9] The inflation measure used is the quarter-over-quarter annualized change of the price index. All data are seasonally adjusted prior to estimations, except the relative oil price variable.

in the estimations (Christiano-Fitzgerald filter, Hodrick-Prescott filter, and linear-quadratic detrended GDP). The baseline estimates are for headline CPI inflation because core inflation excludes a significant share of the CPI basket and the linear-quadratic output gap as in Gali and Gertler (2000). The New Keynesian Phillips curve is estimated with quarterly data from the second quarter of 1996 to the fourth quarter of 2014 (or starting in 2003 in the case of the specifications that include survey-based expected inflation).

The analysis of inflation dynamics using Phillips curves, including the New Keynesian version, suggests that both forward-looking and backward-looking inflation are important determinants of India's inflation (see Tables 1.2 to 1.4). The backward-looking Phillips curves and the specifications with survey-based expected inflation are estimated by ordinary least squares (OLS) for both headline and core CPI inflation. The main results are as follows:

- The backward-looking specifications suggest that lagged inflation is generally an important determinant of inflation (Table 1.2). The output gap is also important, with a coefficient of 0.30. Relative oil prices and the moving average of core inflation have coefficients of 0.08 and 0.05, respectively. In the former, this suggests that for a given level of expected inflation (proxied by the moving average of core inflation), a one-percentage-point increase in real oil prices raises long-term inflation by 0.11 percentage point. For core inflation, the results are somewhat similar to that of headline inflation, but the coefficient on the output gap is smaller (0.18).
- In the specifications with survey-based expected inflation, the coefficient on lagged inflation remains nearly unchanged at 0.32, but the coefficient on expected inflation is twice as large at 0.65, suggesting that forward-looking dynamics may be quite important as well. Despite the shorter sample, both coefficients are significant at the usual significance levels. Somewhat surprisingly, the output gap is incorrectly signed and is not statistically significant.

TABLE 1.2

New Keynesian Phillips Curve: Baseline OLS Estimates for CPI Inflation

Variable	Coefficients	*t*-Statistic
New Keynesian Phillips Curve with lagged inflation		
Expected inflation, CF survey (γ_f)	0.65**	2.80
Output gap (λ)	0.01	0.62
Lagged inflation (γ_b)	0.32**	3.09
Relative oil price	0.10**	2.69
Adjusted $R^2 = 0.19$		

Source: IMF staff estimates.

Note: CF = *Consensus Forecasts*; CPI = consumer price index; OLS = ordinary least squares. The sample period is the second quarter of 1996 to the fourth quarter of 2014. The estimated constant is not shown here. In the restricted generalized method of moments estimation, the coefficients on lagged and forward inflation add up to one and the coefficient on the output gap is imposed.

* Denotes significance at the 10 percent level; ** significance at the 5 percent level.

TABLE 1.3

New Keynesian Phillips Curve: Baseline GMM Estimates for CPI Inflation

Variable	Coefficients	*t*-Statistic
New Keynesian Phillips Curve with lagged inflation		
Expected inflation (γ_f)	0.59**	4.75
Output gap (λ)	0.26	1.47
Lagged inflation (γ_b)	0.49**	4.08
Relative oil price	0.09**	2.68
J-statistic = 7.56 (*p*-value = 0.81),		

Source: IMF staff estimates.
Note: CPI = consumer price index; GMM = generalized method of moments. The sample period is the second quarter of 1996 to the fourth quarter of 2014. The estimated constant is not shown here. In the restricted generalized method of moments estimation, the coefficients on lagged and forward inflation add up to one and the coefficient on the output gap is imposed.
* Denotes significance at the 10 percent level; ** significance at the 5 percent level.

TABLE 1.4

New Keynesian Phillips Curve: "Restricted" GMM Estimates for CPI Inflation

Variable	Coefficients	*t*-Statistic
Open-economy New Keynesian Phillips Curve with lagged core inflation		
Expected inflation (γ_f)	0.45**	8.99
Output gap (λ)	0.10	...
Lagged inflation (γ_b)	0.55**	8.99
Relative oil price	0.07**	2.75
J-statistic = 11.30 (*p*-value = 0.66),		

Source: IMF staff estimates.
Note: ... = not available; CPI = consumer price index; GMM = generalized method of moments. The sample period is the second quarter of 1996 to the fourth quarter of 2014. The estimated constant is not shown here. In the restricted generalized method of moments estimation, the coefficients on lagged and forward inflation add up to one and the coefficient on the output gap is imposed.
* Denotes significance at the 10 percent level; ** significance at the 5 percent level.

For core inflation, the results are again broadly similar, but the coefficient on expected inflation is even larger (Table 1.3).

The standard New Keynesian Phillips curve assumes rational expectations, and is estimated with GMM and instrumental variables to address the endogeneity of expectations. The New Keynesian Phillips curve also reveals interesting dynamics, but the results are more sensitive to whether headline or core inflation is used. A few patterns emerge:

- For headline CPI inflation:
    - First, both backward- and forward-looking inflation are important determinants of inflation dynamics. The coefficients of lagged and future inflation are generally economically and statistically significant. Typically, the

coefficient on expected inflation is about 0.60–0.65, while that on lagged inflation is generally about 0.35–0.40. For most specifications, the hypothesis that each coefficient equals 0.50 cannot be rejected.

  - Second, the output gap coefficient is not always significant. In fact, it is generally wrongly signed, except when core inflation is the dependent variable. In this case, the coefficient on the output gap is close to that of the backward-looking Phillips curve, usually about 0.30. There is strong evidence that international commodity prices exert an effect on inflation above and beyond that incorporated in expectations or past inflation. The coefficients are remarkably similar in magnitude to those of the simple baseline least square estimates (0.05 to 0.15).

- For core CPI inflation:
  - The specifications for core CPI inflation reveal that both lagged and future inflation are generally not that important to inflation dynamics (their coefficients are small). This is consistent with a traditional or nonaccelerationist Phillips curve. Here, core inflation appears to be determined primarily by the output gap and supply shifters, with coefficients of 0.4 and 0.10, respectively.

To address the lack of precision of the output gap coefficient, an additional estimation procedure was applied to the New Keynesian Phillips curve for headline CPI inflation.[10] The coefficient on the output gap was restricted to the "average" of the OLS and GMM estimates (that is, λ was set equal to 0.1); the other coefficients were estimated freely (Table 1.4). The results suggest that both backward- and forward-looking components are important, with coefficients similar to those of the baseline estimates. The average coefficient on the output gap is also broadly in line with other studies that employ a Bayesian multiple equation estimation framework. For instance, Anand, Ding, and Tulin (2014) estimate the output gap coefficient at 0.25. All in all, these results suggest that given the generally small magnitude of the output gap series and the overall relatively short sample, there is too much variability in the data to allow pinpointing the coefficient on the output gap with precision.

Other robustness dimensions were also explored, including using different output gap measures, lagging the output gap, adding growth in addition to the output gap (or using the change in the output gap), entering the exchange rate and oil prices separately, and so on. None of these alters the results described thus far in a meaningful fashion. With respect to the exchange rate, when the nominal effective exchange rate is used (instead of the bilateral exchange rate with the U.S. dollar) and entered separately from the oil price, the coefficient on the exchange rate tends to be larger than that of the oil price (both in log first differences).

[10] In fact, simple Wald tests on the output gap show that the hypothesis that it lies somewhere in the 0–0.3 range cannot be rejected.

Figure 1.5 Inflation and Fitted Inflation from the New Keynesian Phillips Curve, 1997–2014
(Percent, annualized)

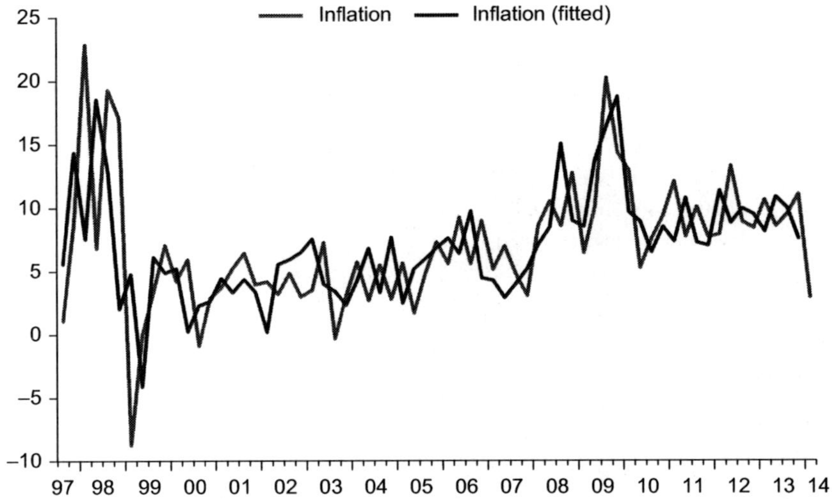

The in-sample fit of the estimated Phillips curves and New Keynesian Phillips curves appears good. The empirical New Keynesian Phillips curve estimated by GMM, including forward and backward inflation, the output gap, and the relative oil price, does a reasonably fine job at capturing the turning points in headline CPI inflation. The in-sample Theil inequality coefficient for the sequence of one-step-ahead forecasts is about 0.27 (also indicating a reasonably good fit, especially when compared against the 0.33 for a random walk model).[11] Despite small coefficients on the relative oil price, the fit is marginally worse when the relative oil price variable is not included in the empirical model. In contrast, the model fit does not improve significantly whether the output gap is included or not (Figure 1.5).

THE CHANGING NATURE OF THE INFLATION OUTPUT TRADE-OFF: EVIDENCE FROM QUANTILE REGRESSIONS

The following analysis explores whether the slope of the Phillips curve changes when the level of inflation changes, or along the empirical distribution of inflation. This complements the Phillips curve estimations and is related to the threshold analysis presented in Box 1.1. Several papers have looked at nonlinear or "kinked" Phillips curves, often motivated by findings of downward wage rigidity in

[11] The Theil statistic lies between zero and one. For reference, a model with a perfect fit would have a Theil statistic of zero.

BOX 1.1 Inflation Thresholds

The literature on inflation thresholds is also related to the issue of whether inflation has moved to higher plateaus, as it attempts to determine whether inflation beyond a certain level (the threshold) has more damaging effects on growth.

Econometric evidence puts the "inflation thresholds" at 5–6 percent for India. Pattanaik and Nadhanael (2011) find evidence of a threshold of about 6 percent, and Mohanty and others (2011) of about 5½ percent. They use three methodologies to check the robustness of the results and control for a number of factors in their reduced-form growth regressions.[1]

Two standard methodologies are used to identify the inflation threshold. They are similar to those generally used in the literature, and are applied only to confirm the robustness of the results because sample sizes and variable selection are often different. These estimations also provide motivation for the estimation of the Phillips curves at segments in the distribution of inflation.

The first approach follows Sarel (1996) and is based on a spline regression. First, a dummy variable is defined ($D=1$ if $\pi_t > \pi_t^*$ and zero otherwise, where π_t is inflation and π_t^* is the posited threshold). Then a reduced-form regression relating growth to inflation, the threshold dummy, and other controls is estimated. Because π_t^* is unknown, the reduced form is estimated for different levels of π_t^*. The threshold is identified at the level at which the root-mean-square error of the regression attains its minimum over a grid of π_t^*s. The coefficient on the threshold dummy yields the difference between the effect of inflation on growth above and below the threshold, and the sum of coefficients on π_t and D also changes sign at π_t^*.

The second methodology generalizes the reduced-form approach and is based on a bivariate vector autoregression. In addition to identifying the threshold, the effects on growth of a shock to inflation and a shock to inflation above the threshold can also be presented.

The results are in line with those of Mohanty and others (2011) and Pattanaik and Nadhanael (2011). Using quarterly data from 1996–2014, the inflation threshold is estimated at 5.5–6.0 percent. In the case of the single equation estimation, both GDP at factor costs and GDP at factor costs excluding agriculture are used with no change in the estimated threshold. Control variables in the reduced-form regression include nonfood-credit-to-GDP ratio (following Pattanaik and Nadhanael 2011) and global growth (as in Mohanty and others 2011).

[1] A number of important issues are also discussed in Mohanty and others (2011). For instance, the authors attempt to control for global growth and the global financial crisis. They also use quarterly data and address the endogeneity in the reduced-form regression.

advanced economies (for example, Akerlof, Dickens, and Perry 1996). In the case of India, Pattanaik and Nadhanael (2011) discuss several aspects that could lead to nonlinear Phillips curves, but do not estimate such relationships. This chapter explores whether the effect of the output gap on headline inflation or inflation inertia changes when inflation rises or is at the top-end of its distribution.[12]

[12] This point can be easily overlooked. We estimate a linear relationship between the change in inflation (assuming an accelerationist Phillips curve) and the output gap. However, the slope of the Phillips curve changes depending on the level of inflation. In the case of the standard least squares regression, the estimated slope gives the effect of output on the conditional expectation of inflation. In quantile regressions, the slope depends on the level of inflation.

To focus on the changing slope of the Phillips curve at different levels of inflation, only accelerationist (or backward-looking) Phillips curves are estimated by a quantile regression Phillips curve. As shown, a simple backward-looking Phillips curve does a reasonable job in terms of in sample fitting as well as forecasting inflation. The posited relationship (constant omitted) is given by:

$$\pi_t = \pi_{t-1} + \gamma(y_t - y_t^*) + \varepsilon_t$$

where the variables are defined as before.

In the case of quantile regressions, the regression model is applied to the entire distribution of the dependent variable, in this case inflation, so the slope parameters can change depending on the level of inflation.[13] The estimated equation is given by:

$$Q_\tau(\pi_t) = \beta_\tau \pi_{t-1} + \gamma_\tau(y_t - y_t^*) + \varepsilon_{\tau,t}$$

where γ is the slope of the quantile regression Phillips curve, but now the coefficients β and γ depend directly on τ, or where inflation is along its own distribution. Other controls are included as before, notably the real oil price. As in the previous section, the sensitivity of the results was assessed along several dimensions, including the output gap measure used, the inclusion of supply shifters, and different measures of expected inflation. The standard errors of the coefficients are calculated based on 100 bootstrap replications. The estimations are shown in Table 1.5.

The estimated quantile regression Phillips curves confirm the importance of the level of inflation in shaping the trade-off between inflation and output. The standard regression estimates show that a 1 percentage point increase in the output gap leads to a 0.2–0.4 percentage point increase in inflation. But for quantile estimates the increase is as large as 0.7 percentage point for higher levels of inflation (the 90th percentile and above). Inflation inertia also rises with the level of inflation. At the lower quantiles of the inflation distribution (10th percentile), the coefficient on lagged inflation is estimated at 0.33, while at the higher quantiles it almost doubles to 0.61. The fact that the coefficient of the output gap rises with the inflation level would imply that a smaller output contraction is needed to reduce inflation, while higher inertia would have the opposite effect. Nevertheless, the estimated magnitude

[13] More formally, in OLS the conditional expectation function is estimated. In the case of quantile regressions, a set of conditional quantile functions are estimated, where the parameters vary according to the quantile in question. In addition to this richer characterization of the relationship between the variables in question, quantile regressions also have the advantage of yielding estimated coefficients that are robust to outliers and nonnormal distributions of the regression error term.

TABLE 1.5

Phillips Curve: Quantile Regression Estimates

Quantile	Lagged Inflation	Output Gap
0.10	0.33*	0.14*
0.25	0.30*	0.21*
0.50	0.47*	0.31*
0.75	0.59*	0.22*
0.90	0.61*	0.72

Source: IMF staff calculations.
* denotes signficance at the 10 percent level.

of the coefficients and the reliability of the estimates suggest that the inertia effect dominates.

As before, the measure of the output gap used matters for the results. These are not estimated with precision and are not robust to alternative measures of the output gap. At the same time, the results just discussed are broadly in line with those in the empirical literature on the sacrifice ratio showing that a higher level of inflation is generally negatively associated with the sacrifice ratio (Ball 1994). But these findings stand in contrast with some of the results reported using data on India by Battacharya, Patnaik, and Shah (2011) and Patra and Kapur (2010).[14]

Overall, the quantile regression Phillips curve estimation results also point to the changing nature of inflationary inertia for different levels of inflation. In addition to the changing slope of the Phillips curve, the coefficient of lagged inflation also rises along the distribution of inflation. In other words, inflation becomes more inertial at higher levels. This is consistent with anecdotal evidence that wage indexation has become more widespread, and with survey evidence showing that inflation expectations had become entrenched until their recent drop in 2014.

CONCLUSIONS

This chapter estimates an inflation model based on the New Keynesian Phillips curve to shed light on India's inflation dynamics. The main findings are summarized as follows:

- After being low and stable and comparing well to other emerging market economies, India's inflation has increased since the mid-2000s and has

[14] As already noted, the baseline trade-off also depends on which measures of inflation and output gap are used in the estimation.

become fairly persistent. Nevertheless, empirical evidence for a structural break is mixed and only holds for CPI inflation and not for WPI inflation.

- Both backward-looking and forward-looking inflation are important to explain inflation, with weights that are not statistically significantly different from 0.5. Uncovering the sources of inflation inertia is important for understanding inflation dynamics. The output gap is also empirically important, but its statistical significance is not robust to the choice of variables (headline or core inflation) or empirical specifications. International commodity prices help deliver a good fit, and their effect on core and headline inflation goes beyond the impact on expectations.
- Finally, the inflation threshold appears to be related to the output-inflation tradeoff. Quantile regression estimates of standard accelerationist Phillips curves indicate that both the degree of inflationary inertia and the slope of the Phillips curve change with the level of inflation. While the coefficient on the output gap generally increases with the level of inflation in some specifications, across nearly all estimations inflation becomes more inertial at higher levels of inflation.

REFERENCES

Akerlof, George, W. Dickens, and G. Perry. 1996. "The Macroeconomics of Low Inflation." Brooking Papers on Economic Activity 1, Brookings Institution, Washington.

Anand, Rahul, Ding Ding, and Volodymyr Tulin. 2014. "Food Inflation in India: The Role of Monetary Policy." IMF Working Paper 14/178, International Monetary Fund, Washington.

Ball, Laurence. 1994. "What Determines the Sacrifice Ratio?" pp. 155–93 in *Monetary Policy*, edited by N. G. Mankiw. Chicago: University of Chicago Press.

———. 2015. "Monetary Policy for a High-Pressure Economy." Center on Budget and Policy Priorities, Washington.

Basu, K. 2011. "Understanding Inflation and Controlling It." *Economic and Political Weekly* 46 (41).

Battacharya, Rudrani, Ila Patnaik, and Ajay Shah. 2011. "Monetary Policy Transmission in an Emerging Market Setting." IMF Working Paper 11/5, International Monetary Fund, Washington.

Chand, R. 2010. "Understanding the Nature and Causes of Food Inflation." *Economic and Political Weekly* 45 (9): 10–13.

Christiano, L., and T. Fitzgerald. 2003. "The Band Pass Filter." *International Economic Review* 44 (2): 435–65.

Gali, Jordi, and Mark Gertler. 2000. "Inflation Dynamics: A Structural Econometric Analysis." NBER Working Paper 7551, National Bureau of Economic Research, Cambridge, Massachusetts.

———. 2005. "Robustness of the Estimates of the Hybrid New Keynesian Phillips Curve." *Journal of Monetary Economics* 52 (6): 1107–18.

Gokarn, S. 2011. "Food Inflation: This Time It's Different." *Monthly Bulletin*, Reserve Bank of India, January.

Lo, Andrew, and Craig MacKinlay. 1988. "Stock Markets Do Not Follow Random Walks: Evidence from a Simple Specification Test." *Review of Financial Studies* 1: 41–66.

Mishra, Prachi, and Devesh Roy. 2011. "Explaining Inflation in India: The Role of Food Prices." Unpublished. National Council of Applied Economic Research, India Policy Forum, New Dehli.

Mohanty, D. 2013. "Indian Inflation Puzzle." Speech at the Dr. Ramchandra Parnerkar Outstanding Economics Award, Mumbai, January 31.

Mohanty, D., A. Chakraborty, A. Das, and J. John. 2011. "Empirical Threshold in India: An Empirical Investigation." RBI Working Paper 18/2011, Reserve Bank of India, Mumbai.

Pattanaik, Sitikantha, and G.V. Nadhanael. 2011. "Why Persistent High Inflation Impedes Growth: An Empirical Assessment of Threshold Level of Inflation for India." Working Paper 17/2011, Reserve Bank of India, Mumbai.

Patra, M., and M. Kapur. 2010. "A Monetary Policy Model for India without Money." IMF Working Paper 10/183, International Monetary Fund, Washington.

Patra, M., D. Khundrakpam, J. Kumar, and A. George. 2013. "Post-Global Crisis Inflation Dynamics in India: What Has Changed?" *India Policy Forum* (10): 117–202.

Sarel, M. 1996. "Non-Linear Effects of Inflation on Economic Growth." IMF Staff Papers 43, International Monetary Fund, Washington.

Shah, Ajay. 2011. "Are the Inflationary Fires Subsiding?" Blog, November 7.
http://ajayshahblog.blogspot.com/2011/11/are-inflationary-fires-subsiding.html.

Stock, James, and Mark Watson. 2007. "Why Has U.S. Inflation Became Harder to Forecast?" *Journal of Money, Credit and Banking* 39 (1): 3–33.

Tulin, Volodymyr. 2015. "India's Food Inflation: Causes and Consequences." India Selected Issues, IMF Country Report 15/62, International Monetary Fund, Washington.

Walsh, James. 2011. "Reconsidering the Role of Food Prices in Inflation." IMF Working Paper 11/71, International Monetary Fund, Washington.

CHAPTER 2

Reconsidering the Role of Food Prices in Inflation

JAMES P. WALSH

This chapter analyzes the dynamics of food and nonfood inflation to assess the appropriateness of minimizing or excluding food inflation in measures of core inflation, particularly in developing economies such as India.

Core inflation indices can be derived in many ways, but the end result in most advanced economies is to minimize or eliminate volatile categories, which often means excluding food and energy. Although central bankers acknowledge the greater role of food prices in emerging market economies, core inflation measures excluding food price changes are also widely cited and can inform policy decisions.

It is not clear, however, that the characteristics of both food and nonfood prices that justify the minimization of food price inflation in advanced-economy core measures apply in developing economies, particularly in India. This is not only a question of the greater weight of food in the consumer basket, but also of the differences in the statistical properties and relationships between food and nonfood prices.

This question is particularly important given the rising volatility and importance of food price changes. During 2003–07, when global commodity prices rose suddenly and rapidly, nonfood inflation also quickly accelerated in many countries. This underscored the importance of looking at the relationship between food prices and headline inflation, and raised questions about whether a focus on core measures of inflation might lead policymakers to underestimate the medium-term impact of changes in food prices.

Of course, policymakers look at various measures of inflation, and no central bank ignores developments in an important and volatile subcomponent of inflation. But as this chapter discusses, discounting food price developments relative to nonfood price developments can lead policymakers not only to underestimate the headline level of inflation that affects inflation expectations, but also the level of inflation in the nonfood basket in countries where the transmission of food price shocks to nonfood prices is a significant factor.

THE ROLE OF CORE INFLATION: BENEFITS AND ISSUES

Measures of core inflation are generally designed in various ways to address a primary challenge for central bankers: how to set policies consistent with medium-term goals, even though data measure only current developments. This difficulty is particularly pronounced for inflation, where monthly developments are highly volatile and central banks must infer whether sudden changes reflect a transitory shock or are evidence of a change in trends. Higher levels and volatility of inflation, as commonly observed in developing economies, can create even greater uncertainty about underlying developments. Thus, while most central banks target headline inflation, policy decisions are often partially informed by other measures of inflation designed to provide a clearer image of underlying price developments than the headline price index.

The desirable characteristics of such a core measure of inflation are difficult to pin down, and different practitioners arrive at different conclusions. In a seminal paper, Bryan and Cecchetti (1993) focus on determining a measure of inflation that maximizes the signal-to-noise ratio, and suggest measuring inflation based on a truncated distribution of the changes of its components. The goal of such a procedure is to eliminate transitory developments in inflation to focus on persistent trends, which are of primary interest to monetary policy practitioners. By eliminating those components whose changes are the most extreme, the measure adjusts for the skewed distribution of component price changes, and provides an estimate of the underlying longer-term trend. In an analysis of how their index differs from headline inflation, Bryan and Cecchetti (1993) calculate the probability that a given component will be at the center of the distribution of price changes; that is, the probability at any given time that one component of the index will be representative of inflation overall. Relative to their weight in the overall price index, shelter and medical care, which are relatively stable, are very likely to display the median price change. Energy and food consumed at home, which are relatively volatile, are among the least likely components. Thus, while the index is not explicitly constructed as a consumer price index (CPI) less food and energy, food and energy in the end assume less importance in this measure than in headline inflation owing to their higher volatility and skewness.

On the other hand, Cutler (2001) builds on a slightly different concept of a core measure of inflation by emphasizing persistence. Noting that policymakers are interested in inflation developments that are likely to have important medium-term effects, she estimates the persistence of inflation across the components of the United Kingdom's retail price index, and weighs components by their relative persistence.[1] This measure places a low weight on energy and seasonal food items, but a high weight on nonseasonal food items, which in the United Kingdom display relatively persistent prices. In this case, the relatively low persistence of food inflation justifies its lower weight in a core index. Bilke and Stracca (2008) construct a similar index for the euro area, but find that food prices are relatively persistent, resulting in a higher weight in their index than in headline CPI.

While these measures effectively reduce the importance of food inflation developments in measures aimed at deriving medium-term inflation from noisy

---

[1] Except for goods with estimated autocorrelations below zero, which are weighted at zero.

contemporaneous data, Cecchetti (2007) cautions against going too far. He suggests that a core inflation measure that excludes food and energy can be a less effective focus for policymakers than headline inflation. Setting aside the volatility or persistence of the two components, he notes that means are also important: if noncore inflation rises faster than core inflation over a sustained period, then stripping out faster-moving components of inflation cannot be said to provide a more accurate picture of overall inflation, and the estimates of current inflation provided by a core measure will be biased significantly downward.

Rich and Steindel (2007) go beyond this to assess whether some measures of inflation in the United States can be thought of as "core" measures at all. They posit the important characteristics of a core measure of inflation are its transparency, displaying dynamics (including both a short-term "close coherence" and a long-term mean) similar to the headline series, and an ability to provide information about past and future developments of the broader series. In assessing four different models for U.S. inflation—including the widely cited aggregate inflation series excluding food and energy, as well as some methodological improvements posited in the literature—they find that the core measure excluding food and energy does not perform particularly well as a core inflation series. While its dynamics are roughly similar (though not as close as might be expected) to headline inflation, its predictive value is weak. This result is particularly important, given that food inflation in the United States is far more transitory and less significant in the creation of overall inflation expectations than in some other economies.

Álvarez and others (2005) look at the persistence of inflation across components in the euro area and compare these results to similar studies for the United States. As with earlier studies, they find that in both regions food prices are less persistent than nonfood prices (particularly services), but that across all categories prices in the euro area are markedly more persistent than prices in the United States. Given this heterogeneity across developed economies, where food dynamics can be expected to be of relatively little importance in overall inflation dynamics, it is reasonable to question whether it is justifiable to discount food price inflation as transitory in developing economies.

The mechanism transmitting food price shocks to nonfood inflation can also be important. Cecchetti and Moessner (2008) assess how the rise in commodity prices since 2003 has fed into overall inflation, and find that in many countries headline inflation is not reverting to core to the same degree that it did in earlier periods. This implies that a secular increase in commodity prices, including prices for food, around the world may now be affecting nonfood prices. These effects are likely to be even more pronounced in countries where food is an important component of the overall consumption basket.[2]

---

[2] This is particularly true given that administered prices, particularly of fuels, which the government sets rather than the market, also generally account for a larger share of the consumption basket in poor countries than in rich countries, and that administered prices are far more prevalent in developing economies.

The run-up in food prices preceding the global financial crisis sparked a literature on the implications of food price inflation for the conduct of monetary policy more generally. Catão and Chang (2010) point out that a distinctive role for food in household utility and the presence of high food-price volatility can have important implications for the welfare effects of different monetary policy regimes. They find that these factors strengthen the case for targeting broad CPI instead of a measure of core inflation, and that policies that offset at least some changes in food prices, even those of food imported from abroad, can be welfare-enhancing. Anand and Prasad (2010) also conclude that in an environment of credit-constrained consumers, a narrow policy focus on nonfood inflation can lead to suboptimal outcomes. Both of these assumptions are more likely to approximate reality in developing economies than in rich ones.

In fact, both the theoretical and empirical literature on core inflation are focused on rich countries, where the dynamics of food inflation are likely to be substantially different from those in developing economies or emerging markets. Reducing the weight of food prices in core inflation or setting it to zero can be justified if food prices are less volatile than nonfood prices, their persistence is relatively low, or their impact on headline inflation is small or fleeting. However, if these assumptions do not hold, then headline inflation could be a better guide or even, as Bilke and Stracca (2008) find, a core measure that overweights food inflation.

The following analysis uses a novel dataset that allows the distinction between food and nonfood inflation to be drawn for a very wide sample of 91 countries (data described in Annex 2.1). It examines the extent to which these assumptions of transitory and volatile food prices with little long-term effect on nonfood prices hold, in both developed and developing economies.

FOOD AND NONFOOD INFLATION

How Does the Distribution of Food and Nonfood Shocks Differ?

Differences in the distribution of food and nonfood shocks can be significant at two important points. First, as Cecchetti (2007) notes, excluding food from a core measure of inflation is only justified when the long-term mean of food inflation is equal to the long-term mean of nonfood inflation. If this is not the case, then core inflation will systematically underestimate headline inflation. In other words, if policymakers are interested in the overall price level, ignoring food price dynamics only makes sense if these do not affect the long-term price level; if they do, then they have to be taken into account.

Second, it is also important to look at the volatility of food price shocks. If these are more volatile than nonfood price shocks, they add to the noise-to-signal ratio that policymakers contend with in assessing inflation. The larger and more frequent these shocks to food inflation are, the likelier it is that they not only lead to erroneous diagnoses of the level of underlying inflation, but also that these

Figure 2.1. Average Food and Nonfood Inflation, 1985–2008
(Percent)

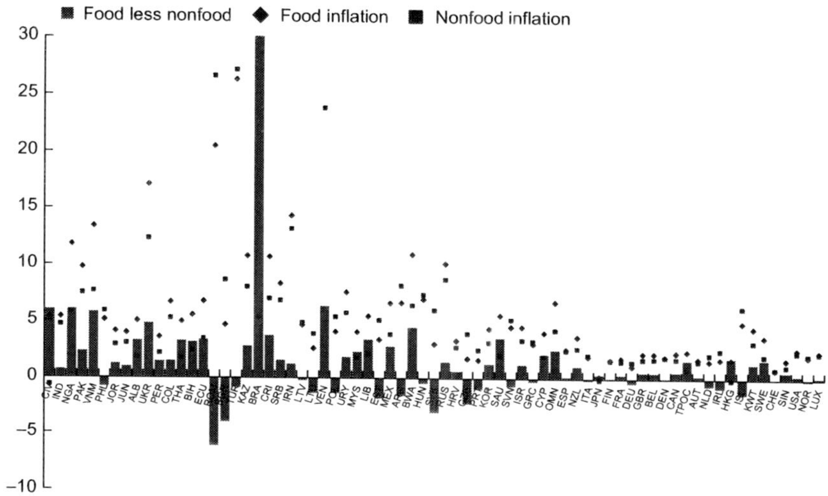

Source: IMF staff calculations.
Note: Data labels in the figure use International Organization for Standardization country codes.

shocks can affect nonfood prices. This propagation mechanism may not exist everywhere, and this possibility is discussed later in the chapter. If food shocks tend to be small, then even the long-term effect is likely to be minimal. However, if food shocks are larger and more volatile than nonfood shocks, then even if the propagation mechanism is weak, food shocks may have serious knock-on effects on nonfood prices.

Figure 2.1 shows average annualized monthly food and nonfood inflation, and the difference between the two, for all the countries in the sample, sorted by average income per capita during the sample period. There are more countries in which food inflation runs higher than nonfood inflation than there are countries where nonfood inflation is higher, particularly among lower-income countries. Countries with higher average food inflation comprise two-thirds of the sample, but the difference is significant at the 10 percent level in only 20 percent of countries. In fact, differences are negligible among almost all high-income countries, but can be substantial among poorer countries. Thus, in rich countries, a measure of inflation that excludes food prices will on average show the same level of inflation as the headline measure. But in poorer countries, where food prices on average rise faster than nonfood prices, a measure of inflation that excludes food prices will show lower inflation than the headline index, even in the long term.

The higher mean of food inflation is interesting for another reason: a higher mean level of inflation would imply that food prices will rise relative to nonfood prices over time. In rapidly growing low-income countries, this is something we

Figure 2.2. Standard Deviation of Food and Nonfood Inflation, 1985–2008
(Percent)

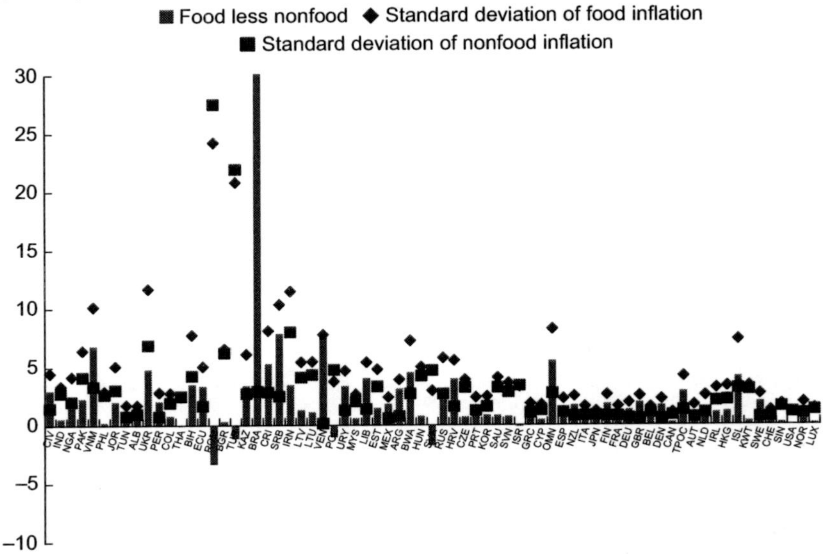

Source: IMF staff calculations.
Note: Data labels in the figure use International Organization for Standardization country codes.

might expect, as consumers with rising incomes consume more food and drive up food prices relative to other goods. Similarly, this differential should narrow as countries become richer, both as tastes shift away from food and as the composition of retail food prices shifts away from commodities and more toward labor and other costs. In fact, of the countries for which the difference between food and nonfood inflation is significantly different, none are advanced economies; the richest is Saudi Arabia. Other causes are also plausible, such as the relatively low tradability of nonstaple foods, the labor intensity of agriculture, and the Balassa-Samuelson effect (Balassa 1964; Samuelson 1964). This effect is also visible in Figure 2.1, where the inflation differential is greater among the low-income countries in the sample.

Figure 2.2 shows the volatility of food and nonfood inflation for the countries in the sample, ranked again by income per capita. Food price inflation is also more volatile than nonfood price inflation in 65 of the 71 countries in the subsample for which long-term data are available.[3] This higher volatility of food price inflation necessarily makes underlying trends harder to discern, supporting the

[3] Three of the six exceptions are countries in central and eastern Europe (Poland, Romania, Slovakia) while the difference for many other countries in the region (such as Bulgaria, the Baltic states, and Hungary) are also quite low, even though the volatility of food inflation is relatively high. The reasons for this are beyond the scope of this chapter, but these countries are outliers in this respect.

Figure 2.3. Skewness of Food and Nonfood Inflation, 1985–2008
(Percent)

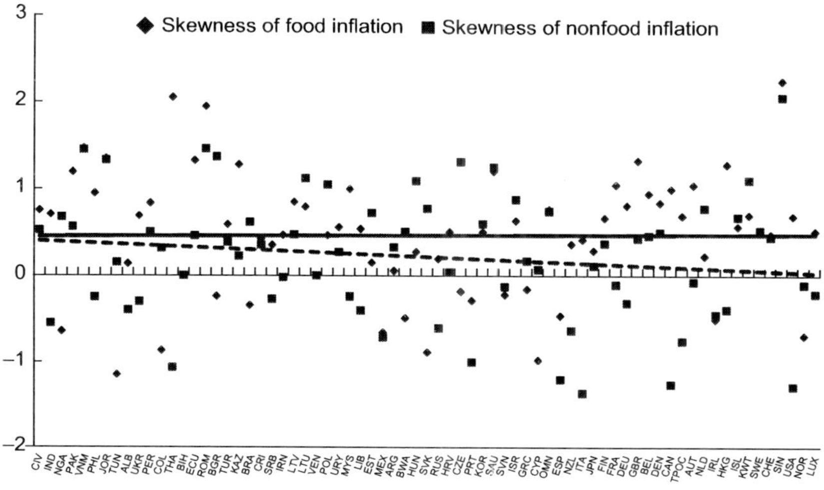

Source: IMF staff calculations.
Note: Data labels in the figure use International Organization for Standardization country codes.

exclusion of food prices from core indices aimed at maximizing this ratio. However, as mentioned, this greater volatility also means that the shocks transmitted from food to nonfood inflation can in some cases be quite large, and if the propagation mechanism between food and nonfood prices is strong, these large shocks can result in large upward shifts in nonfood prices. Such developments would not be clear from a nonfood core measure until the transmission to nonfood prices had already occurred.

Both food and nonfood price inflation also tend to be right-skewed (Figure 2.3), meaning that unusually large shocks are more common than unusually small ones. As can be seen by the negatively sloped best-fit line for nonfood inflation, this skew becomes smaller at higher income levels: the poorer a country is, the more likely its large nonfood price shocks will be positive rather than negative. For food inflation, however, skewness is relatively constant across the sample. Thus food prices tend to have larger positive shocks than negative ones in both rich and poor countries, but for nonfood prices this effect is stronger in poor countries. Under the Bryan and Cechetti (1993) methodology, based on U.S. data, the weights of food and energy prices are reduced in trimmed-means core measures of inflation, partly because of their greater skewness relative to other items. But among poorer countries, this difference in skewness is not nearly as pronounced, and a trimmed-means estimator might produce a very different result—and possibly one that would not drastically reduce the weight of food prices.

The innovations to inflation are also interesting. The standard deviations of changes in inflation (that is, the second derivative of the price level) are shown in

Figure 2.4. Standard Deviation, Changes in Food and Nonfood Inflation, 1985–2008
(Percent)

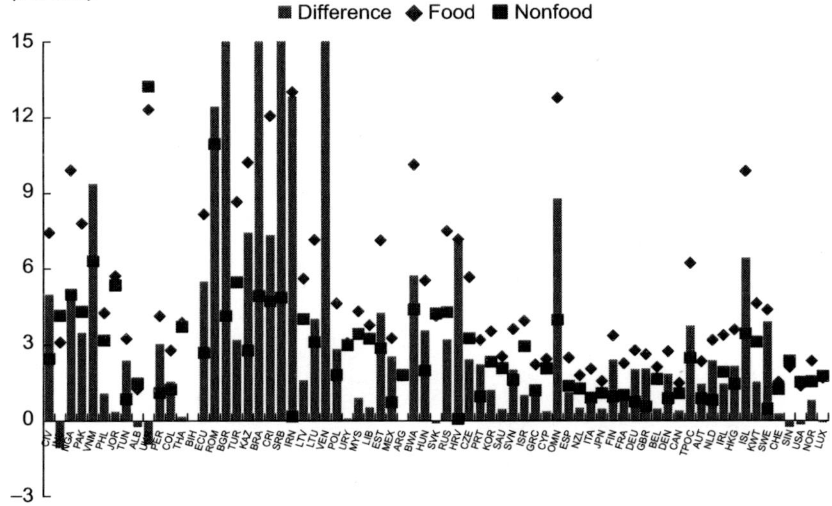

Source: IMF staff calculations.
Note: Data labels in the figure use International Organization for Standardization country codes.

Figure 2.4. Not only is food inflation more volatile than nonfood inflation, but even innovations to food inflation are more volatile. This underscores the argument that if transmission to nonfood prices is sufficiently strong, then food price shocks—which in low-income countries are not only on average larger and more volatile than nonfood price shocks, but are also skewed to the right—can feed strongly into nonfood inflation.

In all, food inflation tends to be higher and more volatile than nonfood inflation, and skewed to the right, with all of these effects on average stronger in lower-income countries. In addition, changes to food inflation over time are themselves more volatile than changes to nonfood inflation; again with the effect stronger among poor countries.

How Does the Persistence of Food and Nonfood Shocks Differ?

The distribution of food price shocks, particularly their higher volatility, clearly has implications for their effect on nonfood and overall inflation. But another model for core inflation measures is the one used by Cutler (2001) based on the persistence of shocks. Longer-lived shocks will result in inflation remaining elevated for a longer period after a shock hits, and also lead to a longer window during which food price shocks can be transmitted to nonfood prices.

The argument that food price shocks are not persistent is another reason policymakers often discount them in assessing the level of inflation. Even if food price shocks tend to be larger and more volatile, and extreme food shocks more likely than nonfood shocks, if these shocks dissipate quickly, then their effect on headline inflation will not be significant beyond the short term. On the other hand, persistent food price shocks are much more likely to feed into inflationary expectations. This necessitates earlier action by policymakers to keep expectations from rising on the basis of what could still prove to be a transitory but nevertheless persistent shock.

Measuring persistence is not straightforward. In a summary of the literature, Pivetta and Reis (2007) discuss a variety of methods for estimating inflation persistence, all of which have advantages and disadvantages. They posit three methods of inflation persistence, each of which will overestimate persistence in some cases and underestimate in others.

The basis for each of these persistence measures is the estimation of a baseline autoregressive equation of the form:

$$\pi_t^X = \rho_1 \pi_{t-1}^X + \cdots + \rho_q \pi_{t-q}^X + \varepsilon_t^X \qquad (2.1)$$

in which π_t^X represents inflation for X, a basket either of food or nonfood items, as time t. This equation can also be written as a lag polynomial:

$$\pi_t^X = L(q)(\pi_t^X) + \varepsilon_t^X \qquad (2.2)$$

in which $L(q)$ is a polynomial with the same number of lags appearing in equation 2.1.

For each country in the sample, equation 2.1 was estimated for food and nonfood inflation, nine times, with q ranging between 1 and 9. The model chosen for the calculations that follow was the one with the highest Akaike information criterion among the nine estimated models for each price index. The AR(q) models were estimated using the standard maximum likelihood ARIMA technique.

Sum of Autoregressive Coefficients

The first persistence measure is the sum of autoregressive coefficients (SARC). For this measure, the AR(q) measure chosen above for each of the inflation indices is estimated, and the ρ coefficients in the equation are summed.

The SARC is a widely used method for assessing persistence, first proposed with some modifications in Andrews and Chen (1994), who present it as a better single-number estimate of long-term dynamics than unit root tests. However, it also has shortcomings, particularly those that relate to oscillating dynamics. If some of the ρ coefficients are positive and others are negative, the sum will be close to zero despite what could be near-infinite dynamics.

TABLE 2.1

Sum of Autoregressive Coefficient Results

	CPI	CPI-Food	CPI-Nonfood
Mean	0.194	**0.182**	0.021
Median	0.274	**0.243**	0.000
Standard deviation	0.558	**0.494**	0.556
Skewness	−1.066	**−1.668**	−1.573
Kurtosis	1.753	**3.412**	6.594

Source: IMF staff calculations.
Note: CPI = consumer price index.

Table 2.1 and Figure 2.5 show the distribution of the SARC measures for the countries in the sample. Both measures show positive and negative persistence for some countries, but, on average, persistence in nonfood prices is far less, because more countries have negative sums for nonfood prices and also because those countries that have positive sums for food prices tend to have much higher values. SARC estimates for both food and nonfood inflation have high standard deviations, and outliers tend to be on the negative side.

To some extent, this lower degree of persistence among nonfood prices is likely an artefact of credible monetary policy. If central banks accommodate food price shocks, but do not accommodate nonfood price shocks, this will appear in the data as a greater persistence of food price inflation. Figure 2.6 shows that

Figure 2.5. Histogram of Sum of Autoregressive Coefficients Estimates

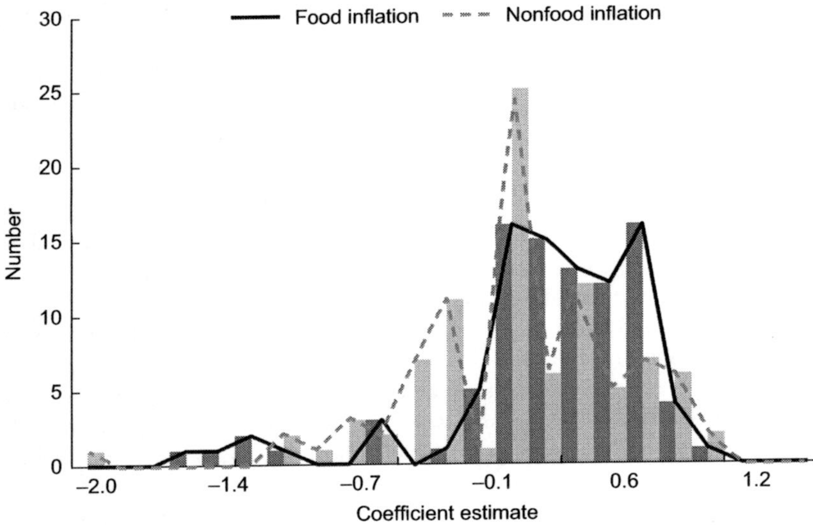

Source: IMF staff calculations.

Figure 2.6. Persistence of Food and Nonfood Inflation by GDP per Capita: SARC Measure

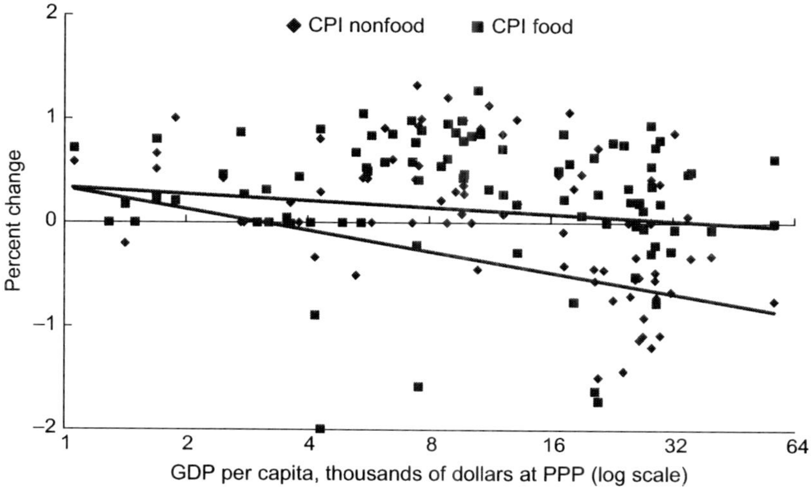

Source: IMF staff calculations.
Note: PPP = purchasing power parity; SARC = sum of autoregressive coefficients.

advanced economies, where central bank credibility is likely to be highest, not only have the least persistent nonfood shocks, but that the persistence of these shocks is negative: exactly the expected outcome if central banks act to reverse the impact of nonfood price shocks on overall inflation. However, in those economies, the effect of food price shocks on nonfood price shocks is on average smaller: they are less volatile and persistent than in poorer countries, and, as detailed later, present less of a risk to nonfood price shocks. Accommodating food price shocks is therefore unlikely to endanger price stability. In middle- and low-income countries, the situation is different. Here, improving the outcome of monetary policy might involve reducing the persistence of nonfood inflation by reacting more forcefully to nonfood price shocks, but, given the greater risk food price shocks represent to nonfood inflation, it might also involve reacting more forcefully to food price shocks as well.

Interestingly, both food and nonfood prices are less persistent than overall inflation. This result, which is robust to all the persistence measures discussed here, may seem counterintuitive. But overall CPI is a weighted average of food and nonfood CPI. Because both of these display persistence, and (as shown later) the two series transmit shocks between them, it is not surprising that overall inflation shows more persistence than either of its subindices. Similar results are presented for a decomposition of U.S. CPI in Clark (2003).

The distribution of SARCs is also found to be related to income. As shown in Figure 2.6, persistence of both food and nonfood inflation is highest among lower-income countries, and both fall with income. Interestingly, on average, food and nonfood inflation are equally persistent among the poorest countries, but for the richest countries nonfood inflation persistence falls to close to zero, while food inflation persistence is negative.

Largest Autoregressive Root

The second measure for inflation persistence calculated here is the largest autoregressive root (LAR). The lag polynomial displayed in equation 2.2 can be factored:

$$L(q) = (1 - \theta_1 L - \theta_2 L^2 \; \cdots \; - \theta_q L^q) \tag{2.3}$$

$$L(q) = \left((1 - \beta_1 L) \cdots (1 - \beta_{q-1} L)\right) \tag{2.4}$$

where the β_i coefficients are ordered according to their size, with β_1 the largest. In the long term, the effect of a shock on inflation will be dominated by this largest root: in the case where ρ is one, the series has a unit root, and all shocks are permanent. The advantage to the LAR measure is that it effectively measures how close a given inflation series is to having a unit root; that is, how close to permanent a given shock will be. A disadvantage is that the other roots beyond the unit root are ignored, while they matter too in practice. For example, a series with a β_2 coefficient of 0.8 will display more persistence than one with 0.2.

For each of the food and nonfood CPIs in the sample, the underlying lag polynomials were factored and the largest real root selected. The results are presented in Table 2.2 and Figure 2.7.

Table 2.2 shows that overall the mean and median of the LARs for food inflation are higher than those for nonfood inflation and, as above, the mean LAR for CPI is higher than for both of its subcomponents. Figure 2.7 shows that as with the case of the SARC estimate, the higher range of LAR estimates has more observations for food inflation than for nonfood inflation, while lower estimates have a (lesser) preponderance of nonfood inflation estimates.

None of the food or nonfood inflation series analyzed here have unit roots, though some of the largest roots are relatively high. Three countries have LAR

TABLE 2.2

Largest Autoregressive Root Results

	CPI	CPI-Food	CPI-Nonfood
Mean	0.425	**0.438**	0.347
Median	0.448	**0.442**	0.356
Standard deviation	0.304	**0.239**	0.288
Skewness	–0.585	**–1.170**	0.527
Kurtosis	0.240	**2.801**	0.729

Source: IMF staff calculations.
Note: CPI = consumer price index.

Figure 2.7. Histogram of Largest Autoregressive Root Estimates

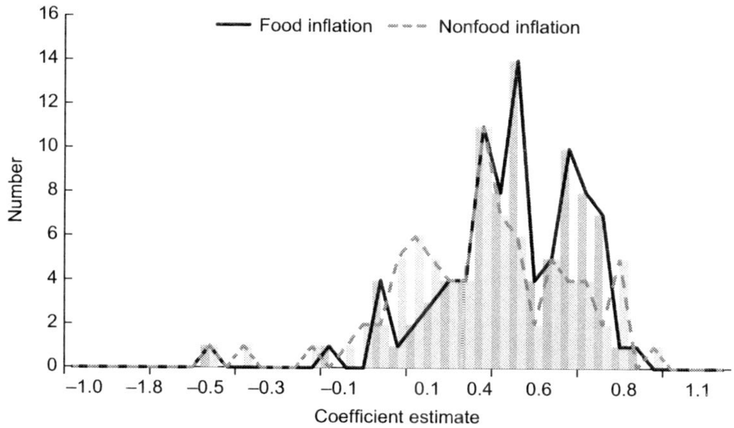

Source: IMF staff calculations.

Figure 2.8. Persistence of Food and Nonfood Inflation by GDP per Capita: LAR Measure

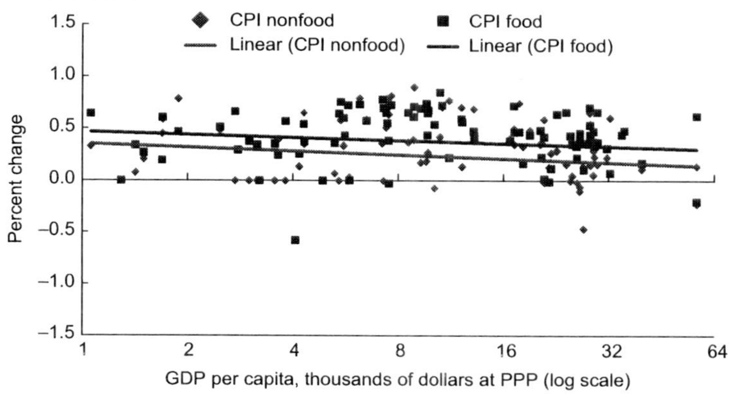

Source: IMF staff calculations.
Note: CPI = consumer price index; LAR = largest autoregressive root; PPP = purchasing power parity.

estimates for food inflation greater than 0.75: Ecuador, Mexico, and South Africa. But seven have LAR estimates for nonfood inflation above that level: Bulgaria, Colombia, Iran, Pakistan, Poland, Romania, and Turkey.[4]

Figure 2.8 shows the LAR measure relative to (log) GDP per capita. As in the SARC measure, the persistence of both food and nonfood inflation falls with

[4] For the former command economies, such as Bulgaria, Poland, and Romania, data generally extend back to the early 1990s. Inflation has now fallen dramatically in these countries, but the sample average remains quite high.

income. Given the differences in calculation methods between the SARC and the LAR, it is not surprising that the results are slightly different. The overall pattern, however, is similar: the correlation between the SARC and LAR measures for CPI is 83 percent, while that for food inflation is 70 percent and for nonfood inflation 61 percent.

Half-Life

The third method for estimating persistence is calculating the impulse half-life. For this method, an impulse response function for each of the AR(q) models estimated in the previous section is derived. The number of periods required to reduce the impulse response function below 0.5 from an initial unit shock is the half-life. Unlike the previous two methods, this produces integral measures of persistence, and the distribution of results is quite different. Nevertheless, as Table 2.3 shows, the mean and median half-lives of shocks-to-food CPI exceed those of nonfood CPI.

But even according to this measure, food inflation is more persistent. In most countries, both food and nonfood inflation revert quickly, and half-lives are quite small. In 53 countries (58 percent of the sample), the half-life of a shock to non-food inflation is only one month (Figure 2.9). For food inflation, this is true for only 35 countries (38 percent of the sample). For one-third of the countries, half the effect of a unit shock to food prices has not dissipated after two months, but this is true for nonfood prices in only one-fifth of the sample.

This persistence measure, as with both measures previously discussed, is strongly related to income (Figure 2.10). The half-lives of almost all the higher-income countries in the sample are bunched in a range below six months, while the range for middle-income countries in particular is far wider. This is particularly true for food prices.

For all three of these measures, SARC, LAR, and half-life, the persistence of food price shocks is nontrivial in many countries. Under such circumstances, a core index based on persistence should not eliminate the food component of price inflation, though it is an empirical question whether merely reweighting components might yield a lower weight than the consumer-expenditure weight used in CPI baskets.

TABLE 2.3

Half-Life Results

	CPI	CPI-Food	CPI-Nonfood
Mean	3.967	**3.033**	0.915
Median	2.000	**1.000**	0.000
Standard deviation	10.455	**7.315**	12.534
Skewness	8.713	**7.425**	3.677
Kurtosis	80.471	**61.974**	45.570

Source: IMF staff calculations.
Note: CPI = consumer price index.

Figure 2.9. Histogram of Half-Life Estimates
(Months)

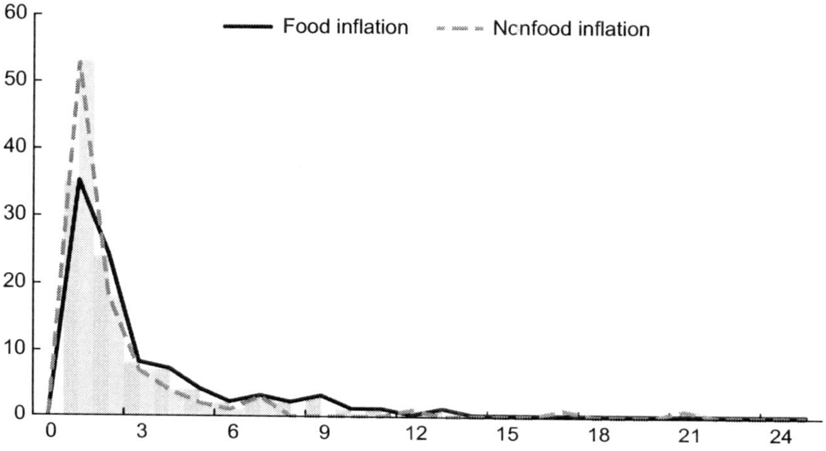

Source: IMF staff calculations.

Figure 2.10. Persistence of Food and Nonfood Inflation by GDP per Capita: Half-Life of Unit Shock
(Months)

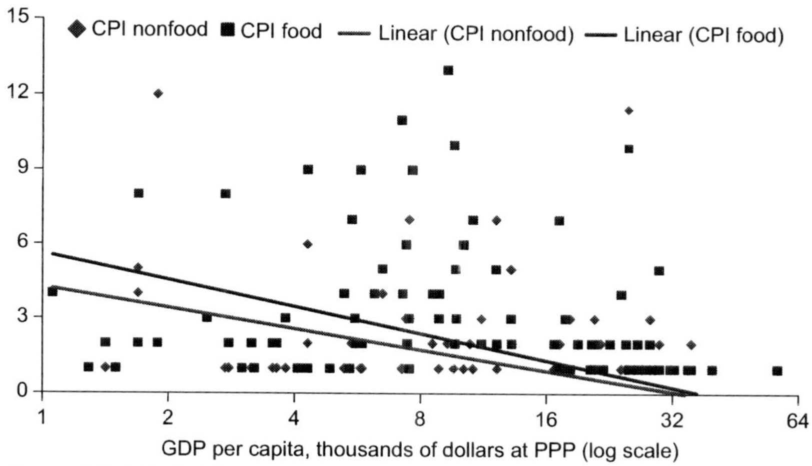

Source: IMF staff calculations.
Note: CPI = consumer price index; PPP = purchasing power parity.

This empirical question is particularly important in low-income countries. All three measures show a greater persistence of inflation, especially food price inflation, among poorer countries. In many of these countries, excluding food price shocks under an untested assumption of low persistence is unjustified.

HOW DOES THE TRANSMISSION OF FOOD AND NONFOOD SHOCKS DIFFER?

The third component of food inflation dynamics that might differ between poor and rich countries is the transmission of shocks between food and nonfood inflation. After all, if a supply shock to food prices does not propagate into nonfood prices, a monetary policy response to the shock is unlikely to be as efficient as, for example, ensuring sufficient food supply to vulnerable individuals at the new higher prices. But if food prices propagate strongly into nonfood prices, particularly given the evidence presented of their greater magnitude, volatility, and persistence in poor countries, then an earlier monetary response might be optimal to limit the increase in nonfood inflation.

To assess these effects, we estimate a two-equation vector autoregression for food and nonfood prices, and derive impulse response functions:

$$\pi_t^F = \beta^{FF}\pi_{t-1}^F + \beta^{NF}\pi_{t-1}^N + \varepsilon_t^F \tag{2.5}$$

$$\pi_t^N = \beta^{FN}\pi_{t-1}^F + \beta^{NN}\pi_{t-1}^N + \varepsilon_t^N \tag{2.6}$$

where π_t^F is food inflation and π_t^N is nonfood inflation. The equations are estimated jointly, using standard maximum likelihood techniques for seemingly unrelated equations.

The derived impulse response functions are very heterogeneous, as be expected given the heterogeneity of persistence measures. Figure 2.11 shows the four estimated impulse responses, averaged across the top and bottom halves of the sample sorted by income, along with the cumulative differences between the two.[5]

Panel 1 of Figure 2.11 shows the figure of most interest: the effect of food price shocks on nonfood prices. The first-round effect is much larger in the poorer countries than in the richer ones, and though the slower response in the rich countries eventually eliminates some of this difference, as the declining cumulative impulse response functions shows, the large difference persists. The impulse responses among the poor countries are also generally far more volatile: the average standard deviation of impulse responses among the poorer half of the sample is 0.043, while it is 0.038 for the richer countries.

The response of each inflation index to its own shock is also of interest. In both cases, the cumulative response among the poor countries is stronger than in the rich countries. In the long term, a 1 percent shock to nonfood prices increases the nonfood price level by 1 percent in the rich countries, but by almost 2.5 percent in the poorer half of the sample. Given the results showing that three other measures of persistence also yield higher estimates for the poor countries than the rich ones, this is not surprising. With food prices, on the other hand, shocks dissipate

[5] The cumulative impulse responses show the long-term effect on price levels. For example, a cumulative difference of 0.5 fifteen periods after the shock would imply that the price level in poor countries is ½ percent (0.005) higher than in rich countries.

Figure 2.11. Responses to Food and Nonfood Price Shocks

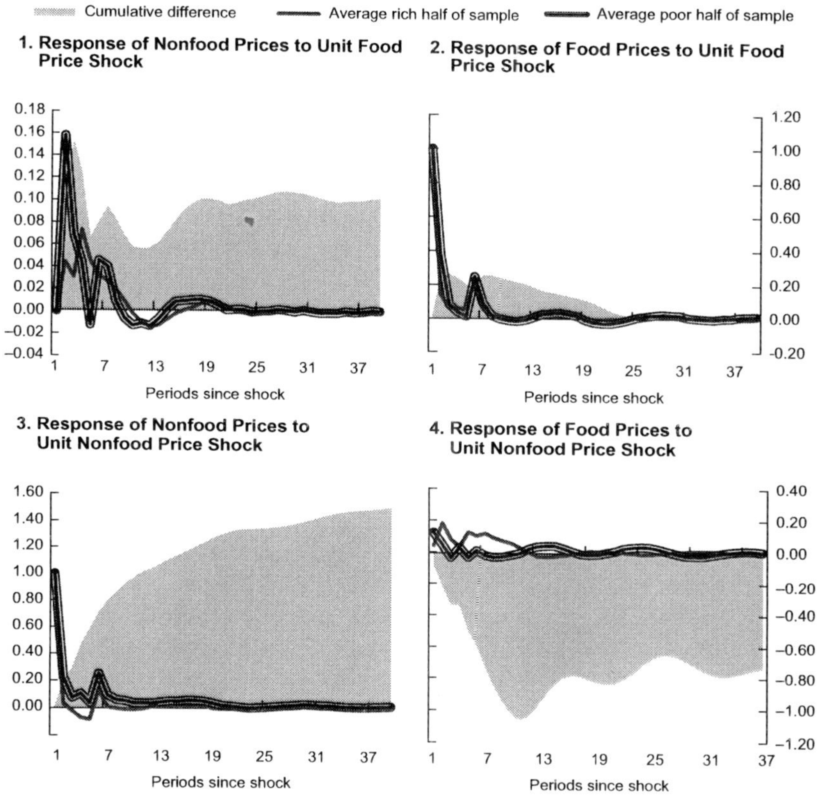

Source: IMF staff calculations.
Note: CPI = consumer price index; PPP = purchasing power parity.

more, with the long-term effect of a 1 percent food price shock in the rich countries about 0.8 percent, but in the poor countries about 0.9 percent.

Shocks to nonfood prices can have an effect on food prices. As shown in panel 4 of Figure 2.11, these effects are stronger among the rich countries than among the poor countries. This is different from the other three linkages, and likely has to do with the greater capital content of food in rich countries than in poor ones: an increase in the cost of electricity or construction costs would have a larger effect on the prices of goods sold in grocery stores than in markets.

CONCLUSION

Taken together, the results in this chapter imply that eliminating food prices from core inflation may provide an incorrect picture of underlying inflation trends, especially in low-income countries, for three primary reasons.

First, a core measure of inflation must have the same medium-term mean as the headline measure. However, food inflation in many countries is higher than nonfood inflation, making it likely that a core inflation measure excluding food prices will show lower inflation, even in the long term, than headline inflation. This is of particular concern among poorer countries, where in some cases food inflation is significantly higher than nonfood inflation.

Second, excluding food prices from core measures (or assigning them a lower weight) because of their perceived transience is often unjustified. In the sample analyzed here, food inflation in many cases is quite persistent, and in many countries more so than nonfood prices. This relationship is particularly pronounced in poorer countries where food is a large share of the consumption basket. In such countries, the slow dissipation of food shocks could lead to higher expectations not only for food inflation, but also for overall inflation. Given the higher volatility of food price shocks, a core inflation measure that excludes food prices will miss these shocks. Because they only slowly dissipate through the headline index, inflation expectations will be affected and could rise even though traditional measures of core inflation are unaffected.

Third, food inflation in many countries is transmitted into nonfood inflation in a significant and important way. This is, again, particularly so in developing economies. In both rich and poor countries, large upward food price shocks are propagated into nonfood prices relatively quickly. However, this effect is much more pronounced in poor countries than in rich ones. In rich countries, a 1 percent shock to food prices results on average in a 0.15 percent increase in nonfood prices, but in poor countries the average is about 0.3 percent.

This effect is aggravated by the high volatility of and right skew to food prices. With large price shocks more likely to occur among food prices than among nonfood prices, discounting food price developments in countries where food price shocks are transmitted strongly or quickly to nonfood prices can lead to an underestimate of the medium-term effect of those shocks.

Given these effects, core inflation indices that minimize or even eliminate food prices from a headline index are likely to be misspecified in many developing economies. Policymakers should thus return to first principles in constructing core price indices for assessing medium-term developments. Whether these are based on reducing the weight of the more volatile components of the price index or that of the more transient components, it is not clear that such a calculation will result in the construction of a core price index that underweights food price inflation.

For policymakers in many countries, food inflation is therefore not something that can be broadly disregarded as a phenomenon only tenuously linked to underlying medium-term inflation developments. Although this issue assumed some salience before the global financial crisis as food prices increased dramatically during 2003–07, the rapid disinflation brought on by the crisis caused these concerns to recede. Now, as food prices have begun to rise again globally, policymakers are again faced with the question of the extent to which a divergence between headline inflation and measures of inflation excluding food prices represents a development calling for an active response.

The evidence in this chapter implies that if the transmission of food price shocks into nonfood prices is strong, as it is in many low-income countries, then central banks should be aware of the impact that food prices may have on the broader price index. In some cases stronger policy action may be warranted earlier in a tightening cycle, though this will depend on circumstances. Food inflation is indeed quite volatile, and central banks, particularly in countries with weak mechanisms for monetary transmission, should not overreact to transitory shocks by tightening policy prematurely. The right response will also depend on the central bank's broader exchange rate and monetary policy regimes, and analyzing how the inflation dynamics are influenced by varying policy regimes is itself an important area for further research. But in all cases, looking at how rapidly food price shocks affect nonfood inflation can help central banks be vigilant about stemming an incipient rise in nonfood inflation that could be spilling over from food prices.

ANNEX 2.1. DATA USED

The data used in the sample are consumer price indices (CPI) for 91 countries.[6] The headline CPI index is used, along with the widest definition of food used in these countries, excluding alcoholic beverages where this distinction is made. In other words, the subindex for "food" is used, but in cases where the subindex is "food and beverage," this is also used. Nonfood CPI is calculated from total CPI, the weight of food in the CPI, and food CPI. Inflation is calculated on a month-over-month basis. Other macroeconomic data used in the analysis come from the IMF's World Economic Outlook database.

It is quite possible that the dynamics discussed for food prices apply equally strongly to energy prices. However, these are excluded from this analysis for a number of reasons. First, constructing comparable energy price indices across countries is less straightforward than constructing one for food prices. All countries in this analysis have a category for food, but not every country has one for energy; and some important items, such as gasoline, are classified differently in different countries. Second, and perhaps more important, government administration of energy prices is more widespread than for food prices. This is particularly important in many developing economies. Although the effects of changes in administered energy prices are as significant as changes in market-determined prices, including them here would be problematic: energy price shocks in rich countries tend not to be persistent, a commonly cited reason for their exclusion from core indices. But they are extremely persistent in countries with administered prices. If persistence is the only measure for inclusion in a core index, this would argue for including administered energy prices in a core index, even when changes to administered prices lead to sudden large increases in prices. These difficulties argue for treating energy prices outside a cross-country framework.[7]

Finally, there is a trade-off between using seasonally adjusted and non-seasonally adjusted data. The analysis below uses non-seasonally adjusted data. Not all countries publish seasonally adjusted CPI data, particularly for components, and including seasonally adjusted and non-seasonally adjusted data would tend to reduce the volatility of one group of countries relative to the other. In theory, all CPI data could be seasonally adjusted for the analysis, but with a heterogeneous sample of countries this is highly problematic. Given the wide variety of important seasonal factors in many countries that do not fall in the same month each year (such as Ramadan or Lunar New Year), applying a blanket seasonal adjustment measure such as X12 that looks only at monthly factors across the entire sample would be inappropriate for many countries.

---

[6] For India, wholesale price index data are used, because this is the only national price index with a monthly frequency available and it is the headline index most commonly cited by the central bank and in the media.

[7] It is true that food subsidies and price controls in both rich and poor countries establish floors or ceilings for many commodities. But even in countries with heavily regulated food markets, prices for most consumers and most products vary over time to a greater degree due to market forces than, for example, administered gasoline or heating-oil prices.

REFERENCES

Álvarez, Luis J., Emmanuel Dhyne, Marco M. Hoeberichts, Claudia Kwapil, Hervé le Bihan, Patrick Lünnemann, Fernando Martins, Roberto Sabbatini, Harald Stahl, Philip Vermeulen, and Jouko Vilmunen. 2005. "Sticky Prices in the Euro Area: A Summary of New Micro Evidence." ECB Working Paper 563, European Central Bank, Brussels.

Anand, Rahul, and Eswar S. Prasad. 2010. "Optimal Price Indices for Targeting Inflation under Incomplete Markets." NBER Working Paper 16290, National Bureau of Economic Research, Cambridge, Massachusetts.

Andrews, Donald W. K., and Hong-Yuan Chen. 1994. "Approximately Median-Unbiased Estimation of Autoregressive Models." *Journal of Business and Economic Statistics* 12 (2): 187–204.

Balassa, B. 1964. "The Purchasing Power Parity Doctrine: A Reappraisal." *Journal of Political Economy* 72: 584–96.

Bilke, Laurent, and Livio Stracca. 2008. "A Persistence-Weighted Measure of Core Inflation in the Euro Area." ECB Working Paper 905, European Central Bank, Brussels.

Bryan, Michael F., and Stephen G. Cecchetti. 1993. "Measuring Core Inflation." In *Monetary Policy.* Chicago: University of Chicago Press.

Catão, Luis A. V., and Roberto Chang. 2010. "World Food Prices and Monetary Policy." IMF Working Paper 10/161, International Monetary Fund, Washington.

Cecchetti, Stephen G. 2007. "Core Inflation is an Unreliable Guide." VoxEU, March 1.

Cecchetti, Stephen G., and Richhild Moessner. 2008. "Commodity Prices and Inflation Dynamics." *BIS Quarterly Review* December: 55–66.

Clark, Todd E. 2003. "Disaggregate Evidence on the Persistence of Consumer Price Inflation." Working Paper RWP 03-11, Federal Reserve Bank of Kansas City, Kansas City.

Cutler, Joanne. 2001. "Core Inflation in the UK." External Monetary Policy Committee Unit Discussion Paper 3, Bank of England, London.

Pivetta, Frederic, and Ricardo Reis. 2007. "The Persistence of Inflation in the United States." *Journal of Economic Dynamics and Control* 31 (4): 1326–58.

Rich, Robert W., and Charles Steindel. 2007. "A Comparison of Measures of Core Inflation." *Economic Policy Review* 13 (3).

Samuelson, P. 1964. "Theoretical Notes on Trade Problems." *Review of Economics and Statistics* 46: 145–54.

CHAPTER 3

Food Inflation in India

PRACHI MISHRA AND DEVESH ROY

Investigating the primary drivers of food price inflation in India is important given its high level and persistence. As Cecchetti (2007) argues, ignoring food and energy prices, particularly in recent times when they have consistently risen faster than other prices, could bias estimates of medium-term inflation. In India, food inflation is particularly important because the poor, a large part of the country's population, spend over 50 percent of their income on food, based on the 2004–05 round of the National Sample Survey. The poor are also typically net buyers of food and have incomes that tend to be fixed.[1] However, there is little systematic empirical evidence of the long-term evolution of food inflation in India at a disaggregated level.

This chapter analyzes food inflation in India using a high-frequency commodity-level dataset spanning the past two decades. First, we document stylized facts about the behavior of food inflation. We establish that low food inflation was a rare occurrence in the Indian economy in the past two decades (specifically 1988 to 2014). Long-term food inflation has followed a U-shaped pattern, with a rising trend since the early 2000s. Domestic and international food prices have been only moderately correlated, though there is significant variation across commodities based on their tradability. Furthermore, we find food inflation to be consistently higher than nonfood inflation.

Next, we explicitly quantify the contribution of specific commodities to food inflation. The findings suggest that animal source foods (milk, fish), processed food (sugar, edible oils), fruits and vegetables (onions), and cereals (rice, wheat) are typically the primary drivers of food inflation in India. We then conduct case studies of two of the top contributors to food inflation—milk and cereals. Combining the insights from the analyses of overall food inflation and the individual case studies, we suggest several policy implications.

Policy focus needs to be reoriented toward commodities, where demand-supply gaps have been persistent, for example in food items such as milk and milk products. Policies have to be geared not only toward enhancing overall production, but also to smoothing production across time and space. For milk, this

[1] Panagariya (2005) argues more generally that an increase in food prices due to the removal of Organisation for Economic Co-operation and Development subsidies might actually hurt the poor in developing economies, many of which tend to be net buyers. Specifically in India, de Janvry and Sadoulet (2009) estimate a large share of the rural population to be net food buyers.

would entail stocking milk powder in the flush season (October–March) to be liquefied during the lean season (April–September), and the transport of milk powder from surplus to deficit areas.

Domestic interventions such as minimum support prices, which are aimed at increasing production, might themselves be contributing to food inflation. For example, rising minimum support prices for cereals lead directly to higher cereal prices by setting the market floor price, but they also hinder the reallocation of resources (land and labor) to crops in relatively short supply, such as pulses and oilseeds. Minimum support prices and the procurement of grains should ideally be made to adjust to the level of production, with high support prices and larger procurement amid abundant production and the reverse amid comparatively scarce supply.

Trade policies need to be aligned with domestic procurement and stocking policies, which have often worked at cross-purposes. For example, while export restrictions on cereals try to hold consumer prices down, rising minimum support prices and the resulting high stocks tend to raise them.

The debate on trade reforms in agriculture needs to be revisited. The examples of edible oils and, more recently, pulses raise the question of whether the pattern of inflation we observe in most commodities would have been different were trade more liberalized to begin with. In this context the discussion on trade reforms should focus not only on liberalizing import tariffs and export restrictions, but also on easing regulatory barriers. For example, to import livestock products, an applicant must apply 30 days in advance to get clearance from the Department of Animal Husbandry and Dairying. A fast-track window is needed for such clearances.

MEASURING FOOD INFLATION IN INDIA

Any price index can in principle be calculated using producer, consumer, or wholesale prices, with each serving a different purpose. The producer price index measures the average selling prices received by domestic producers of goods and services. This contrasts with other inflation measures, such as the consumer price index (CPI) which measures average prices from the consumer's perspective. Seller and consumer prices may differ; for example, due to taxes, subsidies, and distribution costs. The wholesale price index (WPI) ideally measures average prices in the wholesale market; that is, where goods are sold in bulk. These price indices are used to measure the average change over time in selling prices received by producers (producer price index inflation), or prices paid by consumers (CPI inflation), or the average price change in the wholesale market (WPI inflation).

The WPI is historically the most commonly used price index for measuring inflation in India.[2] However, the term "wholesale" is misleading in that the index

[2] Following the recommendations of the Patel Committee Report, the Reserve Bank of India adopted in February 2015 the CPI as the key measure of inflation (RBI 2014, 4).

does not necessarily measure prices in the wholesale market. In practice, the WPI in India measures prices at different stages of the value chain. As discussed in Srinivasan (2008), based on the National Statistical Commission, "in many cases, these prices correspond to farm-gate, factory-gate, or mine-head prices; and in many other cases, they refer to prices at the level of primary markets, secondary markets or other wholesale or retail markets."

The weights used in the WPI are revised every decade. The latest series is based on 2004/05 as the base year, and includes 676 commodities. Figure 3.1 shows the weights used in the WPI: food's total weight is 24.3 percent, of which 14.3 percent is for primary foods and the rest for processed food. Fuel's weight is close to 15 percent. In the nonfood, nonfuel category, the three largest weights are chemicals (12 percent), metals (10.7 percent), and textiles (7.3 percent). The WPI does not include services.

As well as the WPI, four consumer price indices are also officially published. These correspond to different segments of the population: industrial workers (CPI-IW, base year 2001), agricultural laborers (CPI-AL, base year 1986–87), rural laborers (CPI-RL, base year 1986–87), and urban nonmanual employees (CPI-UNME, base year 2001). A nationwide measure of CPI that combines rural and urban areas became available in January 2011 (base year 2010). The weights used for the new CPI are derived from the 61st (2004–05) round of the National

Figure 3.1. Wholesale Price Index Weights
(2004–05 = 100)

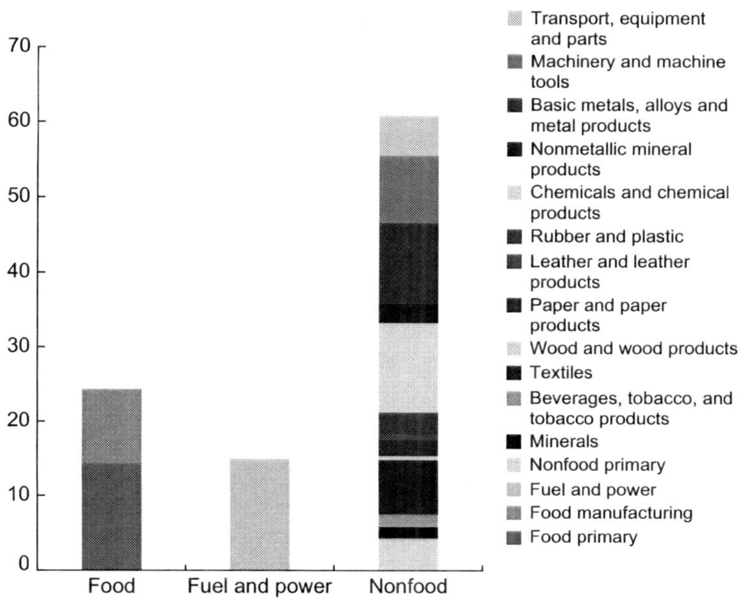

Source: Ministry of Commerce and Industry.

Figure 3.2. Consumer Price Index Weights
(2001 = 100)

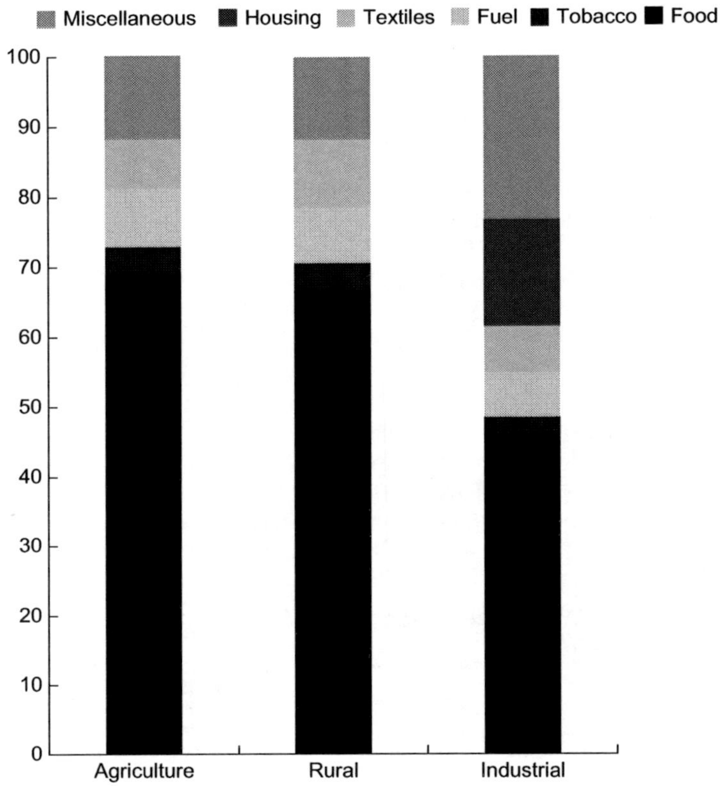

Source: Ministry of Commerce and Industry.

Sample Survey.[3] The CPI-IW includes only six subindices: clothing, food, fuel and lighting, housing, tobacco and intoxicants, and miscellaneous. CPI-AL and CPI-RL are published with only five subindices and exclude housing.

The commodity coverage for the latest CPI measures has been broadened, and includes 23 items. In addition to housing, six subcategories of services are included. Importantly, the CPI gives a much larger weight to food compared to the WPI (Figure 3.2). The weight on food in the CPI ranges from 46–69 percent, depending on the segment of workers the index refers to, and hence is more likely to capture the recent surges in food prices after 2005.[4] The CPI is arguably a better

[3] The CPI weights for CPI-AL and CPI-RL are based on consumption expenditures from the National Sample Survey Organisation, whereas those for CPI-IW and CPI-UNME are based on family expenditures in selected urban centers only (Srinivasan 2008).

[4] The weight on fuel is lower in the CPI than in the WPI (6.4 percent in CPI-IW).

measure than the WPI to study changes in prices of final goods demanded by consumers. The analysis in this chapter, however, relies largely on the WPI, because the CPI is not available at a disaggregated commodity level (even the most recent nationwide index is much more aggregated compared to the WPI). Wherever possible—for more aggregated trends—the CPI is also be used.

Several papers point out the deficiencies of the price indices used in India for measuring inflation (for example, Srinivasan 2008). Recommendations to improve the indices include converting the WPI into a producer price index and expanding the scope of both the WPI and CPI to include services. The CPI, even in its latest incarnation (2010 as base year) has limited coverage of goods and services (total of 23 items), and hence is not amenable to any serious disaggregated analysis. Therefore, if the CPI were to become the primary index for policy purposes (as is the norm in most countries), expanding its coverage beyond a mere 23 items is imperative.

We use WPI data at the monthly frequency, covering July 1988 to February 2014. The WPI index (2004–05 as base year), with 676 items (112 food items), is only available from April 2004. To create one comparable series for the WPI over 1988–2011, we project the 2004–05 series backward using the growth rates in the price indices based on the 1993–94 series (covering 435 commodities) and 1981–82 (447 commodities) series. Although we confirmed that using either series does not significantly change the trends in overall inflation, caution should be exercised in comparing *aggregate* inflation trends based on the changing basket of commodities over time.

The food price index can be specified using the following formula:

$$I_t^F = \frac{\sum_j (W_{j0}^F * I_{jt}^F)}{\sum_j W_{j0}^F} \tag{3.1}$$

where I_{jt}^F is the price index of the jth food item at time t, W_{j0}^F is the weight assigned to the jth food item in the food price index (not the overall price index). The weight of the jth food item is given by

$$\frac{W_{j0}^F}{\sum_{j=1}^n W_{j0}^F}$$

where W_{j0}^F is the expenditure on the jth food item calculated using base-year prices and quantities.

The top 25 food items with the highest WPI weights are shown in Figure 3.3.[5] Inflation is calculated on a year-over-year basis. Although food and fuel prices may show similar dynamics, the focus of this chapter is on food prices; hence we exclude fuel. The term "nonfood" denotes the items excluding food and fuel.

[5]The weights at the disaggregated commodity level are not published online for the 1993–94 and 1981–82 indices; the weights for aggregate categories are available from a report from the Ministry of Commerce and Industry. All price data are publicly available on the website of the Ministry of Commerce and Industry.

Figure 3.3. Top 25 Food Items with the Highest WPI Weights
(2004–05 = 100)

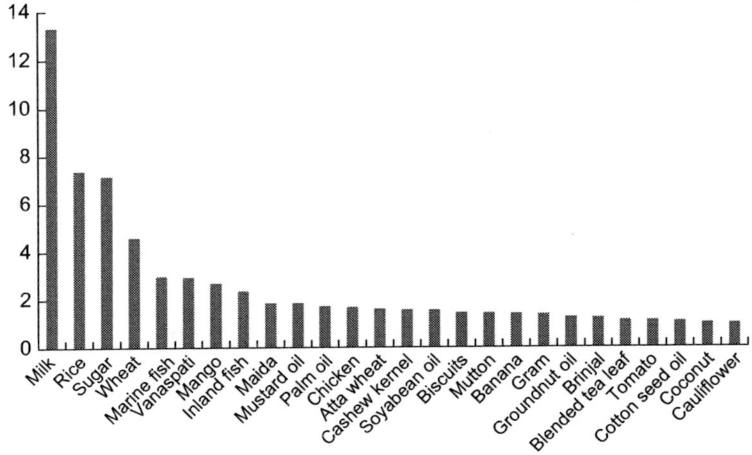

Source: Ministry of Commerce and Industry.
Note: WPI = wholesale price index.

BROAD TRENDS IN FOOD INFLATION

In this section, we examine the behavior of food inflation and its relationship with nonfood and aggregate inflation. The goal is to systematically document stylized facts about the importance of food in inflation, using some descriptive statistics.

There have been three peaks of food inflation in the past two decades—1991, 1998, 2010—when average annual year-over-year (calendar year) inflation rates reached 17.9 percent, 11.1 percent, and 14.2 percent, respectively (Figure 3.4). Indeed, if we look at the peaks of monthly year-over-year inflation reached during a given year, the three peaks were higher—20.8 percent in 1991, 18.1 percent in 1998, and 20.2 percent in 2009–10 (Figure 3.5, panel 1). Panel 2 presents the number of months for which food inflation was higher than nonfood inflation. In most years, for the majority of months, food inflation has been higher than nonfood inflation. We will look closely at the contributors to food inflation in the latter two peaks, but the lack of disaggregated commodity-level data on prices prior to 1994 precludes a deeper analysis for 1991.

Domestic and International Food Prices

How integrated are domestic food prices with their international counterparts? In this section, we make a first pass at this question, which has become particularly relevant since the global food price crisis in 2008. We find only a moderate correlation between domestic and international food prices (close to 0.5), as panel 1

Figure 3.4. Inflation Rate: Food and Nonfood
(Percent)

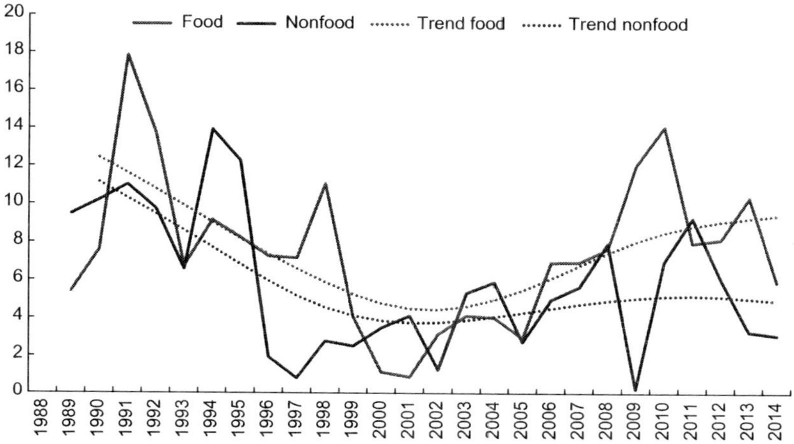

Source: Ministry of Commerce and Industry; and authors' calculations.
Note: This figure shows the average year-over-year inflation rates based on the wholesale price index. The trends are estimated based on a Hodrick-Prescott filter, with a smoothing parameter of 100.

of Figure 3.6 shows.[6] Yet, at the commodity level, variation in the degree of comovement between domestic and international prices is significant (shown in Table 3.1). In general, the relationship is weaker for staples like rice and wheat compared to, say, edible oils and sugar. This may reflect, in part, the government's reluctance to allow any significant pass-through from international to domestic prices of staples, as discussed in detail in the section on short-term factors. But broadly, the degree of comovement depends on the actual or potential tradability of the commodity.[7] Highly tradable products like edible oils therefore exhibit a high degree of comovement between domestic and international prices.

Another interesting and consistent pattern that emerges across commodities is that the degree of comovement between domestic and international prices is stronger when international prices are low than when they are high (for example, in the case of rice and wheat shown in panels 2 and 3 in Figure 3.6). This may suggest that the government is more unwilling to allow the pass-through when prices are higher (see Misra and Misra 2009).[8]

[6]This is consistent with research done at the Reserve Bank of India (for example, Misra and Misra 2009).

[7]For example, if an export ban is in place on a potentially exportable commodity, then a rise in international prices can put upward pressure on domestic prices through different channels, such as illegal trade or political pressure to raise support prices.

[8]One relevant question is whether the Reserve Bank of India pursues a policy of monetary accommodation in response to rising international food prices. We did not find any documentation for this. We also looked at the correlation between repo rates and international food prices: the correlation coefficient is positive but small.

Figure 3.5. Behavior of Food and Nonfood Inflation

1. Food and nonfood inflation peaks
(Percent)

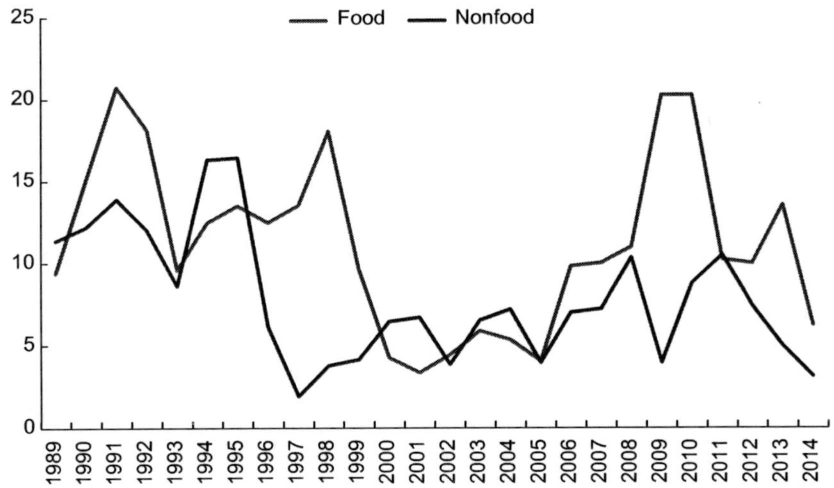

2. Number of months with food inflation higher than nonfood inflation

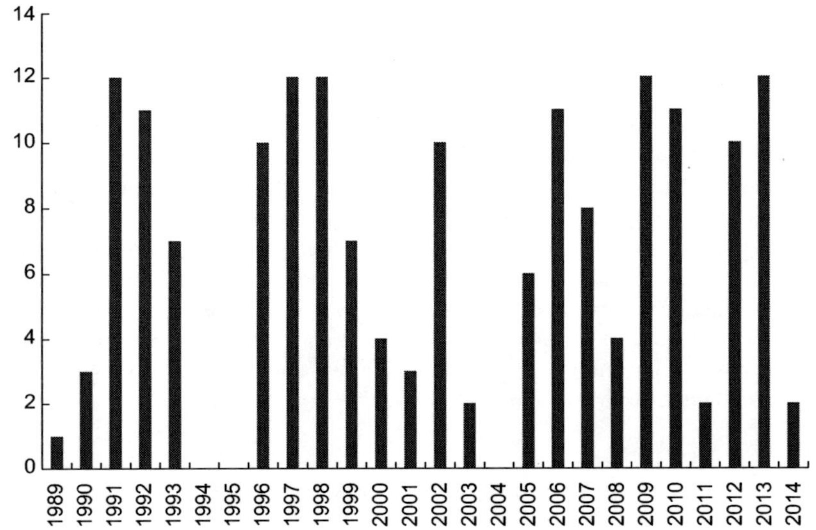

Sources: Government of India; Ministry of Commerce and Industry; and authors' calculation.
Note: Panel 1 shows the peaks in any month in a year for the year-over-year inflation rates based on the wholesale price index (WPI). The WPI figure for 2011 is based on January–May; for consumer price index, from January–April. Panel 2 uses year-over-year inflation rates based on the WPI. The index figure for 2011 is based on January–May.

Figure 3.6. Relationship Between Domestic and International Cereal Prices

1. Domestic and international food prices, 1990–2013

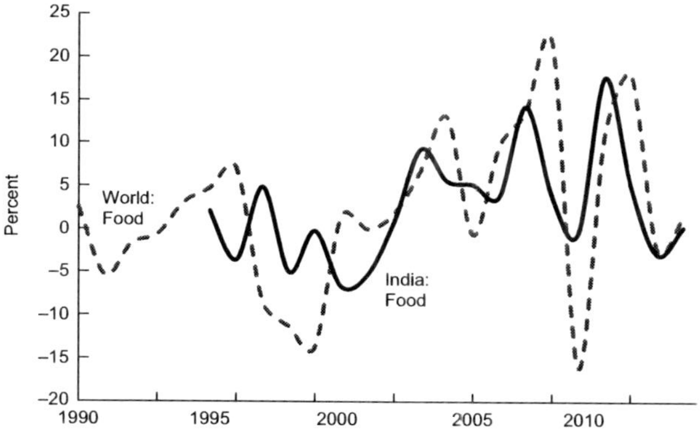

2. Rice: domestic and international prices
(Price indices; 2005 = 100)

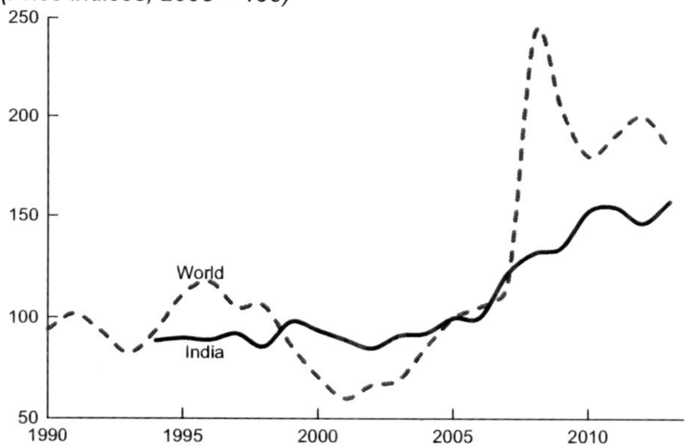

3. Wheat: domestic and international prices
(Price indices; 2005 = 100)

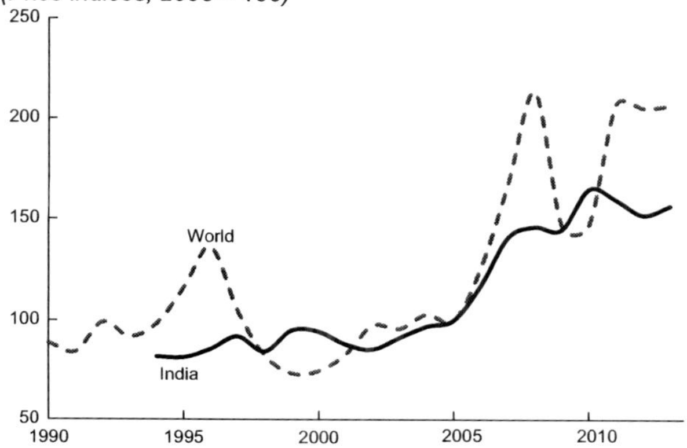

Source: IMF, Commodities database.

Note: Panel 1 shows the evolution of world and domestic food prices. The world prices are for 13 food items; domestic prices are based on the wholesale price index and are a weighted average of the 13 items for which the world prices exist.

TABLE 3.1

Correlation between Domestic and World Food Price Inflation

Overall	**0.47**
Rice	0.14
Wheat	0.30
Maize	0.15
Sugar	0.62
Edible oils	0.88
Chicken	0.32
Fish	0.55

Source: IMF, Commodities Database.

Note: The database covers 13 food items. The domestic food price inflation is based on a weighted average of the wholesale price index for the same 13 items.

WHICH COMMODITIES DRIVE FOOD INFLATION?

Two main factors determine the contribution of different commodities to food inflation: the weight of each commodity in the overall food basket, and the change in prices of these commodities. To begin with, we look at broad trends in inflation of primary and manufactured food items. From Figure 3.3 we know that primary food items constitute a bigger weight in the Indian food basket. At the same time, the inflation rate for primary food items is typically also higher than for manufactured items (Figure 3.7). For example, in 2010 the difference was as high as 10 percentage points. Moreover, the long-term trend in inflation for primary products is always above that for manufactured food items. Hence, given both high weights and high inflation rates, we can expect primary commodities to be contributing to a larger extent to overall food inflation (Figure 3.8).

To dig deeper into the specific commodities that contributed to food inflation, we look at all 112 commodities in the 2004–05 food basket and use a simple methodology to quantify their contributions. Recall in equation 3.1, we defined the food price index using a Laspeyres formula. Taking first differences of equation 3.1, and dividing by I_{t-1}^F, we get:

$$\frac{\Delta I_t^F}{I_{t-1}^F} = \sum_i \frac{W_i^F}{\Sigma_i W_i^F} * \frac{\Delta I_{it}^F}{I_{it-1}^F} * \frac{I_{it-1}^F}{I_{t-1}^F}$$

Or,

$$\pi_t^F = \sum_i \frac{W_i^F}{\Sigma_i W_i^F} * \pi_{it}^F * \frac{I_{it-1}^F}{I_{t-1}^F} \tag{3.2}$$

Figure 3.7. Food Price Inflation Rate: Primary and Manufactured Products
(Percent)

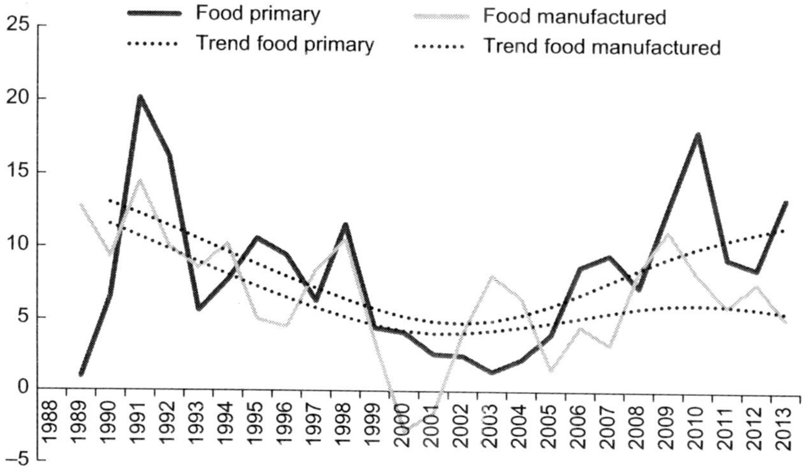

Sources: Ministry of Commerce and Industry; and authors' calculations.
Note: This figure shows the average year-over-year inflation rates based on the wholesale price index. The trends are based on a Hodrick-Precott filter with a smoothing parameter of 100.

Figure 3.8. Food Price Inflation Rate: CPI and WPI

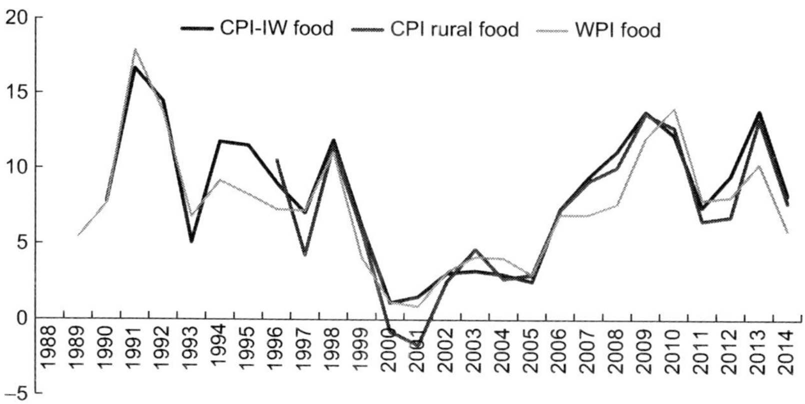

Source: Ministry of Commerce and Industry.
Note: This figure shows the average year-over-year food inflation rates. CPI = consumer price index; WPI = wholesale price index. The WPI figure for 2011 is based on January–May; for the CPI, from January–April. CPI-IW, CPI-AL, CPI-RL, and CPI-UNME are the CPI for industrial, agriculture, rural, and urban non-manual employees, respectively.

where W_i^F is the weight for i in the food basket in the base period. π_t^F denotes the aggregate food inflation rate and π_{it}^F denotes the inflation rate for commodity i at time t. Hence, the contribution of item i in explaining food inflation is given by:

$$C_{it}^F = \frac{W_i^F}{\Sigma_i W_i^F} * \pi_{it}^F * \frac{I_{it-1}^F}{I_{t-1}^F} \tag{3.3}$$

C_{it}^F is a product of three factors: the share of commodity i in the food basket, the inflation rate of i, and the ratio of the price index of i to the overall food price index in the previous period. Hence, commodities with higher weights and high inflation are the natural candidates for being among the biggest contributors to overall food inflation. However, commodities with very high weights in the food basket could also contribute significantly, even though the rise in their prices is not very significant. The converse could be true as well—there could be commodities with relatively low weights that experience a sharp increase in prices, and could contribute to overall food inflation.

Based on this logic, we classify all the commodities in the food basket into four bins: (1) high inflation and high weight, (2) high inflation and low weight, (3) low inflation and high weight, and (4) low inflation and low weight. High and low are defined as above and below the median of inflation and weight, respectively. The commodities falling in the high-inflation, high-weight bin are the most likely candidates for the biggest contributors to food inflation. Although the list of commodities varies, the high-inflation, high-weight commodities can be broadly classified into four groups: animal source food; fruits and vegetables; staples such as rice and wheat; and processed food, including sugar and edible oils.

In what follows, from equation 3.3, we compute C_{it} for each of the 112 commodities in the food basket. We first take the annual averages of the individual commodity indices as well as of the overall food index, and then calculate the respective inflation rates. We use the weights in the 2004–05 basket for the calculations. Finally, as a check, we make sure that the following identity holds in the data:

$$\sum_i C_{it}^F = \pi_t^F$$

The top 50 contributors and their contributions for some selected years—1998, 2008–2013—are shown in Annex 3.1, and the top five contributors in each of these years are shown in Figure 3.9. The contributors to food inflation are typically concentrated in a few commodities, with the contribution of the top five to overall food inflation typically close to half (reaching 56 percent in 2012). The top contributors are commodities in the high-inflation, high-weight bin: these

Figure 3.9. Contribution of Leading Commodities to Food Inflation
(Percent)

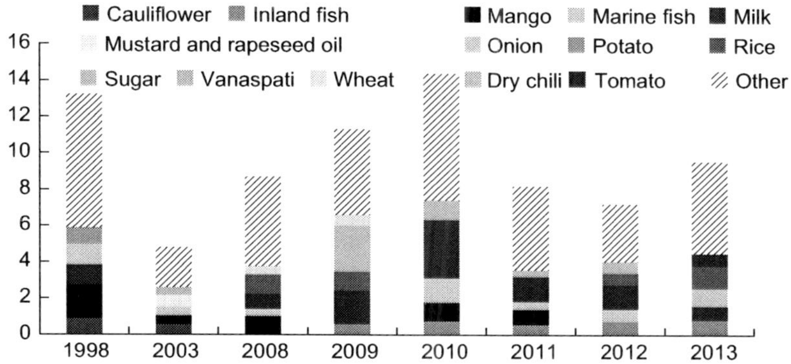

Sources: Ministry of Commerce and Industry; Government of India; and authors' calculations.

include milk and fish in the category of animal source food; onions, potatoes, cauliflower, and mangoes in fruits and vegetables; sugar and edible oils (mustard, rapeseed oil, vanaspati [hydrogenated vegetable cooking oil]) in processed food; and rice and wheat in cereals.

Some variation in the top group has also occurred. While fruits and vegetables were the biggest contributor in 1998, and both animal source foods and processed foods were equally important in 2009, animal source foods have been the leading candidate since 2010. The leading individual items contributing to food inflation have also varied—milk in 2010–12, sugar in 2009, rice in 2008, and mangoes in 1998. Cereals, especially rice, re-emerged as the leading contributor to food inflation in 2013.[9] On the other side, milk has been important over the entire period, and its significance has increased, with its contribution increasing three times by 2010.

WHAT FACTORS EXPLAIN THE RISE IN FOOD INFLATION? CASE STUDIES OF COMMODITIES

Here, we examine in detail the factors that could explain the inflation patterns for commodities, which we have already identified as primary contributors to food inflation during the past two decades. These factors can be classified into long-term factors and those that are more important in the shorter term. The long-term factors include both structural factors and government policies. In particular, we consider the following:

---

[9] Because mango is a seasonal fruit, the inflation figures are based on the few months for which data are available.

- Demand-side factors such as those related to the changing structure of demand away from cereals toward high-value items such as livestock products. This can be attributed to rising incomes and changing lifestyles, such as from urbanization.
- Supply-side factors such as changes in production and productivity. On the supply side, the performance of the agricultural sector in India has been subpar. The sector managed an average annual growth rate of merely 3 percent, and with high volatility, in the 20 years since 1990. In particular, India now has lower yields per hectare of cereals than most comparable countries, including Bangladesh, China, Pakistan, and Sri Lanka.[10]
- Long-term policies such as the cereal-centric focus of the government through a system of producer support prices and maintenance of grain reserves. These long-term structural factors contribute toward built-in inherent inflationary pressures, making the system vulnerable to price increases from short-term shocks.

In addition to longer-term structural factors and policies, short-term factors also contribute to inflation. These include (1) short-term shocks, such as negative shocks from natural disasters like droughts and floods, and positive income shocks, such as rural employment guarantee schemes; (2) domestic policy interventions such as revisions to minimum support prices; (3) trade policy responses such as easing export restrictions; and (4) movements in international commodity prices.

We identified four groups as leading contributors to food inflation: animal source food, fruits and vegetables, processed food, and cereals. We now analyze the trends in inflation for selected items under these groups that we identified as important.

Animal Source Food: Milk

Milk was the most important contributor to food inflation from 2010 to 2012, and has consistently been among the top three contributors since 2008. Moreover, its contribution has followed an upward trend, increasing almost three times from 1998 to 2010. Figure 3.10 shows the evolution of the inflation rate and production of milk over time. Two stylized facts emerge from this figure: the inflation rate for milk has been rising since 2005, with particularly sharp increases in 2009 and 2010; and it appears to have moderated since 2011. In addition, there were price spikes during the lean season relative to the flush season (Figure 3.10, panel 2). We classify the factors responsible for explaining the inflationary patterns in milk as long term and short term.

---

[10] For example, for rice, data from the Food and Agriculture Organization for 2008 suggest that yields in China, at 6.5 tons per hectare, are almost double India's 3.4 tons. Even yields in Bangladesh are higher at 3.9 tons per hectare.

Figure 3.10. Behavior of Milk Prices and Their Key Determinants

Sources: FAOSTAT database; Government of India; Ministry of Commerce and Industry; and authors' calculations.
Note: The dotted line in the first panel shows the Hodrick-Prescott filtered trend.

Long-Term Factors

Milk production globally has undergone a sustained increase, with India now the world's biggest milk producer. The country's production more than doubled from 1990 to 2012 (Figure 3.10, panel 3), and accounts for about 17 percent of the world's total milk production (Kumar and Staal 2010). Moreover, India's per capita availability of milk increased from 176 grams per day in 1990 to 290 grams per day in 2012 (Economic Survey Statistics 2012–13). This is comparable with the world per capita availability of 289 grams per day for 2011 (Mani 2013). Even so, estimates show that India's milk productivity is quite low. Annual milk yield per dairy animal in 2003 was about one-tenth of that achieved in the United States and about one-fifth of New Zealand's (Hemme, Garcia, and Saha 2003).

Indian dairy policies have always protected dairy farmers grouped in cooperatives from low-priced dairy imports (Rakotoarisoa and Gulati 2006). These policies included both domestic support and high trade protection measures. Domestic support has been in the form of subsidies under the government's Operation Flood program launched in 1970, which were part of the plan expenditure.[11] The program is important not only for increasing overall milk supply, but also for smoothing price differentials across time and space, as the program aims to create a national milk grid.

Long-term government trade policy in milk and milk products has also played a role in sustaining inflationary pressures. Trade protection before 1990 mainly took the form of quotas and canalization, whereby all imports were controlled by the National Dairy Development Board. However, the importation of milk powder, under the earlier General Agreement on Tariffs and Trade, was allowed at a rate of zero percent and there was a surge in imports of milk powder. The zero-duty bound rate was subsequently renegotiated and tariff rate quotas imposed since 2000.

India currently allows imports of milk and milk products using a system of tariff rate quotas and import permits. Nonfat dry milk imports, subject to quotas of up to 10,000 metric tons, attract a 60 percent basic duty; and above-quota butter oil imports at a 30 percent basic duty. The tariff rate for imports below 10,000 metric tons is 15 percent. For dairy, India allows exports only of nonfat dry milk.

Domestic policy long subjected the dairy industry to licensing. This was progressively "de-canalized" after 1991 when the private sector, including multinational companies with milk processing and manufacturing plants, were allowed

---

[11] Any expenditure incurred on programs that are detailed under the current Five Year Plan of the central government as advances to states for their plans is called plan expenditure. Provision of such expenditure in the budget is called Plan Expenditure. The system would have changed with the dissolution of the Planning Commission and the implementation of the Finance Commission recommendations for a new revenue-sharing formula between states and the central government.

entry.[12] These supply-side measures increased milk production, yet estimates suggest that in 2004 only 20 percent of milk was distributed through coordinated channels despite these organizational changes. Since 2000, the share of distribution through the organized sector has increased, but only marginally. Of total marketed milk, 75 percent is still handled by informal or traditional milk marketing chains (Kumar and Staal 2010). As a result, even though production increased, the dominance of the informal sector in milk marketing precludes smoothing of supply over time and across space—and this could partly explain the sustained inflationary pressures in milk. The government has approved three new programs to increase productivity and strengthen milk marketing chains; namely, the National Dairy Plan in 2012, the Intensive Dairy Development Programme in 2013, and the Dairy Entrepreneurship Development Programme in 2013. If implemented effectively, these programs could help mitigate milk inflation.

High inflation in milk can also be attributed to a substantial increase in demand. Based on data from different rounds of the National Sample Survey, demand for livestock products has risen significantly (Gandhi and Zhou 2010),[13] with the expenditure share of livestock products increasing 21 percent in 2004/05. Furthermore, within this category, milk and milk products have the largest share, at nearly three-quarters, in both rural and urban areas.

The demand for milk and milk products is most sensitive to changes in income. Based on estimates of expenditure elasticity, demand for milk is projected to grow at about 10.6 percent per year from 2004/05, much larger than the rate of growth in its production, of about 4.2 percent between 2005 and 2010 (Figure 3.10, panel 2).

Overall, inflationary pressures in milk can thus be attributed to rising demand, which has outpaced increases in production, and, importantly, to the skewed structure of dairy supply chains in favor of the informal sector and the resulting inability to smooth the supply of milk over time and across regions.

Short-Term Factors

In addition to longer-term structural factors and policies, we identify key short-term shocks, positive and negative, which could have contributed to the observed patterns of inflation in milk. Two developments since 2005/06 that constitute positive household income shocks are worth mentioning: the National Rural Employment Guarantee Scheme was introduced, with the first phase starting in early 2006; and the Sixth Central Pay Commission was implemented, starting in early 2009. Both brought significant increases in the disposable incomes of

---

[12] In 1992 limited controls were brought back through the Milk and Milk Products Order because of concerns about excessive capacity in milk production, and the sale of adulterated and contaminated milk (Rakotoarisoa and Gulati 2006). In June of that year the registration of milk processing units was reintroduced, and this was an entry barrier for the private sector. In March 2002 the government made important amendments to the order so that it would basically restrict itself to regulating food safety, quality, sanitary, and hygiene conditions of registered milk processing units (Jha 2004).

[13] Gokarn (2010) also presents evidence for rising demand for proteins—both animal-based, such as milk, and plant-based, such as pulses—due to rising incomes and changing lifestyles.

households. Combined with the high income elasticity of milk, these developments could help explain the rising trend in its inflation since 2005, and the spikes in 2009 and 2010. Furthermore, the droughts in 2009 in north India, which raised the price of fodder and the cost of milk production, could also have reinforced the inflationary pressures from the input side.

The moderation in the milk inflation rate since 2011 could be owing to three main factors. First, the improved supply of fodder reduced the costs of milk production and eased inflationary pressures. Second, the slowdown in the economy may have checked the rising demand for milk and milk products. Third, recent government trade policy responses may have played a role. The government allowed duty-free imports of 30,000 metric tons of skimmed milk powder and 15,000 metric tons of butter oil in February 2011, which may have eased supply pressures. At the same time, it imposed an export ban on milk powder and casein, which was lifted in June 2012. Since both exports and imports of milk and milk products constitute a very small share of production (less than 1 percent), these trade measures could, at most, have played only a marginal role in easing inflationary pressures in milk. And since the drop in the inflation rate to single digits is fairly recent, it remains to be seen how far these measures will remain successful in taming inflation.

Cereals: Wheat and Rice

Cereals have generally been among the top 10 contributors to overall food inflation. In some years, rice in particular has been the top contributor, as in 2008 and 2013. Cereals are important to study for three main reasons. First, the government intervenes extensively in the cereals markets, along the supply chain in pricing, procurement, stocking, transport, and distribution. The government is also more proactive in fending off inflationary pressures on cereals than it is with other commodities. Second, cereal prices can put pressure on prices of other food items; for example, through substitution in production away from noncereals. And third, rural wages are linked to cereal prices; hence a rise in these prices could raise production costs for other food items and for nonfood products.

Figure 3.11, panel 1 shows the evolution of the inflation rate for rice and wheat, and its potential correlates. The following four facts emerge from the data: (1) inflation peaked in 1999 for both wheat and rice: in 2006, 2008, and 2012 for wheat, and in 2008 and 2013 for rice; (2) during the peak of the global food price crisis, Indian cereal prices remained comparatively low; (3) the correlation of domestic prices of rice and wheat with international prices is weak; and (4) inflation rates for both wheat and rice picked up from 2011 after declining since 2009.

Long-Term Factors

The production of cereals, wheat in particular, has increased (Figure 3.11, panel 1). Between 1990 and 2012, rice production grew an average 1.8 percent

Figure 3.11. Behavior of Cereal Prices

1. Cereals: production, trade, inflation, and importance in terms of budget shares over time

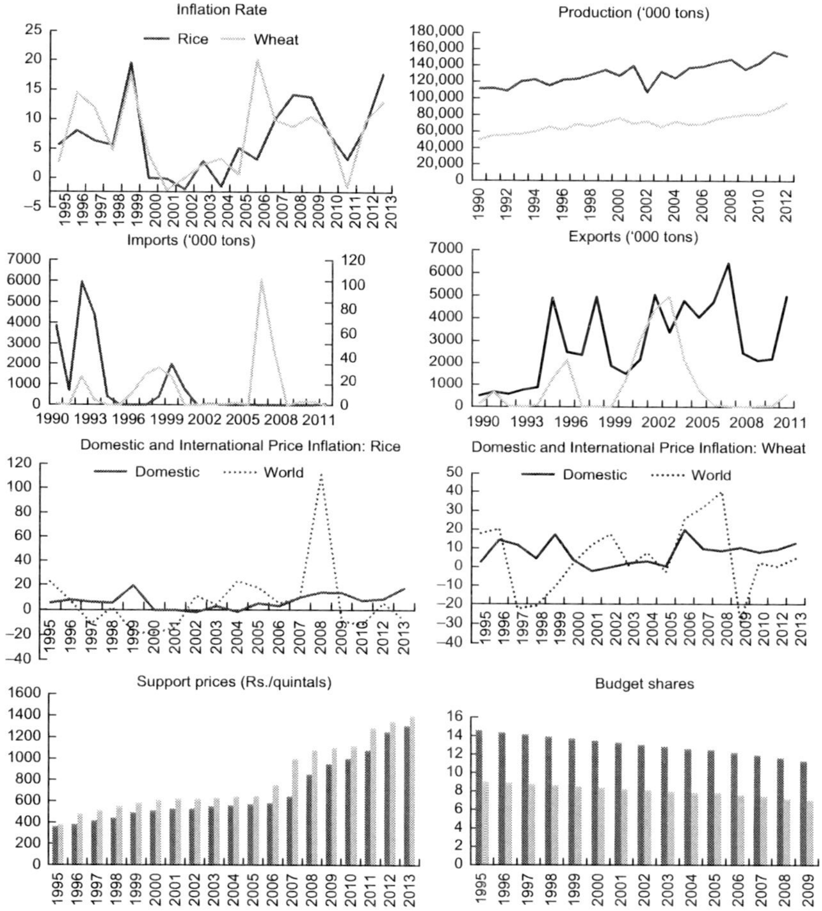

2. Cereals: rice and wheat—monthly inflation rate

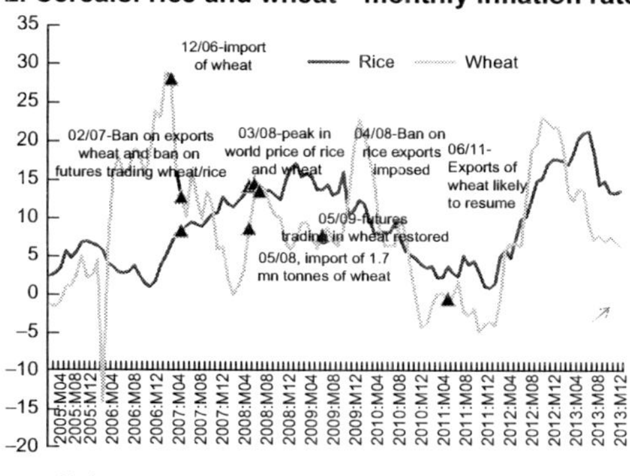

Source: Ministry of Commerce and Industry.

and wheat 3.2 percent annually. However, the adoption of technology in cereal production and better seed varieties by farms has been slow.

Overall, the significant increases in productivity achieved during the Green Revolution have stagnated. Average annual growth in production in the 1990s and 2000s increased only marginally for rice, and declined for wheat. This has been attributed to, among other causes, excess use of fertilizers (particularly urea, which is heavily subsidized) and to falling groundwater levels caused by suboptimal crop choices.

Until about 2009 coarse cereals performed much better than wheat and rice, with an increase in yields of nearly 4 percent in the past decade. Other lagging crops, such as oilseeds and pulses, also outperformed cereals in yields (pulses only marginally). In fact, yield growth across all principal crops is exceeded by cotton, where yields grew as much as 11 percent in the past decade (attributed to the spread of *Bacillus thuringiensis* cotton). Among the major crops that performed worse than the main cereals are sugarcane and some pulses in the disaggregated category.

However, recent years have been exceptional for cereals production in India, particularly for wheat. Wheat production increased 7.5 percent in 2011 and 9.2 percent in 2012, due to higher planting following the government's policy encouraging a steady increase in minimum support prices and generally favorable weather conditions.

On the domestic policy side, the government has intervened heavily in the cereals markets through three main policies: procurement, stocking, and releases through the public distribution system.

The procurement system, in the form of minimum support prices, aims to ensure a reasonable income for farmers and adequate availability of food grains to consumers at reasonable prices. As such, it plays an important role in determining food inflation. The minimum support price acts as a floor and serves as a benchmark for inflation. For it to be effective, the support price has to rise above the market clearing price or the government will not find sellers. Hence, any increases can create inflationary pressures. Gaiha and Kulkarni (2005) showed a strong positive correlation between the minimum support price for rice and wheat and the WPI and CPI-AL after controlling for time trends and levels of income. Although the minimum support price is aimed at providing incentives to farmers, it has often been below international prices. The implication here is that it could act as an implicit tax on farmers, given regulations on exports. Furthermore, as the fiscal costs of the procurement system have spiraled, it has had the long-term effect of reducing public investment in agriculture (Gaiha and Kulkarni 2005).

The government maintains both buffer stocks and strategic grain reserves (the latter since 2008), and uses stockpiling and the release of reserves as tools for price stabilization. On the disbursement side, by keeping issue prices to the public distribution system more or less fixed, the government has tried to stabilize prices for consumers. However, the public distribution system is plagued with leaks and corruption (Kotwal, Murugkar, and Ramaswami 2011) and is inadequate for shielding consumers from price pressures.

Because of a steady increase in the minimum support price and record production, government food grain (wheat and rice) procurement increased strongly from 2007 to 2012. However, government wheat procurement in 2013/14 fell 34 percent because of high open market prices and speculation that domestic production was lower than officially claimed (Singh 2014).[14]

On the trade side, exports of both wheat and non-basmati rice were banned until the mid-1990s (the ban on rice exports was lifted in 1994 and on wheat in 1995). Starting in 2006, there was again a ban on exports of wheat. Meanwhile, the import tariffs on rice (70 percent) and wheat (50 percent) are prohibitive.

With significant public intervention, the government made small reforms to food policies in the 1990s. It more or less removed restrictions on the interstate movement of commodities and proposed to do away with the Essential Commodities Act and replace it with an emergency act.[15] Because agriculture is a state matter, the government has advised states to amend laws such as the Agriculture Produce Marketing Committee Act. In reality, however, most of the restrictive policies have remained unchanged (see Jha, Srinivasan, and Ganesh-Kumar 2010).

Short-Term Factors

Weather is a primary short-term factor contributing to inflation in cereals. A drought in 2009 in north India, for example, was a negative shock, mainly affecting rice production, which fell 8.3 percent in that year (Figure 3.11, panel 1). However, the weather for wheat production in the four years after 2009 has been favorable.

Although the support-price system is a long-term factor in inflation, as already discussed, we now consider revisions in the minimum support price as a short-term cause of inflation. In principle the minimum support price is based on the cost of cultivation calculated by the Commission for Agricultural Costs and Prices, which accounts for all expenses in cash and in kind, rent paid for leased land, the imputed value of family labor, and interest costs on working and fixed capital. Since 1997–98 minimum support prices have often been set higher than

---

[14] High wheat procurement aggravates food grain storage problems, particularly in the origination states of Punjab, Haryana, and Madhya Pradesh. The government's current roofed storage capacity, including leased space, is estimated at 53–54 million metric tons, wherein higher value rice gets priority over wheat for storage. Large quantities of government wheat are kept in the open under tarpaulin and plinth storage, including temporary open storage space during the procurement period (May–July). Storage under these conditions results in significant losses due to damage from rain, temperature fluctuations, rodents and pests, and pilferage (Singh 2014). Government estimates show that over the past eight years, the unit cost of wheat has doubled owing to leasing of warehouses.

[15] According to the Essential Commodities Act, if the government believes it is necessary or expedient to do so for maintaining or increasing supplies of any essential commodity (there is a long list of products containing, among other things, cereals and sugar) for securing their equitable distribution and availability at fair prices, or for securing any essential commodity for the defence of India, it may, by order, provide for regulating or prohibiting the production, supply, and distribution, as well as trade and commerce in such products.

the cost-of-cultivation benchmark (for political reasons). In 2001–02, for example, the weighted average cost of cultivation of eight wheat-producing states was Rs 4.83 per kilogram, while the minimum support price was set at Rs 6.20 per kilogram (Gaiha and Kulkarni 2005).

The minimum support price generally gets revised upward every year, but the magnitude of the increase can vary, sometimes substantially. For example, the minimum support price for both wheat and rice increased one-third in both 2008 and 2009. The increases, moreover, have tended to be higher in high-inflation years to maintain procurement levels. For wheat, the sharp increases in the minimum support price by 15 percent in 2006–07 and 33 percent in 2007–08 coincided with the steady rise in the inflation rate throughout 2006 and the first half of 2008 (Figure 3.11, panel 1). Ideally, the minimum support price should be low so as to reduce procurement in high-inflation years and high in low-inflation years to increase procurement and stock up, as argued by Basu (2010). The absence of any downward revision in the minimum support price, and the lack of adjustment for inflationary pressures, are important factors for inflation in cereals. For example, domestic rice prices have shown a strong upward trend since the beginning of 2012/13 because of significant increases in the minimum support price for paddy rice, coupled with relatively tight domestic supplies (strong government procurement and exports). Domestic prices have weakened since August 2013, perhaps owing to a reduction in export demand (Singh 2014).

Another government domestic policy for tackling price increases is the restriction on futures trading. For example, to reduce incentives for hoarding, the government banned futures trading in rice and wheat in February 2007 (Figure 3.11, panel 2).

Among the main short-term measures to address inflationary pressures in cereals, the government has used trade policy; that is, allowing imports and restricting exports during times of adverse production shocks. The peak in wheat inflation in November 2006 of nearly 30 percent was followed by immediate action with the government importing nearly 6 million tons of wheat, putting significant downward pressure on prices. Concomitant with the May 2008 peak in the inflation rate of nearly 14 percent, the government again imported 1.7 million tons in that month. Export bans were placed on wheat in February 2007, immediately after the inflation rate peaked, and on non-basmati rice in April 2008 during high and rising inflation. Overall, the trade policy response for cereals has been marked by prompt government reaction to rising inflation—in stark contrast to the trade policy response to other commodities, particularly sugar and milk.

With bumper production, the most recent trend in trade in cereals has been more on the export side. Wheat exports took off in August 2012 (the 2007 wheat export ban was lifted in 2011) after the government announced exports of wheat from its own stocks. However, weak international prices affected government wheat exports during 2013/14, forcing it to lower the minimum export price from $300 per ton to $260 per ton in November 2013. Overall, India's wheat exports have not been price competitive in international markets in recent years.

For rice, the government lifted the export ban on non-basmati rice in September 2011, which had been in effect since April 2008. India has since become the world's leading exporter of rice. Export figures for 2013 indicate total rice exports of 10.5 million tons in that year. Exports of basmati rice continue without quantitative restrictions subject to a minimum export price, which changes from time to time. In July 2012 the government removed the minimum export price requirement on basmati rice; the import duties on rice were lifted in March 2008, although there have been no rice imports since then (Singh 2014). The increase in exports of cereals since 2012 is a consequence of increased production and excessive stocks. But this cannot by itself be considered a cause of inflation, which can be predominantly explained by domestic interventions such as the system of support prices.

CONCLUSIONS AND POLICY IMPLICATIONS

This chapter uses a disaggregated commodity level and a high frequency dataset to provide a forensic account of food inflation in India over the past two decades. Our analysis comprises several elements. First, we show that the long-term trend for food inflation has followed a U-shaped path over this period, with a clear reversal of a declining trend starting in the early 2000s. Second, there is evidence for only a moderate correlation between international and domestic food prices, albeit with significant variation across commodities, based on tradability. For example, edible oils exhibit a higher degree of pass-through from international prices. Moreover, the correlation tends to be lower when world prices are high than when they are low.

Rather than treating food as a monolith, we disaggregate it into its different components. We explicitly quantify the contribution of specific commodities to food inflation. Although there is some variation over time, the top contributors are typically milk, fish, sugar, rice, wheat, onions, potatoes, and, to a lesser extent, edible oils.

Finally, we conduct case studies of specific items from the list of top contributors to study the inflation patterns and the factors explaining them. The chapter focuses on milk for animal source foods, and wheat and rice for cereals. The experiences of each of these commodities tell a distinct story about the factors that could be explaining inflation patterns and policy responses. For milk, persistent demand-supply gaps owing to changing consumer tastes, coupled with the nature of the milk supply chain (which prevents smoothing of milk supply over time and across space), could play an important role in explaining persistent milk inflation. For cereals, inflation is more likely a story of excessive domestic interventions, including procurement, stocking, and distribution.

Some unifying messages emerge from the case studies. We find that long-term structural factors and lasting government policies, as well as short-term exogenous shocks and temporary government responses, could explain the patterns of inflation across commodities. Given the built-in inflationary pressures resulting from the existence of long-term factors, short-term shocks can accentuate the effect on inflation. The intensity and speed of government responses also determines how quickly and to what extent inflationary pressures are reined in. Moreover, commodity-specific policies have both direct effects on the targeted sectors and possible spillovers to other sectors. For example, the cereal-centric policies of the government have effects on the supply of high-value items like fruits and vegetables.

The findings in this chapter have several policy implications. A case can be made that in the context of a developing economy like India, both the central bank and other branches of the government can play a meaningful role in tackling inflation. Important policy lessons also emerge for various government departments from the commodity-level analysis. Trade barriers are typically very high and often prohibitive for most food items, including for the top drivers of food inflation. Yet, in the case of the commodities we studied, trade policy (such as export bans, duty-free imports, and so on) has been used as a shock absorber to cool inflationary pressures. One exception (not discussed in this chapter) is edible oil, which was liberalized in the mid-1990s and where inflation has been quite muted. A similar story emerges for pulses, where increased imports moderated inflation. Both raise the question of whether the patterns of inflation we observe in most commodities would have been different were trade more liberalized to begin with.

The case studies further suggest that the effectiveness of trade policy as a stopgap tool to curb inflation depends on the timing of the response. For example, political expediency resulted in a rapid response to inflation in onions and cereals. But the response for milk and sugar was much delayed. Promptness in the implementation of trade policy measures is crucial for two reasons. First, it takes time to build new trade relationships if none existed before (as noted earlier, for clearance to import livestock products, 30-day advance notice is required). Second, international prices, particularly for large buyers like India, could change, affecting import prices.

Based on the case studies, one clear policy message to emphasize is that curbing inflationary pressures could be a rationale in itself to reduce long-lasting import barriers—both tariff and nontariff—in agriculture.[16] Temporary and targeted export regulations could still be warranted from the perspective of controlling inflation, although the long-term application of export regulations needs to be avoided, because it could generate perverse incentives against raising production and productivity.

This chapter's overarching message is that the multiplicity of instruments (different forms of support prices, domestic subsidies, and futures trading, to name a few), as well as the number of government agencies involved, makes the task of controlling inflation a daunting challenge. The in-depth case studies suggest that,

---

[16] Interestingly, India negotiated zero-bound tariffs for a long time for many agricultural commodities, such as rice and dairy products under the Geneva Protocol (1947). The bound tariffs were later renegotiated (as late as 2000) after the Uruguay Round to 80 percent for rice and 60 percent for milk.

in general, policies and institutions primarily created for increasing availability and stabilizing prices—such as relatively closed borders and domestic restrictions—could have actually aggravated the food inflation problem. Therefore, India's persistent food inflation should perhaps reopen the debate over whether a more open and less interventionist stance by the government can stabilize food prices and, hence, overall inflation. The complex web of multiple agencies and multiple instruments, potentially working at cross-purposes, can make the task of enhancing the effectiveness of monetary policy an uphill one.

ANNEX 3.1. TOP 50 CONTRIBUTORS TO FOOD INFLATION

ANNEX TABLE 3.1.1

Contributions by Ranking and Selected Years, 1998–2013 (*Percent*)

Rank	1998		2003		2008		2009		2010		2011		2012		2013	
1	Mango	13.9	Mustard and rapeseed oil	13.7	Rice	12.0	Sugar	22.7	Milk	22.6	Milk	16.8	Milk	18.9	Rice	13.3
2	Onions	8.6	Cauliflower	11.8	Mango	11.7	Milk	16.3	Marine fish	9.3	Mango	9.9	Inland fish	10.2	Onions	10.2
3	Milk	8.3	Marine fish	10.0	Milk	10.0	Rice	9.3	Sugar	7.3	Inland fish	7.0	Marine fish	9.4	Inland fish	8.7
4	Potato	6.8	Mango	9.9	Wheat	5.3	Inland fish	5.1	Mango	7.0	Marine fish	5.6	Sugar	8.9	Milk	7.8
5	Cauliflower	6.7	Vanaspati	8.9	Marine fish	4.3	Wheat	4.9	Inland fish	5.3	Dry chilies	4.3	Rice	8.7	Tomato	7.0
6	Mustard and rapeseed oil	5.9	Soybean oil	7.6	Sugar	4.1	Potato	4.5	Rice	4.1	Soybean oil	3.1	Gram	8.3	Wheat	6.1
7	Soybean oil	4.6	Milk	6.5	Mustard and rapeseed oil	3.0	Cashew kernel	2.9	Turmeric	3.6	Gram	3.0	Wheat	5.9	Tapioca	3.7
8	Tomato	4.4	Groundnut oil	6.0	Vanaspati	3.0	Mutton	2.8	Garlic	2.9	Rice	2.9	Potato	4.0	Brinjal	3.6
9	Rice	3.5	Rice	5.2	Tomato	2.9	Marine fish	2.6	Wheat	2.8	Okra	2.8	Cabbage	3.9	Banana	3.0
10	Cabbage	3.3	Coconut	4.5	Others	2.8	Pigeon pea	2.3	Chicken	2.3	Cashew nuts	2.5	Mustard and rapeseed oil	3.5	Marine fish	2.5
11	Dry chilies	2.9	Wheat flour	4.4	Soybean oil	2.4	Onions	2.3	Banana	1.7	Cotton seed oil	2.5	Groundnut oil	3.2	Wheat flour	2.5
12	Brinjal	2.7	Maida	4.4	Brinjal	2.4	Dry chilies	1.8	Brinjal	1.5	Vanaspati	2.4	Banana	3.0	Chicken	2.4
13	Marine fish	2.5	Unblended tea leaf	3.6	Cotton seed oil	2.3	Turmeric	1.6	Moong	1.4	Coconut	2.4	Others	2.6	Unblended tea leaf	2.0
14	Sugar	2.2	Brinjal	3.5	Cauliflower	2.1	Blended tea leaf	1.5	Mutton	1.4	Maize	2.3	Cotton seed oil	2.2	Mutton	1.9
15	Cotton seed oil	2.0	Cotton seed oil	3.5	Mutton	2.1	Molasses	1.4	Cauliflower	1.3	Mustard and rapeseed oil	2.2	Brinjal	2.2	Cabbage	1.7
16	Groundnut oil	2.0	Rice bran oil	3.4	Tea	2.1	Tea	1.4	Urad	1.3	Grapes	2.2	Soybean oil	2.2	Coconut	1.7
17	Rice bran oil	1.9	Dry chilies	3.2	Blended tea leaf	1.7	Unblended tea leaf	1.4	Beef and buffalo meat	1.2	Cashew kernel	2.1	Mutton	2.2	Ginger	1.5

18	Wheat	1.7	Wheat	2.6	Palm oil	1.5	Tapioca	1.4	Wheat flour	1.2	Orange	1.8	Maize	1.8	Maida	1.4
19	Unblended tea leaf	1.6	Powder milk	2.5	Coriander	1.4	Ghee	1.3	Maida	1.1	Tomato	1.8	Chicken	1.5	Rice bran extraction	1.4
20	Pigeon pea	1.5	Turmeric	2.5	Banana	1.4	Solid brown sugar	1.3	Cabbage	1.1	Jowar	1.6	Black pepper	1.5	Green peas	1.3
21	Inland fish	1.3	Banana	2.5	Papaya	1.3	Urad	1.3	Groundnut oil	1.1	Powder milk	1.5	Tea	1.4	Maize	1.2
22	Orange	1.3	Copra oil	2.2	Coconut	1.2	Moong	1.2	Ghee	1.1	Black pepper	1.5	Palm oil	1.2	Cauliflower	1.1
23	Turmeric	1.2	Blended tea leaf	1.9	Rice bran oil	1.0	Apples	1.0	Egg	1.1	Rice bran oil	1.4	Bajra	1.1	Processed prawn	1.0
24	Chicken	1.2	Tapioca	1.8	Groundnut	1.0	Cashew nuts	1.0	Guava	1.0	Apples	1.4	Blended tea leaf	1.1	Dry chilies	1.0
25	Bagasse	1.1	Onions	1.7	Pigeon pea	1.0	Cotton seed	1.0	Tapioca	1.0	Groundnut oil	1.4	Betelnuts, arecanut	1.1	Bajra	0.9
26	Tea	1.1	Cabbage	1.7	Lentil	1.0	Others	0.9	Tomato	0.9	Lemon	1.4	Groundnut	0.9	Turmeric	0.9
27	Okra	1.1	Pigeon pea	1.3	Ginger	0.9	Bajra	0.9	Vanaspati	0.9	Betelnuts, arecanut	1.3	Egg	0.9	Sugar	0.9
28	Biscuits	1.1	Ghee	1.2	Ghee	0.9	Maize	0.9	Orange	0.8	Coffee	1.2	Okra	0.8	Cattle feed gola	0.9
29	Garlic	1.0	Mutton	1.0	Wheat flour	0.8	Wheat flour	0.9	Papaya	0.8	Mutton	1.2	Powder milk	0.8	Cashew kernel	0.8
30	Black pepper	1.0	Sesame oil	1.0	Unblended tea leaf	0.8	Banana	0.8	Biscuits	0.7	Palm oil	1.1	Ghee	0.8	Unblended tea dust	0.8
31	Sunflower oil	1.0	Orange	0.9	Maida	0.8	Unblended tea dust	0.8	Onions	0.7	Ghee	1.0	Rice bran oil	0.7	Potato	0.8
32	Vanaspati	0.8	Green peas	0.9	Rice bran extraction	0.8	Lentil	0.8	Rice bran extraction	0.7	Papaya	1.0	Cashew kernel	0.7	Blended tea leaf	0.7
33	Grapes	0.8	Canned fish	0.8	Cattle feed gola	0.8	Chicken	0.7	Pigeon pea	0.6	Wheat flour	0.9	Apples	0.7	Papaya	0.7
34	Ghee	0.8	Semolina	0.8	Unblended tea dust	0.7	Khandsari	0.7	Blended tea leaf	0.6	Green peas	0.9	Cattle feed gola	0.7	Moong	0.7

(continued)

ANNEX TABLE 3.1.1 *(continued)*

Contributions by Ranking and Selected Years, 1998–2013 *(Percent)*

Rank	1998		2003		2008		2009		2010		2011		2012		2013	
35	Papaya	0.6	Okra	0.8	Excluding oil	0.7	Cattle feed gola	0.7	Cardamoms	0.6	Tapioca	0.9	Orange	0.6	Cotton seed	0.6
36	Mutton	0.5	Sunflower oil	0.7	Orange	0.7	Maida	0.6	Lychee	0.6	Egg	0.9	Pineapple	0.5	Egg	0.6
37	Cashew nuts	0.5	Bagasse	0.7	Biscuits	0.6	Groundnut	0.5	Cashew kernel	0.5	Sunflower oil	0.8	Besan gram powder	0.5	Guava	0.6
38	Maida	0.4	Groundnut	0.7	Sunflower oil	0.6	Egg	0.5	Powder milk	0.5	Cabbage	0.7	Pork	0.5	Semolina	0.6
39	Sapota	0.3	Cattle feed gola	0.6	Coffee	0.6	Blended tea dust	0.5	Okra	0.5	Copra oil	0.7	Vanaspati	0.5	Garlic	0.5
40	Moong	0.3	Bajra	0.6	Sesame oil	0.6	Garlic	0.5	Maize	0.4	Cotton seed	0.6	Mustard	0.5	Tea	0.5
41	Sesame oil	0.3	Mustard	0.6	Salt	0.6	Papaya	0.5	Processed prawn	0.4	Mixed spices	0.6	Rice bran extraction	0.4	Cashew nuts	0.5
42	Blended tea leaf	0.3	Coffee	0.5	Rice bran	0.6	Biscuits	0.5	Cattle feed gola	0.4	Blended tea leaf	0.6	Solid brown sugar	0.4	Rice bran	0.5
43	Salt	0.3	Maize	0.5	Tapioca	0.6	Green peas	0.4	Pork	0.4	Sapota	0.5	Papad	0.4	Pigeon pea	0.5
44	Solid brown sugar	0.3	Cashew nuts	0.5	Guava	0.5	Mustard	0.4	Wheat bran	0.4	Banana	0.5	Lentil	0.4	Coriander	0.5
45	Khandsari	0.3	Guava	0.4	Mustard	0.5	Rice bran extraction	0.4	Jowar	0.4	Beef and buffalo meat	0.5	Cotton seed	0.4	Vanaspati	0.4
46	Lentil	0.2	Papaya	0.4	Turmeric	0.5	Orange	0.4	Butter	0.3	Food powder	0.5	Sunflower oil	0.4	Dry ginger	0.4
47	Gram	0.2	Dry ginger	0.4	Solid brown sugar	0.5	Vegetable seeds	0.4	Solid brown sugar	0.3	Sugar	0.5	Ragi	0.3	Biscuits	0.4
48	Butter	0.2	Apples	0.4	Dry chilies	0.5	Coffee	0.4	Grapes	0.3	Onions	0.5	Wheat bran	0.3	Others	0.4
49	Mustard	0.2	Coriander	0.4	Groundnut oil	0.5	Powder milk	0.3	Unblended tea leaf	0.3	Vegetable seeds	0.5	Sesame oil	0.3	Sweet potato	0.4
50	Cattle feed gola	0.2	Ragi	0.3	Grapes	0.5	Sapota	0.3	Semolina	0.3	Bajra	0.4	Maida	0.3	Ragi	0.4

Source: Authors' calculations.

REFERENCES

Basu, Kaushik. 2010. "The Economics of Food Grains Management in India." Working Paper, Ministry of Finance, New Delhi. www.finmin.nic.in/WorkingPaper/Foodgrain.pdf.

Cecchetti, Stephen. 2007. "Core Inflation Is an Unreliable Guide." VoxEU, March 1. http://www.voxeu.org/article/why-core-inflation.

de Janvry, Alain, and E. Sadoulet. 2009. "The Impact of Rising Food Prices on Household Welfare in India." Goldman School of Public Policy Working Paper, University of California, Berkeley.

Gaiha, Raghav, and Vani S. Kulkarni. 2005. "Foodgrain Surpluses, Yields and Prices in India." Presentation at the Global Forum on Agriculture: Policy Coherence for Development, Paris, November 30–December 1.

Gandhi, Vasant P., and Zhang-Yue Zhou. 2010. "Rising Demand for Livestock Products in India: Nature, Patterns and Implications." *Australasian Agribusiness Review* 18 (7): 103–135.

Gokarn, Subir. 2010. "The Price of Protein." Address at conference in honor of Kirit Parikh at the Indira Gandhi Institute of Development Research, Mumbai, October 26. http://www.bis.org/review/r101103e.pdf.

Hemme, Torsten, Otto Garcia, and Amit Saha. 2003. "A Review of Milk Production in India with Particular Emphasis on Small-Scale Producers." Working Paper 2, Food and Agriculture Organization, Rome.

Jha, Brajesh. 2004. "India's Dairy Sector in the Emerging Trade Order." Working Paper Series E/243/2004, Institute of Economic Growth, New Delhi.

Jha, Raghbendra. 2005. "Inflation Targeting in India: Issues and Prospects." Working Paper 2005/04, Australian National University, Australia South Asia Research Centre, Canberra.

Jha, Shikha, P. V. Srinivasan, and A. Ganesh-Kumar. 2010. "Achieving Food Security in a Cost-Effective Way: Implications of Domestic Deregulation and Liberalized Trade in India." In *Liberalizing Foodgrains Markets: Experiences, Impact and Lessons from South Asia*, edited by A. Ganesh-Kumar, Devesh Roy, and Ashok Gulati. New Delhi: Oxford University Press.

Kotwal, Ashok, Milind Murugkar, and Bharat Ramaswami. 2011. "PDS Forever?" *Economic and Political Weekly* 46 (2): 72–76.

Kumar, Anjani, and Steven J. Staal. 2010. "Is Traditional Milk Marketing and Processing Viable and Efficient? An Empirical Evidence from Assam, India." *Quarterly Journal of International Agriculture* 49 (3): 213–25.

Mani, Radha. 2013. "India: Dairy and Products Annual." Global Agriculture Information Network Report IN 3119, United States Department of Agriculture, Washington.

Misra, Rajmal, and Sangita Misra. 2009. "Transmission from International Food Prices to Domestic Food Prices: The Indian Evidence." Staff Studies 6, Reserve Bank of India, Mumbai.

Panagariya, Arvind. 2005. "Agricultural Liberalisation and the Least Developed Countries: Six Fallacies." *World Economy* 28 (9): 1277–99.

Rakotoarisoa, Manitra, and Ashok Gulati. 2006. "Competitiveness and Trade Potential of India's Dairy Industry." *Food Policy* 31 (3): 216–27.

Reserve Bank of India (RBI). 2014. First Bi-Monthly Monetary Policy Statement, 2014–15. http://rbidocs.rbi.org.in/rdocs/PressRelease/PDFs/EPFS192BE268D98D3.pdf.

Singh, Santosh. 2014. "Grain and Feed Annual." Global Agriculture Information Network ReportIN 4005, United States Department of Agriculture, Washington.

Srinivasan T. N. 2008. "Price Indices and Inflation Rates." *Economic and Political Weekly* 43 (26 and 27): 115–23.

CHAPTER 4

Understanding India's Food Inflation Through the Lens of Demand and Supply

RAHUL ANAND, NARESH KUMAR, AND VOLODYMYR TULIN

Food inflation in India, unlike in many advanced economies, has had a nontrivial impact on aggregate retail inflation. This reflects, among other things, the large share of food expenditure in total household expenditure and its correspondingly heavy weight in the consumer price index (CPI), inflation expectations which are anchored by food inflation, and wage indexation to consumer price inflation and thereby indirectly to food inflation.

The importance of these factors in shaping India's inflation dynamics and determining the conduct of monetary policy, particularly of large second-round effects of food price shocks, has been documented (Anand, Ding, and Tulin 2014; RBI 2014a). However, there is no consensus on the possible drivers of persistently high food inflation in India. The relative importance of demand and supply factors and the role of related nonmonetary policies—notably the role of minimum support prices and the Mahatma Gandhi National Rural Employment Guarantee Act—are still debated.

Gokarn (2011), in his comprehensive analysis of India's key food price issues since the 1960s, concludes that when food prices rise while supply stagnates or fails to keep up, there is no alternative to curbing food inflation other than raising supply rapidly. Although many studies[1] have investigated demand and supply of the major food commodities in India and projected demand and supply scenarios, even at the commodity level, analysis of food prices in an equilibrating demand-supply framework is practically nonexistent.

This chapter explores the relative role of demand and supply factors and quantifies their impact on the dynamics of food prices in India in a general equilibrium setting. To do this, we adopt a two-stage strategy. First, we estimate individual demand for major food product groups and examine key household consumption patterns using household expenditure surveys. We then construct a general equilibrium model for given output growth scenarios, allowing us to estimate the impact of demand-side pressure on relative food prices. Using this model, we estimate the size of relative food prices since 2006 and simulate possible scenarios

[1] See Ganesh-Kumar and others (2012) for literature review, as well as for medium-term forecasts on India's demand and supply gaps for food grains.

of the contribution of relative food inflation in the medium term. For scenario analysis, the approach of abstracting away from explicit modeling of food supply is not without limitations,[2] and the estimated inflation outcomes are likely to have an upward bias. Nonetheless, as own-price supply elasticities (Kumar and others 2010) are found to be significantly below demand elasticities, effects on prices from shifts in demand are likely to be only minimally mitigated by response of supply, particularly over the near term.

Our results suggest that given the heavy weight of food in household expenditure, robust real income growth in the past decade has resulted in substantial demand-side pressures. Because the supply of key agricultural products did not keep pace with real personal consumption growth, growth in food prices has outpaced nonfood prices by about 3½ percent since 2006/07. And with real personal consumption growth expected to be robust and food supply relatively sluggish in the coming years, it seems that India's inflation dynamics will continue to be shaped by the relative food price trend.

Our estimates suggest that in the absence of a stronger food supply growth response, relative food inflation can contribute about 1¼ percentage points to headline inflation annually. If private consumption picks up to 7 percent and supply growth response remains at its historical level, food inflation is likely to exceed nonfood inflation by 2½–3 percentage points per year. Monetary policy will therefore need to react appropriately to both supply shocks and underlying inflation trends, particularly in the context of the flexible inflation targeting adopted in February 2015. Achieving a long-term inflation target of 4 percent will hinge on enhancing food supply, market-based pricing of agricultural produce, and reducing price distortions. Our simulation analysis also indicates that given India's supply-side vulnerabilities, the recommended inflation band of ±2 percent appears broadly appropriate. A well-designed cereal buffer stock liquidation policy could help mitigate inflation volatility. In addition, administered price setting, such as through minimum support prices and supporting policies, will continue to pose challenges for monetary policy management in India. At the current juncture when relative food prices do not appear to be a key driver of headline inflation, ensuring a durable reduction in headline inflation will require the continuation of a relatively tight monetary stance to durably lower core inflation so as to sustainably reduce inflation expectations and anchor them at a lower level.

RECENT INFLATION DYNAMICS IN INDIA

High and persistent inflation has been a key macroeconomic challenge facing India (IMF 2014a, 2014b; Anand, Ding, and Tulin 2014). Elevated inflation coinciding with the growth slowdown has distinguished India from other major emerging market economies in recent years. Though several reasons have been

[2] As in an inelastic supply system, only price but not supply adjusts to equilibrate demand.

Figure 4.1. Headline and Food Inflation
(Year-over-year percent change)

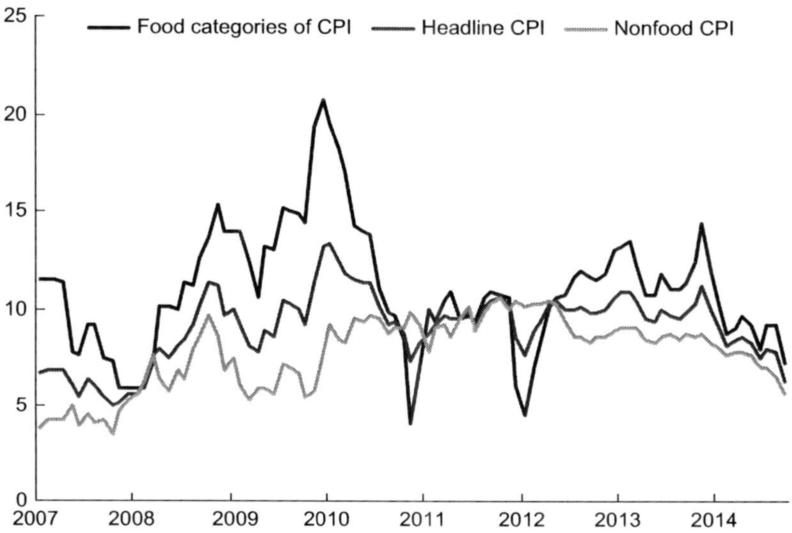

Sources: Haver Analytics; and IMF staff calculations.
Note: CPI = consumer price index.

put forward to explain this persistently high inflation in India, food inflation has been often singled out as a key driver. Indeed, food inflation has exceeded nonfood inflation by about 3½ percentage points on average during 2006/07–2013/14, contributing directly about 1¾ percentage points to headline CPI inflation (Figure 4.1). Furthermore, through its second-round effects on core inflation (Anand, Ding, and Tulin 2014), food inflation has added to the inflationary pressure.

INDIA'S FOOD INFLATION: A TIMELINE

A chronological account of India's food inflation reveals several important events, which have been widely documented and researched (Gokarn 2011; Sonna and others 2014):

- A set of policy interventions commonly known as the Green Revolution caused food inflation episodes to be short-lived and less intense during the 1980s and 1990s. These interventions combined price incentives, input subsidies, technological inputs and infrastructure investments (particularly in irrigation), and, importantly, buffer stocks. The policy interventions helped to raise and stabilize the productivity of cereal cultivation, as well as some other crops (Gokarn 2011).

Figure 4.2. Policy Interventions and Outcomes: Buffer Stocks of Rice and Wheat

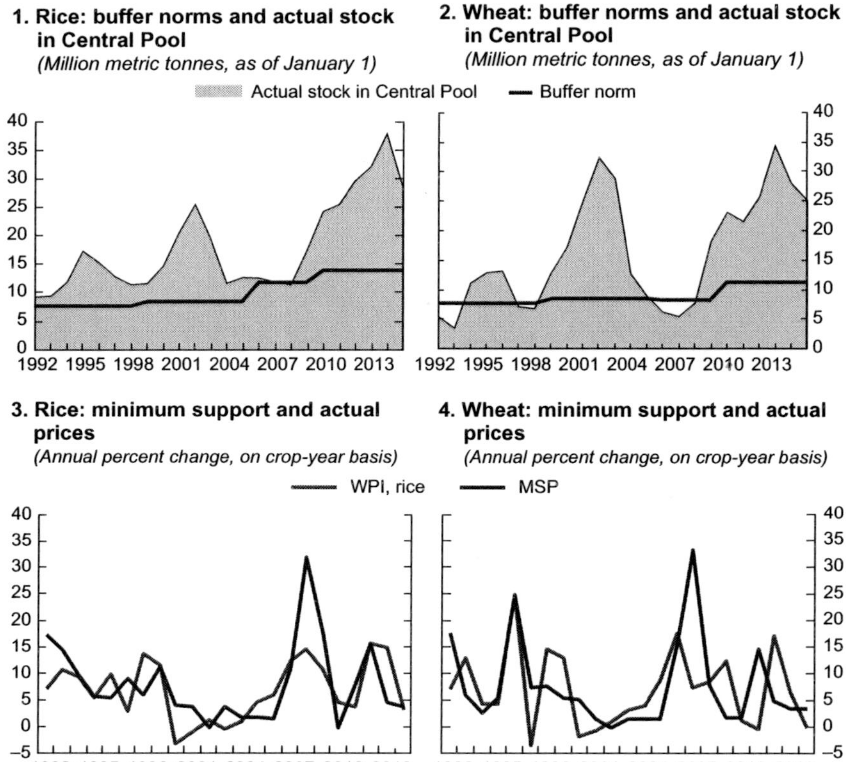

Sources: Food Corporation of India; and IMF staff calculations.
Note: In panels 3 and 4, crop year denotes a 12-month period from July through next June.
MSP = minimum support price; WPI = wholesale price index.

- However, during the 1990s and 2000s, agricultural growth slowed, averaging about 3.5 percent per year. Cereal yields grew by only 1½ percent per year in the 2000s. Amid firming consumer demand, running down buffer stocks helped contain food inflation during the early 2000s, as increases in minimum support prices moderated (Figure 4.2).
- The government's response, beginning in 2007, to a surge in global food prices helped limit the impact on domestic food prices (OECD 2009). However, buffer stocks continued to fall, eventually to significantly below established norms. For example, around mid-2007, the wheat stock in the Central Pool amounted to only about half of the buffer stock norm. Moreover, a series of government measures—such as large increases in food and fertilizer subsidies, and an increase of more than 30 percent in minimum

Figure 4.3. Global Food Commodity Prices
(Index, 2010 = 100, U.S. dollar-based)

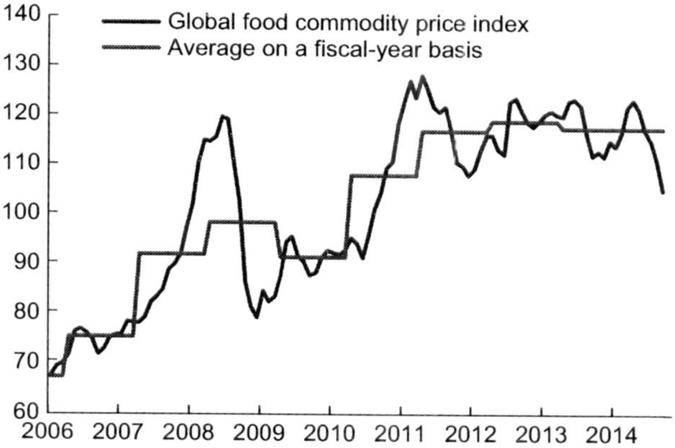

Source: IMF, International Financial Statistics database.

support prices for the 2008/09 season—likely not only postponed, but also prolonged inflationary pressures even after global food commodity prices abated (Figure 4.3). The global commodity price spike of 2007–08 also led to excessive stock hoarding in subsequent years, a shift in the buffer stock policy resulting in sustained inflationary pressure (Figure 4.2).[3]

- Deficient rainfall, as a result of weaker monsoon in 2009, affected the output of key agricultural crops and was an important factor behind elevated food inflation spilling into 2010 (RBI 2014b). Overall, growth in food inflation outpaced nonfood inflation by almost 30 percentage points during 2006–10: food inflation exceeded nonfood inflation on an average by almost 7½ percentage points per year during this period (Figure 4.3).
- Even though 2010 was a good monsoon year, food inflation remained high. Furthermore, despite 2011 being another relatively good monsoon year, food inflation surged again following a minor blip in food prices. This time, nonfood inflation also picked up, averaging 9½ percent during 2010–13, a full 3 percentage points higher than the average of 6½ percent during 2006–09.
- Thus, even as relative food prices staged only a moderate gain during 2010–14, headline inflation remained high, driven by entrenched, elevated inflation expectations (Figure 4.4). This accelerated the inflationary spiral with food inflation feeding quickly into wages and core inflation (Figure 4.5).

---

[3]In the aftermath of the surge in global commodity prices, not only food importers but also the largest exporters, namely China and India, became wary of overreliance on international grain markets, particularly in times of food emergency, which led to large-scale grain procurement and hoarding.

Figure 4.4. India: Food versus Nonfood Inflation
(Index, 2006 = 100)

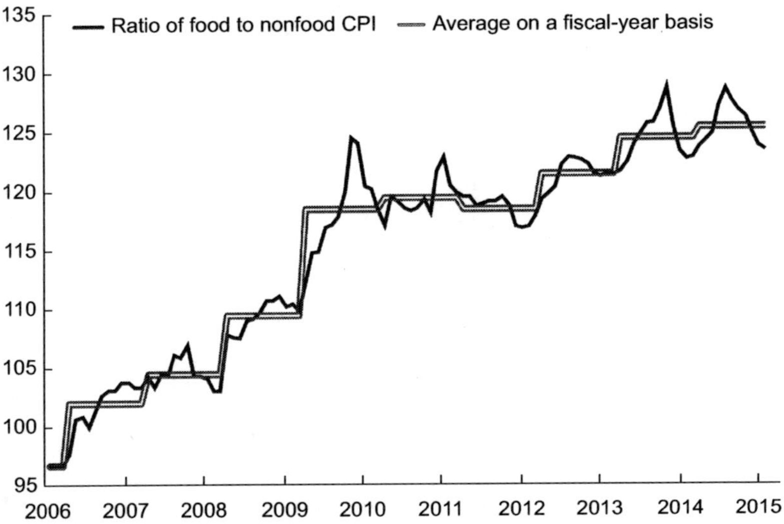

Sources: Haver Analytics; and IMF staff calculations.
Note: Monthly data; CPI = consumer price index.

Figure 4.5. Food Inflation and Household Inflation Expectations
(Percent)

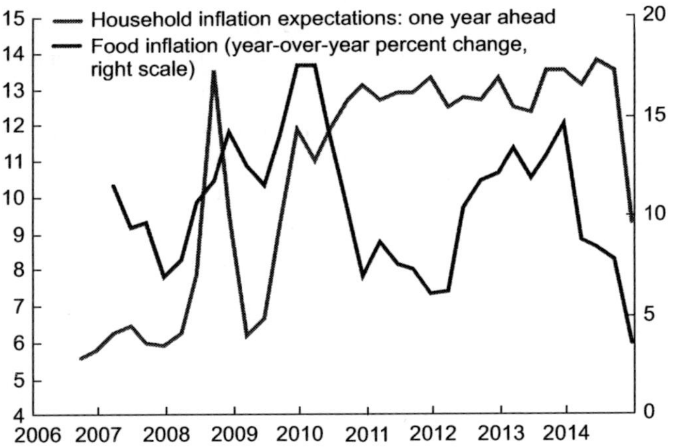

Source: Reserve Bank of India.

Figure 4.6. India: Private Consumption
(Annual percent change)

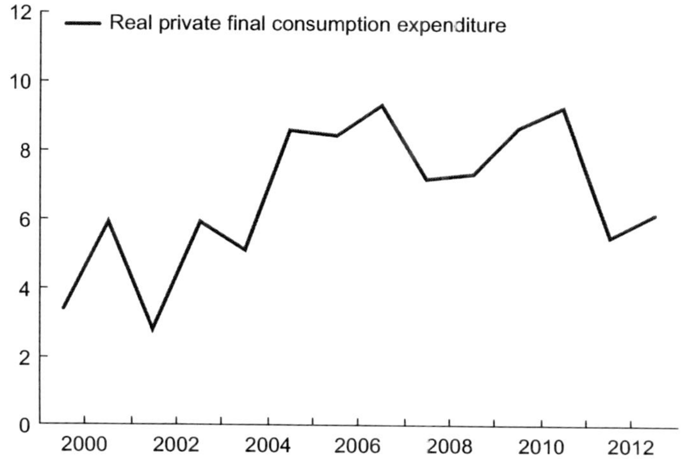

Sources: Haver Analytics; and IMF staff calculations.

INDIA'S FOOD INFLATION: THE SUPPLY-DEMAND ANGLE

While a number of supply-side factors could be responsible for food price pressures, they need to be scrutinized in the context of India's growing food demand.

Underpinned by robust economic growth, India's private consumption growth rose to about 8½ percent during 2005/06–2011/12 from a 5 percent average growth rate during 1998/99–2004/05 (Figure 4.6). Moreover, private consumption growth was essentially unaffected by the global financial crisis. However, following a slowdown in the economy, private consumption growth declined in 2012/13 and 2013/14; demand-side pressures on food inflation were thereby reduced.

Agricultural GDP growth remained robust during 2005/06–2007/08, growing at about 5 percent per year (Figure 4.7). However, with private consumption growing at 9 percent during these years, demand-side pressures aggravated by a surge in global commodity prices contributed significantly to the rise in relative food prices (see Figure 4.4). During these three years, food inflation accelerated significantly. For example, wholesale price index (WPI) food inflation[4] jumped to about 8¾ percent per year from an average

[4]WPI food inflation averaged slightly under 5 percent during 1994/95–2004/05 and about 9¾ percent during 2004/05–2013/14. WPI food inflation has been broadly in line with CPI food developments, while providing a longer series of a consistently defined gauge of aggregate food prices.

Figure 4.7. Supply and Demand for Food

(Annual percent change, real)

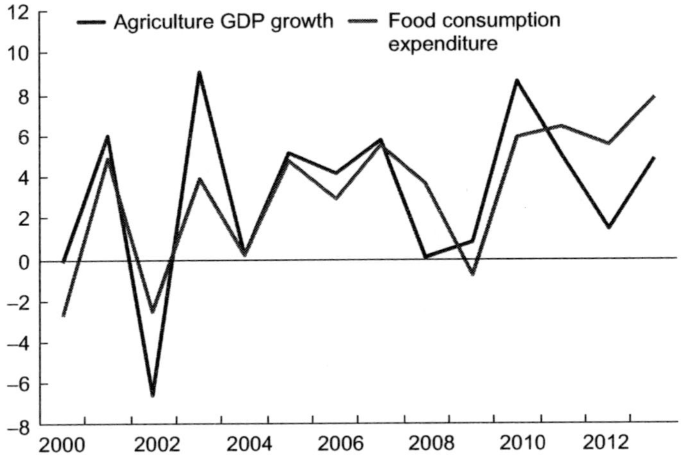

Sources: Haver Analytics; and IMF staff calculations.

of 1¾ percent during 2000/01–2004/05. Furthermore, the surge in relative food prices continued during 2008/09–2009/10. Even though private consumption growth moderated due to the global financial crisis, it remained strong during 2008/09–2009/10. Coupled with weak agricultural GDP growth in those years due to deficient rainfall, it led to a further rise in relative food prices.

As a result of a good monsoon, agricultural GDP growth recovered in 2010/11 and 2011/12 to 8½ and 5 percent, respectively (Figure 4.7). Simultaneously, with a concurrent moderation in private consumption growth due to the economic slowdown, relative food prices remained broadly stable during this period. At the same time, however, nonfood inflation was high and remained firm in the 9–10 percent range, partly as a result of an accommodative monetary stance resulting from a delayed withdrawal of stimulus provided during the global financial crisis (Anand, Ding, and Tulin 2014; Mohan and Kapur 2015).

INDIA'S FOOD INFLATION: A RESULT OF LOOSE MONETARY POLICY

While monetary policy in India was suitably eased to counter the global financial crisis, the subsequent tightening that began in 2010 was not sufficient to rein in inflation, which had become generalized by then. As suggested by Anand, Ding, and Tulin (2014), the short-term interest rate gap vis-à-vis its optimal level, a gauge of the monetary stance, averaged about 100 basis points during 2011–12

Figure 4.8. Interest Rates: Predicted versus Actual[1]

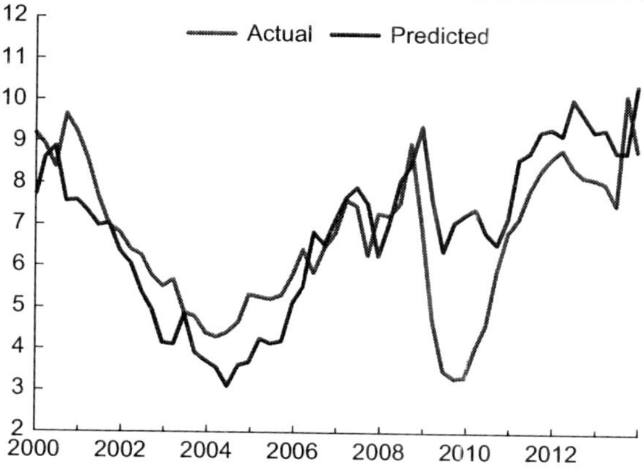

Source: Anand, Ding, and Tulin (2014).
[1]Interest rate corresponds to 3-month Treasury bill yield.

(Figure 4.8). Successive IMF India Staff Reports highlighted the role of an overly accommodative monetary stance in fostering persistently high inflation, which argued for a tighter monetary stance to counter inflation and inflationary pressures (IMF 2011, 2012, 2013, 2014a, 2014b). Concerns over insufficient tightening were also raised in India.[5]

THE MODELING FRAMEWORK

To study the interaction of food demand and supply in determining food prices in India, we use a modeling framework to estimate the demand of key food item groups that incorporates India's household surveys. We then model the supply of these food item groups, and use a general equilibrium framework to analyze the interaction of demand and supply in determining food prices in India.

As highlighted in the previous section, growing income per capita has translated into higher demand for food. Engel's law states that as the average household income increases, the average share of food expenditure in total expenditure declines. The Engel curve for food has been found to be log-linear and stable, both over time and across societies (Banks, Blundell, and Lewbel 1997; Beatty and Larsen 2005; Blundell, Duncan, and Pendakur 1998; Leser 1963; Yatchew 2003).

[5]As, for example, noted by Chakravarthi Rangarajan in his June 23, 2014 interview with the *Economic Times:* "Perhaps, the monetary policy instruments could have been used differently. Tightening in small steps didn't have an impact on inflation. The alternative could have been to raise rates sharply and we could have had a better impact on inflation."

Household Demand Analysis

Our food demand modeling approach relies on a two-stage budgeting framework, which assumes that consumers allocate their income in two steps. In the first, they decide on spending across broad categories of goods or services—our model entails a choice between food and nonfood. Each consumer decides on how much to spend on food items and nonfood items. In the second step, each consumer simultaneously decides on how to allocate the total food expenditure across specific food categories; for example, how much of the food expenditure budget will be spent on pulses versus how much on milk products. We look at six food item groups: cereals; pulses; milk; egg, fish and meat; vegetables and fruits; and a category that includes oil and fats, sugar, condiments, and spices.

The two-stage approach invokes the block independence idea or strong group-separability assumption of the consumer preference theory, which implies that preferences among items within one broad consumption group are not dependent on the quantities consumed within other broad consumption groups. In other words, demand for specific nonfood items is not influenced by demand decisions for specific food items. A simple first-stage budgeting, which involves a choice between only two broad expenditure groups (namely, food and nonfood), allows us to greatly simplify the econometric estimation. The added condition of the expenditure weights—that the budget share on food and nonfood adds up to unity—implies that the first-stage estimation can be reduced to a single equation least squares regression with coefficient restrictions rather than the estimation of a system of equations.

However, when it comes to spending decisions within specific expenditure categories, understanding demand for several food items requires demand modeling using a system of equations approach. This is important given that independent demand equations for various food items will not capture appropriately the demand for individual food items, as different food products can be substitutes or complements with important cross-price effects. A system of equations approach is, therefore, employed to estimate the demand of various food items within the broader food category. Overall, the two-stage budgeting procedure allows us to use reasonable assumptions regarding consumer behavior—the separability of consumer choice with respect to aggregate food and nonfood consumption and the consumption of various food items, while preserving some important characteristics of demand for various food items.

More specifically, to investigate the consumption patterns of Indian households, we employ a two-stage quadratic almost ideal demand system (QUAIDS) model (Banks, Blundell, and Lewbel 1997). QUAIDS is an extension of the almost ideal demand system (AIDS) approach (Deaton and Muellbauer 1980) that includes a quadratic expenditure term to model nonlinearity of Engel curves. In the literature, AIDS-based approaches have been the preferred specification for estimating demand systems, owing to their consistency with consumer theory, exact aggregation properties, and ease of estimation. QUAIDS extensions, which provide a more accurate picture of consumer behavior across income groups, have proven useful in studying consumer food demand patterns, including those in India (Mittal 2010).

The first stage of QUAIDS involves estimating a first-step budgeting equation, whereby consumers make a choice about how much total expenditure will be devoted to food, conditional on the consumption of nonfood goods and services, and the demographic and socioeconomic characteristics of households. The nonlinearity in food expenditure—implying that a relatively lower share of income will be spent on food as income increases—is modeled through a quadratic expenditure term. Because we focus on only two broad categories of consumer expenditure—food and nonfood—the adding-up restriction on the expenditure weights implies that the first-stage estimation is reduced to a single equation least squares estimation. See Annex 4.1 for additional details.

In the second stage, we estimate a system of simultaneous equations, each representing demand for specific food item categories (cereals; pulses; milk; egg, fish, and meat; vegetables and fruits; and others). Here, we specify a QUAIDS system of individual food item demand equations (see for example, Poi 2002, 2008) using the general QUAIDS structure outlined in Box 4.1, where expenditure weights represent expenditure on specific food categories as a share of the consumer's total expenditure on food. In turn, the value of a consumer's total expenditure on food is the predicted value of aggregate food expenditure from the first-stage estimation results. Given consumer choice over multiple food items, the second-stage QUAIDS specification is estimated as a system of nonlinear, seemingly unrelated regressions through iterated feasible generalized least squares, using the Stata routine described in Poi (2008).

Supply Analysis

The consumer demand model we use for estimation and simulation purposes assumes that prices, food prices in particular, are predetermined. The exogeneity of prices, which we assume, is rather common in demand system modeling. From the aggregate economy perspective, this is equivalent to assuming that supply is perfectly elastic in prices, and that it is demand that adjusts to clear the markets.[6] A perfectly elastic supply and market-clearing demand is an appropriate assumption when dealing with traded goods, such as imported foods, in the case of small open economies. Of course, such assumptions may be somewhat unrealistic for the analysis of food supply in a country like India.

Nonetheless, studies of the supply of food commodities production in India suggest that own-price elasticities are low, particularly compared to own-price elasticities of demand (Kumar and others 2010). Therefore, the effect on prices

[6] Inelastic supply assumptions are usually more suitable to analyze demand for goods with fixed prices, as a result of administered price setting.

BOX 4.1 General QUAIDS Specification

In the quadratic almost ideal demand system (QUAIDS) model, a consumer's expenditure shares across the set of expenditure categories are defined by equations 1 and 2:

$$w_{i,j} = \frac{p_{i,j} q_{i,j}}{m_i} \tag{1}$$

$$\sum_{j=1}^{N} w_{i,j} = 1 \tag{2}$$

where $p_{i,j}$ and $q_{i,j}$ are price and quantity of item j purchased or consumed by an individual i, and $w_{i,j}$ is expenditure weight on item j in individual i's total expenditure (denoted by m_i) across all related products $j = \overline{1, N}$. In the first stage of the consumer budgeting choice, $w_{i,j}$ refers to the shares of expenditure on food versus nonfood categories as a part of the consumer's total expenditure. In the second budgeting stage, $w_{i,j}$ refers to expenditure on specific food commodities within the consumer's total expenditure on food. Therefore, a general econometric specification prescribed by QUAIDS for expenditure weights takes the form:

$$w_{i,j} = \alpha_j + \sum_{n=1}^{N} \gamma_{j,n} \ln p_{i,n} + \beta_j \ln \frac{m_i}{P(\mathbf{p}_i)} + \frac{\lambda_j}{b(\mathbf{p}_i)} \left[\ln \frac{m_i}{P(\mathbf{p}_i)} \right]^2 + \vartheta_{i,j} \tag{3}$$

where subscript i represents an individual consumer, while m_i denotes total expenditure per capita. As well, $\mathbf{p}_i$ is the vector of prices faced by consumer i, and $b(\mathbf{p}_i)$ is the Cobb-Douglas price index, defined as:

$$b(\mathbf{p}_i) \equiv \prod_{j=1}^{N} p_{i,j}^{\beta_j} \tag{4}$$

In $P(\mathbf{p}_i)$ is a price index defined as:

$$\ln P(\mathbf{p}_i) \equiv \alpha_0 + \sum_{n=1}^{N} \alpha_n \ln p_{i,n} + \frac{1}{2} \sum_{j=1}^{N} \sum_{n=1}^{N} \gamma_{j,n} \ln p_{i,j} \ln p_{i,n} \tag{5}$$

Note that the term $\frac{m_i}{P(p_i)}$ essentially represents a measure of an individual's real consumption. The quadratic term for the logarithm of consumption allows us to capture the nonlinearity of consumption of specific product categories with respect to total expenditure on related products. $\vartheta_{i,j}$ denotes a residual term, with the vector of residuals $\vartheta = [\vartheta_1, \ldots, \vartheta_N]$ which has a multivariate normal distribution with a covariance matrix of Σ. The adding-up condition given by equation 2, that expenditure shares sum up to one, implies that Σ is singular and requires further restrictions on the coefficients:

$$\sum_{j=1}^{N} \alpha_j = 1, \quad \sum_{j=1}^{N} \beta_j = 0, \quad \sum_{j=1}^{N} \lambda_j = 0, \text{ and } \sum_{j=1}^{N} \gamma_{j,n} = 0 \, \forall n \tag{6}$$

Also, two other conditions are imposed to ensure consistency with the economic theory of demand.

(1) Demand function homogeneity of degree zero in prices and income requires:

$$\sum_{n=1}^{N} \gamma_{j,n} = 0 \, \forall j \tag{7}$$

BOX 4.1 (*Continued*)

(2) whereas Slutsky symmetry implies:

$$\gamma_{j,n} = \gamma_{n,j} \tag{8}$$

In the first stage, we estimate the aggregate food demand equation compared to total expenditure on nonfood categories. As mentioned, the adding-up condition (as there are only two goods of choice implying that the sum of weights must equal one) implies that consumer demand can be estimated within a single equation econometric specification. Imposing additional economic theory-based conditions on demand specification, namely the symmetry of the Slutsky matrix and the homogeneity of demand function of degree zero in prices and income, the general form of QUAIDS specification (3) can be reduced to the following food demand equation, which can be estimated using least squares:

$$\frac{m_i^f}{Y_i} = \alpha_f + \gamma_{f,f}\left(\ln P_i^f - \ln P_i^{nf}\right) + \beta_f \ln \frac{Y_i}{P(\boldsymbol{p}_i)} + \frac{\lambda_f}{b(\boldsymbol{p}_i)}\left(\ln \frac{Y_i}{P(\boldsymbol{p}_i)}\right)^2 + \varepsilon_i \tag{9}$$

where consumer-specific aggregate price indexes $b(\boldsymbol{p}_i)$ and $P(\boldsymbol{p}_i)$ are defined according to equations 4 and 5, which after imposing the mentioned coefficient restrictions, reduce to:

$$\ln b(\boldsymbol{p}_i) = \beta_f\left(\ln P_i^f - \ln P_i^{nf}\right) \tag{10}$$

$$\ln P(\boldsymbol{p}_i) = \alpha_0 + \alpha_f\left(\ln P_i^f - \ln P_i^{nf}\right) + \ln P_i^{nf} + \frac{1}{2}\gamma_{f,f}\left(\ln P_i^f - \ln P_i^{nf}\right)^2 \tag{11}$$

where m^f denotes total per capita expenditure on food; P^f and P^{nf} represent consumer-specific aggregate price index of food and nonfood items, respectively; Y is per capita total consumption expenditure; and ε is an error term.

Substituting aggregate price indexes specifications given by equations 10 and 11 into equation 9, we estimate the resulting food demand function using nonlinear least squares using household-level data. To calculate aggregate price indexes to be used in the first stage of the budgeting procedure, consumer-specific food P^f and nonfood price P^{nf} indexes are approximated using Stone price indexes:[1]

$$\ln P_i = \sum_{j=1}^{N} w_{i,j} \ln p_{i,j} \tag{12}$$

---

[1] Stone's (geometric) price index is a common price index approximation based on a linear approximate AIDS following Blanciforti and Green (1983).

from the shift in demand is likely to be only minimally mitigated by the response of supply, particularly in the near term. For simplicity of scenario analysis and pragmatic interpretation, particularly in the context of policies aimed at raising supply, we rely on simulating out-of-sample general equilibrium dynamics assuming inelastic supply curves (that is, supply remains constant in the short term).

RESULTS AND DISCUSSION

Household Demand for Food

Results of the regression analysis are reported in Annex 4.1, and Box 4.2 explains how to interpret these coefficients.

We focus on six food categories representing key food groups in the Indian household consumption basket: milk and milk products; egg, fish, and meat; pulses; cereals; vegetables and fruits; and a category of other foods that includes oil and fats, sugar, condiments, and spices. The choice of these categories is driven by distinct government policies, such as those related to production, pricing, and provision, toward these sectors. These food categories together correspond to about 43 percent of household consumption expenditure, both in the CPI and in the household survey data.[7] Estimated expenditure weights on key food categories in the latest household survey (National Sample Survey Office 68th round for 2011/12) closely track weights in CPI Combined (Table 4.1), supporting the suitability of household-survey-based analysis to study implications of food demand dynamics for CPI inflation in India.

First-Stage Budgeting Estimation Results: Total Expenditure on Food

Estimates of consumer demand for food from the first-stage budgeting exercise indicate clear heterogeneity in food demand patterns across the income spectrum of Indian households.

The estimates suggest that as income per capita goes up by 1 percent, the demand for food rises by 0.64 percent (Table 4.2). Similarly, a 1 percent increase in food prices results in a 0.62 percent decline in total food expenditure when the consumer is not compensated for the price increase. However, if the consumer is compensated to maintain the same level of welfare, the total expenditure on food goes down by 0.35 percent when food prices rise by 1 percent.

Panel 1 of Figure 4.9 plots the weights of food expenditure (predicted by our model) against the log of individual incomes. As predicted by Engel's law, as income increases, households spend less and less on food (estimated weights on food expenditure declines). Panel 2 suggests that households spending a lot on food (high weight on food expenditure) also have high income elasticity of food expenditure. Panels 1 and 2 together suggest that the demand for food by poorer households goes up by more than for richer households when income per capita rises. Panels 3 and 4 of Figure 4.9 present price elasticities of food for food expenditure weights. The results suggest that the elasticity is relatively large for those who spend a lot on food.

---

[7] Note that CPI expenditure categories, commonly attributed to the food basket, such as beverages (2 percent CPI weight), prepared meals (2.8 percent), and pan, tobacco, and intoxicants (2.1 percent), are excluded from the analysis.

BOX 4.2 Interpreting QUAIDS Coefficients

The quadratic almost ideal demand system (QUAIDS) coefficients are usually interpreted following basic transformation of the estimated raw coefficients of equation 3 in Box 4.1. Specifically, following Banks, Blundell, and Lewbel (1997), differentiating the expenditure shares in the demand equations described in equation 3 with respect to the logarithm of total expenditure (ln m) and the logarithm of prices, food expenditure elasticity, and both compensated and uncompensated price elasticities (μ_j and $\mu_{j,n}$ respectively) can be calculated using expressions 13–15:

$$\mu_j \equiv \frac{\partial w_j}{\partial \ln m} = \beta_j + \frac{2\lambda_j}{b(\mathbf{p})} \ln \frac{m}{P(\mathbf{p})} \tag{13}$$

$$\mu_{j,n} \equiv \frac{\partial w_j}{\partial \ln p_n} = \gamma_{j,n} - \mu_j \left(\alpha_n + \sum_{k=1}^{N} \gamma_{n,k} \ln p_k \right) - \frac{\lambda_j \beta_n}{b(\mathbf{p})} \left[\ln \frac{m}{P(\mathbf{p})} \right]^2 \tag{14}$$

Consequently, the expenditure elasticity for the item j with respect to total expenditure can be computed as:

$$e_j = \frac{\mu_j}{w_j} + 1 \tag{15}$$

where e_j denotes the responsiveness of demand (expenditure) for item j with respect to changes in total expenditure. The value of e_j thus indicates the nature of a food item and how consumers perceive its importance with respect to total food budgets. More importantly for understanding India's future food demand, equation 15 allows us to understand how demand for food, as well for specific food items, is likely to evolve with India's overall economic development. More generally, the value of $e_j > 1$ is associated with so-called normal goods within food expenditure, while values between 0 and 1 correspond to so-called normal necessities. For such goods, demand will increase with overall income and expenditure, but their budget shares will decline. Luxury goods are those with demand elasticity above 1; inferior goods have negative elasticities.

To obtain price elasticities of food, we can use two alternative definitions based on the underlying demand equations: Marshallian (uncompensated) price elasticity, and Hicksian (compensated) price elasticity. The Marshallian price elasticity equation is obtained by maximizing utility subject to the consumer's budget constraint, while the Hicksian demand is derived by solving the expenditure minimization problem, keeping the utility level constant. The Marshallian price elasticity can be obtained using the following transformation:

$$e^{u}_{j,n} = \frac{\mu_{j,n}}{w_j} - d_{j,n} \tag{16}$$

where $d_{j,n}$ represents the Kronecker's delta ($d_{j,n} = 1$ for $j = n$ and $d_{j,n} = 0$ for $j \neq n$). While using the Slutsky equation, the Hicksian elasticities can be obtained using the following expression:

$$e^{c}_{j,n} = e^{u}_{j,n} + e_j w_j \tag{17}$$

TABLE 4.1

Food Expenditure Weights in CPI-Combined and Household Survey Data
(Percent of total household expenditure)

Food Category	CPI Combined	Household Survey (NSSO 68th Round)
Egg, fish, and meat	2.9	3.5
Milk and milk products	7.73	8.4
Cereals and cereal products	14.6	12.9
Pulses and pulse products	2.7	3.4
Vegetables and fruits	7.3	6.9
Other (oils and fats, sugar, condiments, and spices)	7.5	8.1
Total	**42.7**	**43.2**

Sources: Haver Analytics; and IMF staff estimates.
Note: Expenditure on nonalcoholic beverages, paan, tobacco and intoxicants, and prepared meals not included. CPI = consumer price index; NSSO = National Sample Survey Office.

TABLE 4.2

Food Demand Elasticities: First Budgeting Stage *(Sample mean values)*

Income Elasticity of Total Food Expenditure	
0.640	
(0.172)	
Uncompensated (Marshalian) Price Elasticity of Total Food Expenditure	
Food prices	**Nonfood prices**
−0.627	−0.013
(0.185)	(0.023)
Compensated (Hicksian) Price Elasticity of Total Food Expenditure	
Food prices	**Nonfood prices**
−0.353	0.267
(0.086)	(0.122)

Source: IMF staff estimates.
Note: Standard deviations relative to sample mean values in parenthesis.

Second-Stage Budgeting Estimation Results: Expenditure on Specific Food Categories

Using expenditure weights for specific food categories and individual total food expenditure, we now estimate demand functions for specific food categories. Econometric estimates of consumer demand for food from the first-stage budgeting exercise indicate that based on expenditure elasticities for total food expenditure, we can essentially classify the six food categories into three groups (Table 4.3):

- *High income elasticity products*—Includes milk products as well as egg, fish, and meat. On average, expenditure on these items (across all households) will increase disproportionally more than the increase in total food expenditure.
- *Unit income elasticity products*—Includes vegetables and fruits. On average, expenditure on these items (across all households) will rise at the same rate as the increase in total food expenditure.

Figure 4.9. Analysis of Household Total Food Expenditure

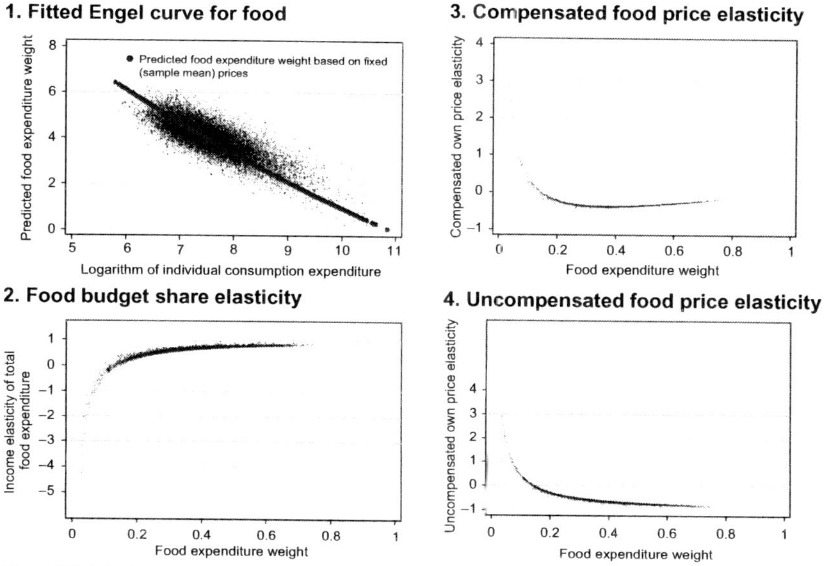

Source: IMF staff estimates.

TABLE 4.3

Food Expenditure Demand Elasticities: Second Budgeting Stage
(Sample mean values, based on actual expenditure weights)

Food Category	
Egg, fish, and meat	1.321
Milk and milk products	1.590
Cereals and cereal products	0.848
Pulses and pulse products	0.666
Vegetables and fruits	1.000
Other (oils and fats, sugar, condiments, and spices)	0.841

Source: IMF staff estimates.
Note: Table shows expenditure elasticity for a given food category with respect to total expenditure on food.

- *Less-than-unity income elasticity products*—Includes pulses, cereals, and the "other products" category. On average, expenditure on these items (across all households) will increase relatively less than the increase in total food expenditure.

The observed patterns are in line with Bennet's law, which states that with rising incomes, food consumption shifts from simple starchy plant-dominated diets toward more nutritious and high-value foods that include dairy products, vegetables and fruits, and especially meat.

The estimates of expenditure elasticities reported in Table 4.3 correspond to their mean values across all households, and thus do not take into account differences in food budgets across households. To gain an insight into the possible impact of increased food expenditure on the aggregate demand for specific food categories, and taking into account differences in food budgets across households, we can reweight estimated elasticities by each household's actual expenditure on each of the food categories. The results reported in Table 4.4 are qualitatively similar, though magnitudes are closer to unity, suggesting that aggregate demand impact for high-elasticity food commodities is somewhat lower than the simple mean elasticity estimates.

Note that in the aggregated expenditure elasticity analysis, we focus on the impact of a uniform percentage change in household total food expenditure. A further insight into implications for aggregate demand for specific food items can be obtained by estimating the sensitivity of demand for specific food groups for increases in total household expenditure. This assumes a uniform percent change in total household expenditure and then accounts for the impact of the interaction of its variation with the variation in total household food expenditure elasticity on each household's total food expenditure, and then on expenditure on specific food items. The results in Table 4.5 indicate a significantly higher increase

TABLE 4.4

Food Expenditure Demand Elasticities: Second Budgeting Stage
(Expenditure-weighted values, based on actual expenditure weights)

Food Category	
Egg, fish, and meat	1.165
Milk and milk products	1.326
Cereals and cereal products	0.845
Pulses and pulse products	0.725
Vegetables and fruits	0.985
Other (oils and fats, sugar, condiments, and spices)	0.848

Source: IMF staff estimates.
Note: Table shows expenditure elasticity for a given food category with respect to total expenditure on food.

TABLE 4.5

Food Expenditure Demand Elasticities: Second Budgeting Stage
(Expenditure-weighted values, based on actual expenditure weights)

Food Category		Relative to Pulses
Egg, fish, and meat	0.592	1.515
Milk and milk products	0.645	1.650
Cereals and cereal products	0.468	1.196
Pulses and pulse products	0.391	1.000
Vegetables and fruits	0.484	1.238
Other (oils and fats, sugar, condiments, and spices)	0.459	1.173

Source: IMF staff estimates.
Note: Table shows expenditure elasticity for a given food category with respect to total household expenditure.

in demand for milk and milk products and the category of egg, fish, and meat compared to pulses (the lowest-elasticity product category), with relative elasticities of 1.7 and 1.5, respectively. Moreover, each of the corresponding budget elasticities for cereals, vegetables and fruits, as well as other food categories is about 1.2 times higher than the budget elasticity of pulses, suggesting that the relative demand pressures for some food categories can be significantly higher as household incomes grow.

Own-price uncompensated demand elasticities reported in Table 4.6 provide some insight into the extent of sensitivity of demand for specific food items to prices. Specifically, holding total household food expenditure constant, demand for milk and related products is least sensitive to changes in milk prices, while the demand for other proteins (in the categories egg, fish, and milk, and pulses) responds almost one to one. This also implies that to induce demand adjustment for milk products—for example in response to a limited supply of milk—a much stronger response of milk prices would be required to equilibrate its supply and demand. The uncompensated cross-price elasticities reported in Table 4.6 indicate some complementarity among most food categories. For example, a 1 percent increase in the price of egg, fish, and meat leads to a decline in the demand for milk by about 0.1 percent. However, some foods also appear to be substitutes. Notably, values of uncompensated price elasticities indicate that cereals are substitutes for proteins: milk; egg, fish, and meat; and also pulses. In other words, when prices of proteins rise while food budgets stay unchanged, consumption is switched to cereals and related products (see also Figure 4.10).

Hicksian price elasticities provide a somewhat different insight into food demand patterns in India. Most of the food categories emerge as substitutes (Table 4.7). To achieve a comparable level of utility following an increase in the price of other products, the demand for most food products goes up, compensating for the decline in the consumption of food items whose prices have risen. Perhaps the only food category that is a noticeable exception is vegetables and fruits with respect to their sensitivity to prices of egg, fish, and meat. As prices of this category of food rise, the demand for vegetables and fruits needs to decline, in part as consumers substitute egg, fish, and meat for other proteins, namely pulses and milk.

TABLE 4.6

Uncompensated (Marshallian) Price Elasticities: Second Budgeting Stage
(Sample mean values, based on actual expenditure weights)

Food Category	Egg, Fish, and Meat	Milk and Milk Products	Cereals and Cereal Products	Pulses and Pulse Products	Vegetables and Fruits	Other
Egg, fish, and meat	**–0.563**	–0.026	–0.044	–0.134	–0.169	–0.080
Milk and milk products	–0.096	**–0.880**	–0.102	–0.216	–0.091	–0.089
Cereals and cereal products	0.020	0.013	**–0.858**	0.008	–0.017	0.028
Pulses and pulse products	–0.045	–0.068	0.015	**–0.704**	0.002	0.047
Vegetables and fruits	–0.254	–0.028	–0.035	–0.052	**–0.754**	0.001
Other	–0.062	–0.012	0.024	0.098	0.030	**–0.907**

Source: IMF staff estimates.

Figure 4.10. Analysis of Household Expenditure on Key Food Categories

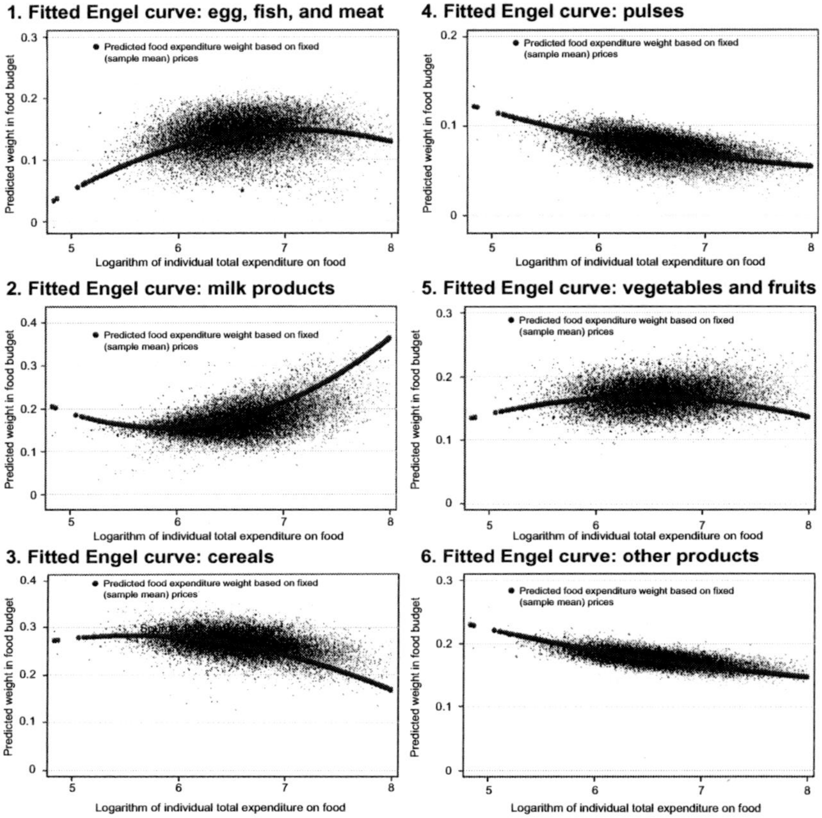

Source: IMF staff estimates.

TABLE 4.7

Compensated (Hicksian) Price Elasticities: Second Budgeting Stage
(Sample mean values, based on actual expenditure weights)

Food Category	Egg, Fish, and Meat	Milk and Milk Products	Cereals and Cereal Products	Pulses and Pulse Products	Vegetables and Fruits	Other
Egg, fish, and meat	**−0.395**	0.142	0.124	0.034	−0.001	0.088
Milk and milk products	0.125	**−0.659**	0.119	0.004	0.129	0.131
Cereals and cereal products	0.255	0.248	**−0.623**	0.243	0.218	0.263
Pulses and pulse products	0.012	−0.011	0.072	**−0.647**	0.059	0.105
Vegetables and fruits	−0.086	0.141	0.133	0.117	**−0.585**	0.169
Other	0.090	0.139	0.175	0.249	0.181	**−0.756**

Source: IMF staff estimates.

Food Subsidies and Some Distributional Aspects

The government procures a substantial portion of the domestic output of cereals. This provides mainly for the needs of the targeted public distribution system (TPDS), other welfare schemes, and maintenance of the buffer stocks. Note that in recent years, the share of public procurement has risen substantially (Figure 4.11), from an average of 25 percent during 2002/03–2007/08 to 32 percent during 2008/09–2013/14. This has prompted criticism of increasing the state's role in the cereals market (CACP 2013). The share of public distribution system (PDS) purchases in consumption has also increased considerably (Figure 4.12). In the case of rural household consumption, the share of rice

Figure 4.11. Procurement Trend of Rice and Wheat
(Percent of annual production)

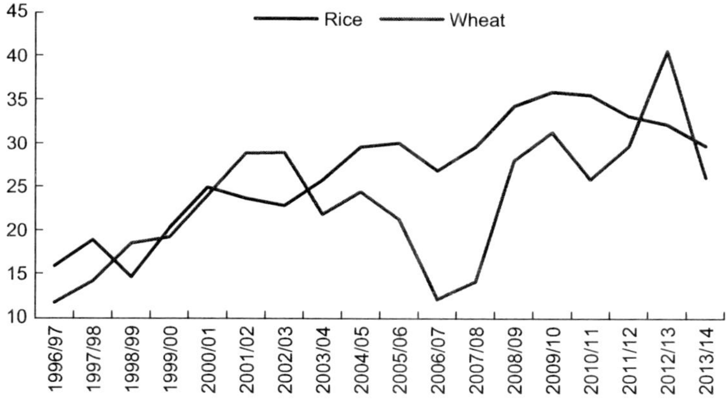

Sources: CEIC; and IMF staff calculations.

Figure 4.12. Share of PDS Cereals Purchases in Food Consumption
(Percent of household consumption, quantity-based)

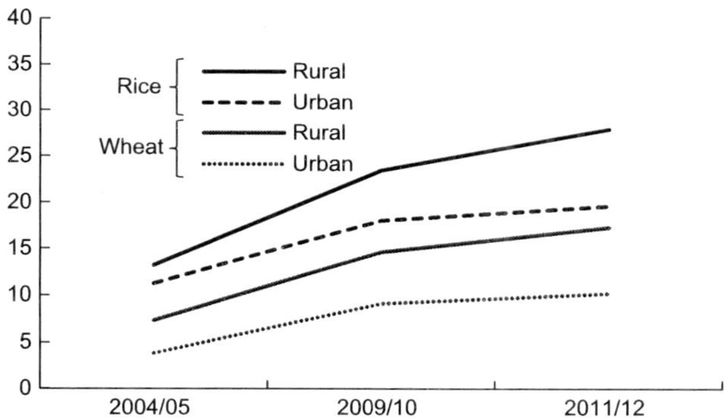

Source: National Sample Survey Office.
Note: PDS = public distribution system.

purchases from the PDS rose from 13 percent in 2004/05 to 28 percent in 2011/12, and the share of wheat rose from 7 percent to 17 percent. For urban households, in the same period, the increase was from 11 percent to 20 percent for rice, and from 4 percent to 11 percent for wheat.

With a sizable share of subsidized cereals in the consumption basket of many households, the average price of cereals (PDS and open market) paid by households is below both open market prices and the minimum support price that a cereal producer can receive through the open-ended public procurement system. As a result of subsidized pricing to consumers (Figure 4.13), the weight on cereals from the PDS in expenditures is significantly less than it would be on the basis of quantity. For example, PDS rice in the CPI Combined, which tracks budget shares, is about 8 percent of the total expenditure on rice, while the quantity of PDS rice is about 25 percent of the total quantity. For wheat, the discrepancy is also nontrivial: 6 percent of expenditure on PDS wheat compared to 16 percent of quantity. These weights imply that on average in 2011/12, the price of PDS rice was about a quarter of the open market price, while the price of wheat from PDS was about a third of its open market price (see also Basu and Das 2014).

The share of rice consumed from the PDS is significantly higher for poorer households, which benefit from the TPDS, in particular the Below Poverty Line and Antyodaya Anna Yojana schemes; and because poorer households essentially face a different set of prices of cereals than the richer households. Our demand specification does not account for possible links between the rupee amount of household budgets and the available prices of cereals. As such, we attribute relatively higher cereal consumption by poorer households to the lower price rather

Figure 4.13. Government Food Subsidies

(Percent of GDP)

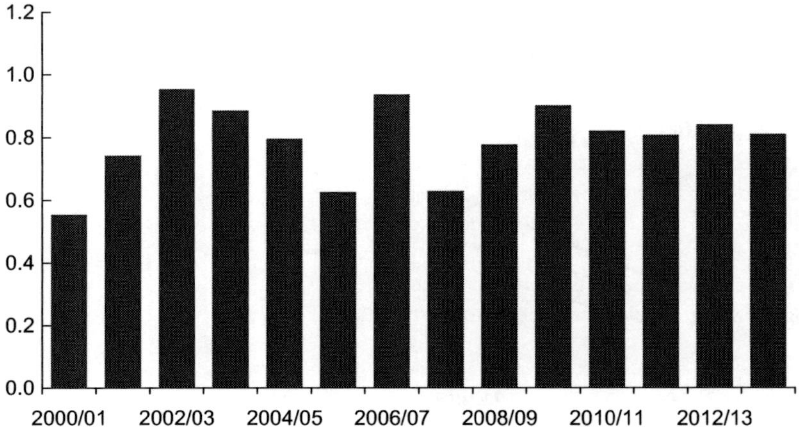

Source: IMF staff calculations.

than to their smaller budgets.[8] In other words, the estimated demand system is conditional on the distribution of cereal prices with respect to the level of household budget, which in practice is ensured through the in-kind nature of the TPDS. Moreover, it does not account for leakages, which are estimated to be large (CACP 2013). As a result, our estimated demand system may not be fully capturing the effects of these distortions, and is only suitable to study demand under the existing food distribution policy and associated subsidies.

BUFFER STOCKS AND MINIMUM SUPPORT PRICES

Buffer Stocks

In this section, we quantify the impact of the buildup of buffer stocks on India's relative food inflation over the past decade. Specifically, we estimate relative food inflation because of the diminished net supply of cereals into the market from the buildup of buffer stocks. We also estimate the impact of a hypothetical (and counterfactual) proactive buffer stock liquidation policy on relative food inflation volatility.

It has been frequently argued that the excessive buildup of buffer stocks for cereals (rice and wheat) contributed to India's inflationary pressures in the past several years (CACP 2013). The cumulative buildup of the buffer stock of rice over a six-year period from 2007/08 to 2012/13 was close to 20 million tons, while average production was about 100 million tons. The buildup of wheat stocks was even more significant; the average wheat stock in the Central Pool during 2012/13 exceeded average stocks in 2007/08 by about 30 million tons, as production averaged 85 million tons per year. The rice intake into the Central Pool averaged 4 percent of annual output during this period, and nearly 7 percent for wheat. As a result, by July 2012, India's stocks of rice and wheat accounted for more than 6 percent and 7 percent of the world's total rice and wheat utilization, respectively (Saini and Kozicka 2014). Since 2010, on average, actual buffer stocks held with the Food Corporation of India were more than double the norms. Several underlying reasons account for this situation, including distortions such as export bans and open-ended procurement. But a key reason appears to be lack of a proactive liquidation policy. The inefficiency of the buffer stock policy has been aggravated by the significant costs of carrying excess stocks, considering that the economic cost to the Food Corporation of India for acquiring, storing, and distributing food grains has been some 40–50 percent more than the procurement prices (Gulati, Gujral, and Nandakumar 2012).

In practice, minimum support price increases are announced in advance of the agricultural season, the actual intake to buffer stock following harvesting has a

[8] For example, the bottom decile of rural households have a budget share of cereals of about one-fourth, and it declines to less than one-tenth for the top decile. In urban India, the share of cereals falls from slightly less than one-fifth to just 3–4 percent for the top decile households.

further impact on inflation dynamics, because it reduces the quantity of cereals available for households' purchases on the open market, especially during a poor output period. Even though minimum support prices essentially provide a floor for open market prices, in part due to an open-ended procurement policy, the actual postharvest buffer stock intake and household demand define the eventual open market prices. Figure 4.14 illustrates a simplified interaction of postharvest short-term supply and demand for cereals. If we abstract away from international trade aspects, we can assume that the postharvest short-term cereal supply curve is vertical. In addition, we assume that the government's decision on the buildup of buffer stocks does not depend on the price paid, which implies a vertical government demand curve. The increase in government demand for buffer stock buildup leads to a parallel rightward shift of the total cereal demand curve. Under these assumptions of fixed supply and fixed government demand, the quantity available for households' open market purchases is reduced by a fixed amount, implying that the inflationary impact of buffer stock intake can be assessed solely using the structure of household demand.

Indeed, the actual monthly price dynamics suggest that WPI cereal inflation during the months of peak buffer stock intake significantly exceeded minimum support price increases (Figure 4.15). For example, by mid-2013 wholesale price inflation for rice exceeded 20 percent compared to the minimum support price growth of about 15 percent. For wheat, the buffer stock intake was even more pronounced, and so was the departure of wholesale price inflation from minimum support prices.

Figure 4.14. Open Market Price and Supply, Household and Government's Buffer Stock Demand for Cereals

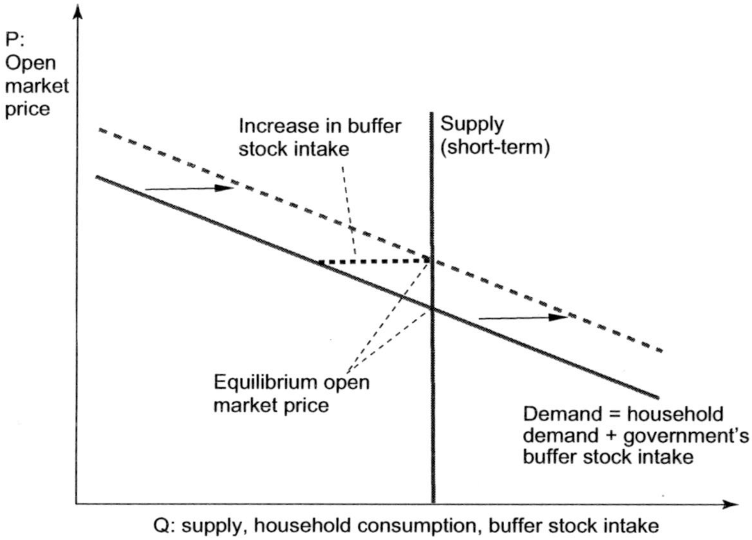

Figure 4.15. Prices and Central Pool Stocks

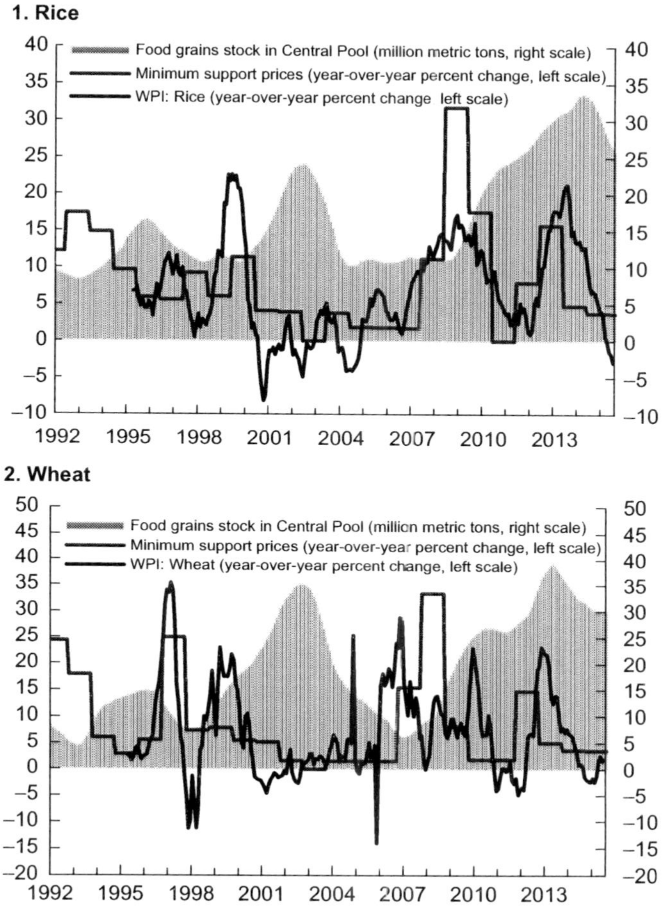

Sources: CEIC; Food Corporation of India; Haver Analytics; and IMF staff calculations.
Note: WPI = wholesale price index.

Therefore, we can in principle consider alternative scenarios of historic relative food price dynamics under different scenarios of the evolution of buffer stocks, conditional on minimum support price policies and output. In other words, the intake and liquidation of stocks can smooth consumption and stabilize prices.

Specifically, we model relative food inflation dynamics under an alternative (counterfactual) scenario with two key properties related to buffer stock policies. First, we take into account the revised buffer stock norms and calculate the inflationary effect of releasing the excess stock relative to the new norm on relative food inflation. In particular, we adopt the government's recently approved buffer norms,

Figure 4.16. Relative Food Inflation: Predicted versus Actual

(Food inflation less actual nonfood inflation, percent)

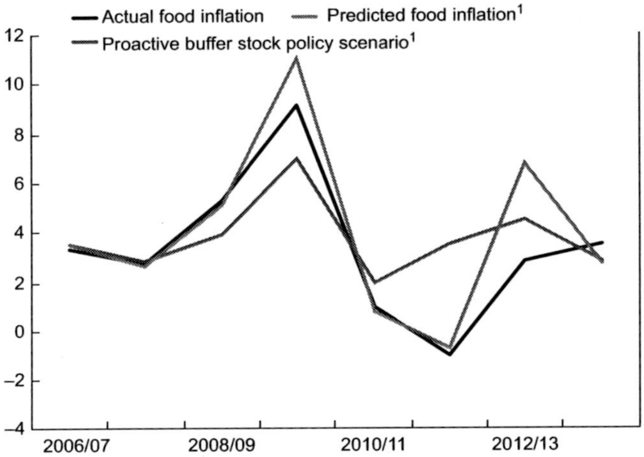

Sources: IMF staff estimates.
[1]Two-year monthly average.

reflecting the needs of the National Food Security Act.[9] Our scenario analysis has a reduced net overall buffer stock intake between 2006/07 and 2013/14 that results in average stocks in the Central Pool during 2013/14 reaching close to the revised norm levels. More specifically, we assume a lower cumulative buffer stock intake between July 2007 and July 2012, by about 15 million metric tons for rice and by about 20 million metric tons for wheat. Our estimates suggest that this would have resulted in a reduction in food inflation by about ½ percentage point per year compared to the actual aggregate stock intake during 2006/07–2012/13, assuming the government had continued to subsidize PDS distribution of cereals.

Second, we consider a proactive cereal liquidation policy, which involves releasing more from the buffer stocks in a year of low production and increasing intake during a good harvest year to stabilize the growth rate of cereal consumption and, therefore, market prices. We estimate the impact of such policy on reducing relative food inflation volatility. Conditional on the implementation of revised buffer stock norms by mid-2013, smoothing the growth rate of cereal consumption at slightly below 1½ percent per year through a proactive intake and release of buffer stocks could have reduced the standard deviation of historic relative food inflation during this period by half—from about 3¼ percentage points to just about 1⅔ percentage points (Figure 4.16). Note that by focusing only on

[9]The revised norms introduce greater differentiation of buffer norms across different quarters of a year, with the maximum combined requirement of about 27.5 million metric tons of wheat and about 13.5 million metric tons of rice to be maintained on July 1. As of July 1, 2012, which was a near-peak stock holding period, Food Corporation of India stocks amounted to 49.8 million metric tons of wheat and 30.7 million metric tons of rice.

modeling the relative food inflation and keeping the path of nonfood inflation unchanged, we ignore potential second-round effects of elevated food inflation on core inflation, which are nontrivial (Anand, Ding, and Tulin 2014). Therefore, our exercise likely understates the additional impact on aggregate retail inflation, particularly at times of elevated food inflation.

Minimum Support Prices

The strong buildup of buffer stocks was undoubtedly aided by strong rises in minimum support prices, which averaged about 13 percent per year, even as headline CPI inflation averaged about 9 percent and WPI inflation slightly above 7 percent. Although minimum support prices are intended to provide a floor for market prices, substantial minimum price increases were generally followed by rising inflation in key agricultural crops (Rajan 2014). This suggests that minimum support price increases have played a role in fueling inflationary pressures, including by chipping away the production of other crops. Nonetheless, incentive schemes, such as minimum support prices, were also found to have contributed to increased cereal production during this period.[10] Growth of cereal production averaged about 1¼ percent per year during 1995/96–2005/06 when the growth of minimum support prices for cereals remained close to headline CPI and WPI inflation. However, since then the growth of cereal production rose to an average of about 2¾ percent per year, while the growth of minimum support prices exceeded headline WPI inflation by about 4½ and headline CPI inflation by about 2 percentage points.

Kozicka and others (2014) argue that minimum support prices likely helped increase cereal production, which helped underpin the rebuilding of buffer stocks of cereals and increase household consumption. Nevertheless, as a policy instrument the role of minimum support prices was much broader, because by design they ensure a remunerative and stable price environment. Thus, even though the buildup of buffer stocks over the past decade was very strong, enabled in part by procurement policies including minimum support prices, it nevertheless appears to have been less than the estimated cereal production gains. And this was caused partly by the strong growth in minimum support prices. The increase in the average buffer stock between 2006/07 and 2013/14 was equivalent to lowering the growth rate of household cereal consumption during this period by about ¾ percentage point per year, which is about half of estimated production gains using the estimates from Kozicka and others (2014). Given the government's policy to make available cereals at subsidized prices, this meant increasing fiscal costs of providing food subsidy.

---

[10] Using estimates of cereal's supply elasticity of about 0.3 for minimum support prices (WPI deflated) reported by Kozicka and others (2014), the impact of these prices on production may have been significant. Specifically, minimum support prices might have accounted for nearly three-quarters of the 1¾ percent average annual increase in rice production and close to about a half of the 3 percent average annual increase in wheat production during this period.

Figure 4.17. Minimum Support Price and Supply, and Household Demand for Cereals

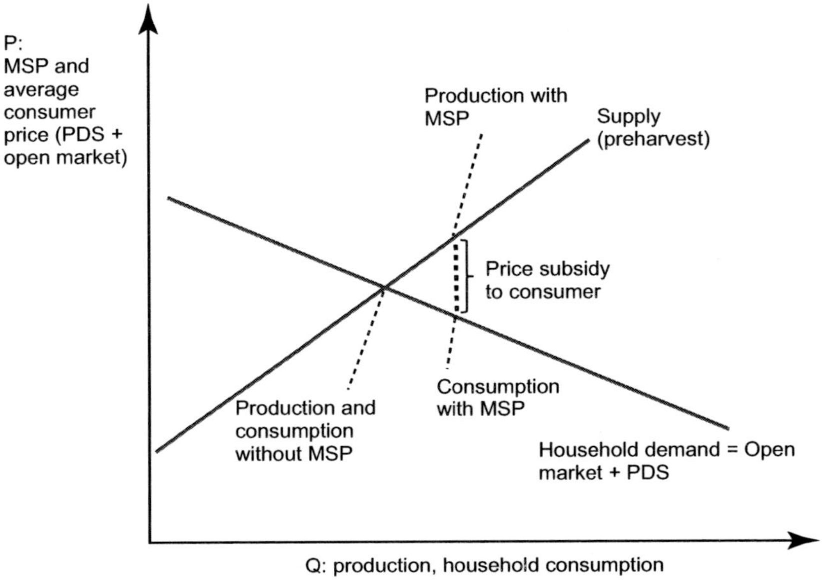

Note: MSP = minimum support price; PDS = public distribution system.

Under the assumptions of (1) a price-floor policy of the minimum support price, (2) minimum support prices resulting in increased production relative to the market equilibrium without government subsidies, and (3) the absence of buffer stock buildup, ensuring postharvest market clearing of an increased supply of cereals necessitates a subsidy to the consumer (Figure 4.17). Indeed, the average consumer prices of cereals purchased at subsidized prices from the PDS and the open market tended to be below minimum support prices, even though the open market wholesale prices of cereals generally exceed these prices (Figure 4.18). For example, cereal expenditure shares and consumption volumes suggest that PDS prices are about a quarter of the retail prices for rice, and a third of the retail prices for wheat.

Thus, from the perspective of consumer demand, if higher minimum support prices lead to higher supply and therefore higher consumption of cereals, higher minimum support prices might also result in lower inflation (quantity weighted) for cereals relative to nonfood inflation. However, the increased availability of cereals may also lead to further demand pressures on other food commodities, including as a result of their reduced supply due to production distortions generated by the minimum support price. Also, given the government's policy to enhance the supply of cereals and make them available to households at subsidized prices, this means increasing the fiscal costs of minimum support price

Figure 4.18. Wholesale and Minimum Support Prices: Paddy and Wheat

(Rupees per kilogram)

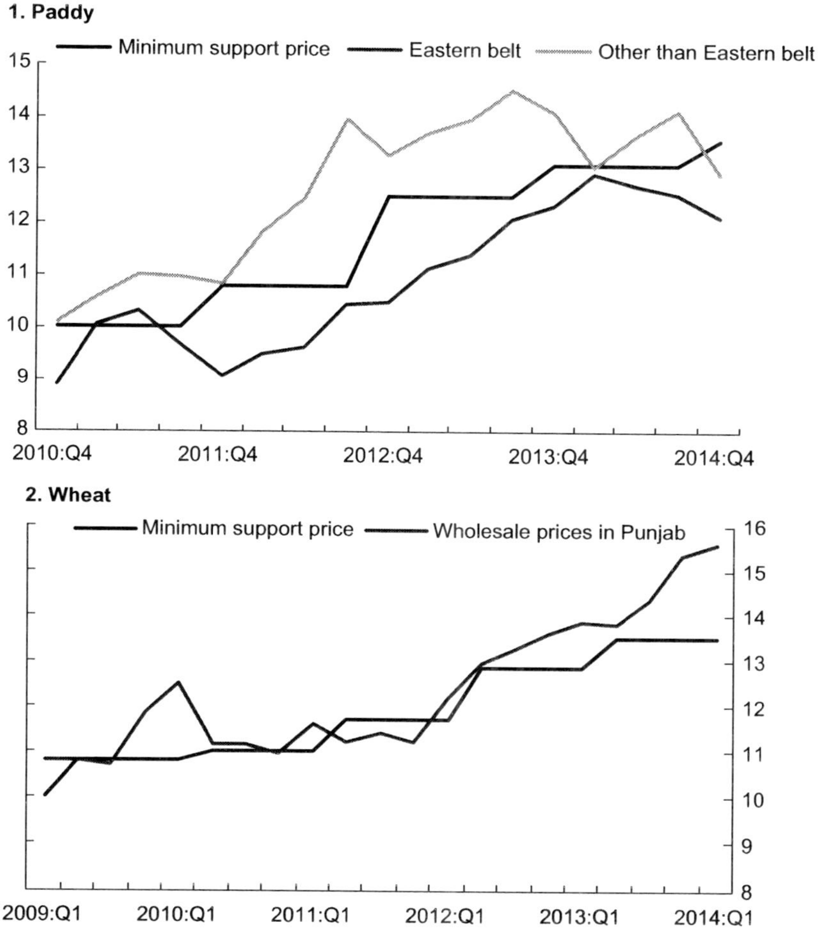

Source: Commission for Agricultural Costs and Prices.

policies. However, it is precisely the minimum support price mechanism, in combination with open-ended procurement, that can generate overall inflationary pressures. Given a relatively large share of cereals in household consumption, an essentially administered setting of their prices as a result of the minimum support price policy, open-ended procurement, and food subsidy policies can lead to generalized inflationary pressures. In other words, even though relative food inflation may end up lower, nonfood and also headline inflation can rise significantly as they become anchored by inflation caused by minimum support prices.

Note that our simulation framework is aimed at explaining relative food inflation for a given level of nonfood inflation rather than establishing a causal relationship. A possible simulation approach, of course, could be to tie food and nonfood prices to administered prices, such as the minimum support price, and then solve for inflation dynamics conditional on cereal price inflation. It is not clear to what extent this is a useful exercise because, while not trivial, products subject to minimum support prices constitute a relatively small share of total consumption. In this case, time-series techniques aimed at identifying causal links may be better suited, as examined in Sonna and others (2014), for example. Controlling for real incomes, demand for protein, and agricultural input costs, they find that a 1 percentage point increase in the production-weighted minimum support price of rice and wheat is associated with about a 0.3 percentage point increase in food inflation. In addition, on the basis of weak exogeneity tests, they conclude that in the short-term, minimum support prices have a statistically significant impact on food inflation. Similarly, Anand, Ding, and Tulin (2014), using a reduced-form dynamic general equilibrium model for India, show that food inflation shocks can lead to a significant increase in core inflation.

Finally, empirical evidence provided by Anand, Kumar, and Tulin (2016) suggests that, except in the short term, minimum support prices of cereals tend to react to changes in Indian farm gate prices of cereals, rather than the other way around. They also find that international market prices influence Indian farm gate prices and minimum support prices, in both the short and long term. The global market price will thus remain important in defining Indian cereal prices in the long term.

IMPLICATIONS FOR MONETARY POLICY

Our modeling framework does not take into account that supply could be responsive to prices. By imposing adjustment only on prices and demand, it may not be ideal to study situations when supply is price elastic. And it may be particularly limiting when analyzing long-term food inflation dynamics.

As discussed, the approach of abstracting away from explicit modeling of food supply is not without limitations,[11] and the estimated inflation outcomes are likely to have an upward bias. Nonetheless, as own-price supply elasticities are usually found to be significantly below demand elasticities, responsiveness of supply to mitigate the impact of demand on prices may be rather limited, particularly over the near term. The Food and Agricultural Policy Research Institute's Elasticity Database, for example, indicates that the price elasticities of rice supply are usually close to 0.2, with a value of 0.25 in Bangladesh, 0.16 in China, and 0.11 in India. The price elasticities of response for wheat are slightly higher, averaging, for example, 0.33 in Australia, 0.43 in Brazil, 0.09 in China, and 0.29 in India. In the case of more recent studies on India, Kumar and others (2010) report similar estimates of own-price elasticities of supply: 0.24 for rice, 0.22 for wheat, and 0.17 for pulses. Supply elasticities for minimum support prices, estimated by Kozicka

[11] As in an inelastic supply system, only price, not supply, adjusts to equilibrate demand.

TABLE 4.8

Projection Assumptions *(Percent per year)*

Food Category	Historic	Preferred	Conservative
Egg, fish, and meat	5.4	6.4	5.4
Milk and milk products	4.6	5.6	4.6
Cereals and cereal products	2.0	3.0	0.8
Pulses and pulse products	4.9	5.9	4.9
Vegetables and fruits	4.7	5.7	4.7
Other	3.4	4.4	3.4
Private consumption, real	7.0	7.0	7.0
Population growth	1.4	1.4	1.4

Source: IMF staff estimates.

and others (2014), are somewhat higher (0.27 for rice and 0.33 for wheat), which might be explained by the low risk related to minimum support prices. Estimates of long-term supply elasticity to a sustained increase in the relative price of cereals are about 0.35 for rice, but 0.72 for wheat (Kozicka and others 2014).

Next, we estimate relative food inflation dynamics under different scenarios for supply growth (Table 4.8). Under the historic scenario for this, average growth rates of domestic food supply in the recent decade, food inflation would exceed nonfood inflation by about 3 percentage points per year, thus contributing about 1¼ percentage points to the headline inflation in excess of underlying nonfood inflation. Under a preferred growth scenario, which assumes that the rates of supply growth of all food categories are raised by about 1 percentage point per year, food inflation would exceed nonfood inflation by only about ½ of a percentage point. We also consider a conservative growth scenario that assumes a growth rate for cereal production at about ¾ percent per year, implying stagnant cereal productivity and/or the absence of policy support. In this scenario, food inflation would exceed nonfood inflation by 4 percentage points per year.

Moreover, taking into account historic food supply growth volatility[12] and absent a proactive buffer stock policy, relative food inflation could contribute close to 1½ percentage points to headline inflation over a two-year period. In turn, a proactive buffer stock intake and liquidation policy for cereals could help reduce the potential contribution of relative food inflation volatility by half over a two-year period.

Our results thus imply that durably achieving a long-term inflation target of 4 percent under India's recently adopted flexible inflation targeting will need policies to enhance food supply. For example, in the absence of increased food supply growth, average long-term nonfood inflation would need to be brought down to about 2½ percent, which is low by historic and international experience and may be too costly in terms of growth and employment. In addition, the band of ±2 percent around the long-term inflation target of 4 percent appears appropriate in light of relative food inflation volatility. It is worth noting that if long-term

[12] Increase in relative food inflation over two years in response to one standard deviation shock to domestic food supply.

average inflation were higher, the upper band would probably be breached more often or would need a more aggressive monetary stance. Our analysis also suggests that administered price setting, such as through minimum support prices and supporting policies, constitute an important impediment to monetary policy transmission and will continue to pose challenges for monetary policy management in India. Finally, a proactive buffer stock policy could be instrumental in containing inflation volatility and limiting the burden on monetary policy in addressing the adverse consequences of food supply shocks, including the second-round effects of food inflation shocks to core inflation.

CONCLUSIONS AND POLICY IMPLICATIONS

During the decade just past, India has seen a prolonged period of high inflation, to a large extent driven by persistently high food inflation. Domestic food demand and supply factors underpin India's food price dynamics. Relative food prices have played a key role in equilibrating India's food demand and domestic supply, given the limited responsiveness of agricultural production, particularly in the short term. The acceleration of India's economic growth during the past 10 years, accompanied by stagnant agriculture growth, resulted in excess demand for food, giving rise to relative food price inflation. Furthermore, the excessive buildup in buffer stocks since 2007/08 and the lack of a proactive liquidation policy increased average relative food inflation and its volatility.

As India's economic growth picks up, food demand pressures will remain strong, particularly for high-value foods, such as dairy products and animal-based proteins. Rising incomes will prompt shifts in food consumption away from simple starchy plant-dominated diets toward more nutritious and high-value foods. Recent steps to contain food inflation will help in the short term, until durable measures to increase food supply are put in place. The recent measures to limit the rise of minimum support prices for key agricultural commodities, wheat and rice in particular; the release of food grains from the Central Pool into the market; and adjusting the buffer norms of food grains to levels significantly below prevailing actual stocks have helped lower cereal (rice and wheat) inflation. However, India's agricultural yields for key food commodities remain significantly below those of many emerging markets; rice yields, for example, are about one-third of China's and about half of Vietnam's and Indonesia's (Himani 2014). The excess demand will likely reemerge; and thus a durable increase in supply, particularly through enhancing agricultural yields for key commodities, will be required to keep food inflation in check. For cereals, the impact of price support and stabilization policies will need to be complemented by policies to enhance agricultural productivity, including along the lines of the FCI Restructuring Committee Report (Government of India 2015).

In the absence of a stronger food supply growth response, relative food inflation can contribute about 1¼ percentage points to headline inflation annually. Indian food inflation is likely to exceed nonfood inflation by 2½–3 percentage points per year, assuming private consumption growth picking up to 7 percent per year and food supply growing at historic rates. Therefore, the sustainability of a long-term inflation target of 4 percent under the recently adopted flexible inflation targeting will depend on enhancing food supply, agricultural market-based pricing, and reducing price distortions. In the interim, monetary policy will need to remain tight to anchor inflation expectations at a lower level. Our simulation analysis also indicates that in light of India's supply-side vulnerabilities, the band around the inflation target of ±2 percent is broadly appropriate. A well-designed cereal buffer stock liquidation policy could help mitigate food inflation volatility. Finally, administered price setting, such as through minimum support prices and supporting policies, will continue to pose challenges for monetary policy management in India, as highlighted in the Patel Committee Report.

ANNEX 4.1. ESTIMATED PARAMETERS OF THE QUADRATIC ALMOST IDEAL DEMAND SYSTEM FOR INDIA

ANNEX TABLE 4.1.1

Regression Analysis of Total Food Demand: First Budgeting Stage

Dependent Variable: Food Expenditure Weight	All Households
α_f	0.9147661***
	(0.0139673)
$\gamma_{f,f}$	0.0040952**
	(0.0019713)
β_f	–0.1710632***
	(0.0030094)
λ_f	0.0035315***
	(0.0002866)
α_0	–0.3615261***
	(0.0871973)
R^2, degrees of freedom adjusted	0.96
Number of observations	138,055

Source: IMF staff estimates.
*** denotes significance at the 1 percent level; ** at the 5 percent level.

ANNEX TABLE 4.1.2

Regression Analysis of Food Demand: Second Budgeting Stage

Dependent Variable: Specific Food Category Expenditure Weights within Total Expenditure on Food[1]			
α_1	0.0088237	β_1	−0.0906848 ***
	(0.0105971)		(0.0056052)
α_2	0.7792011 ***	β_2	0.2985137 ***
	(0.00788)		(0.0037655)
α_3	0.0045011	β_3	−0.1362998 ***
	(0.086211)		(0.0049977)
α_4	0.0335076 ***	β_4	0.0004809
	(0.0041138)		(0.0023344)
α_5	0.0460594 ***	β_5	−0.0685883 ***
	(0.0084452)		(0.0045569)
$\gamma_{1,1}$	0.0508396 ***	$\gamma_{3,3}$	0.0509947 ***
	(0.0014078)		(0.002251)
$\gamma_{1,2}$	−0.0362661***	$\gamma_{3,4}$	−0.0012684 **
	(0.0025156)		(0.0005724)
$\gamma_{1,3}$	0.0130379 ***	$\gamma_{3,5}$	0.0045374 ***
	(0.0011217)		(0.0010383)
$\gamma_{1,4}$	−0.0070304 ***	$\gamma_{4,4}$	0.0173077 ***
	(0.000379)		(0.0003484)
$\gamma_{1,5}$	−0.0119021 ***	$\gamma_{4,5}$	−0.0032853 ***
	(0.0007133)		(0.0003766)
$\gamma_{2,2}$	0.1561513 ***	$\gamma_{5,5}$	0.0433831 ***
	(0.0033231)		(0.0012753)
$\gamma_{2,3}$	−0.0676573 ***	λ_1	−0.0172765 ***
	(0.002574)		(0.0007423)
$\gamma_{2,4}$	−0.0105381 ***	λ_2	0.0355227 ***
	(0.0010885)		(0.0004995)
$\gamma_{2,5}$	−0.0331631 ***	λ_3	−0.0147488 ***
	(0.0022921)		(0.000792)
γ_4	0.00311 ***	λ_5	−0.0098896 ***
	(0.0003492)		(0.0006421)
Backed-out remaining QUAIDS coefficients:			
α_6	0.1279071 ***	β_6	−0.0034218
	(0.0058365)		(0.0033796)
$\gamma_{1,6}$	−0.0086787 ***	$\gamma_{2,6}$	−0.0085266 ***
	(0.0005484)		(0.0001568)
$\gamma_{3,6}$	0.0003557	$\gamma_{4,6}$	0.0048146 ***
	(0.0008364)		(0.0003004)
$\gamma_{5,6}$	0.0004301	$\gamma_{6,6}$	0.0116050 ***
	(0.0005029)		(0.0004804)
γ_6	0.0032823 ***		
	(0.0005151)		
Additional coefficient restrictions:			
$\gamma_{2,1} = \gamma_{1,2}$, $\gamma_{3,1} = \gamma_{1,3}$, $\gamma_{3,2} = \gamma_{2,3}$, $\gamma_{4,1} = \gamma_{1,4}$, $\gamma_{4,2} = \gamma_{2,4}$, $\gamma_{4,3} = \gamma_{3,4}$,			
$\gamma_{5,1} = \gamma_{1,5}$, $\gamma_{5,2} = \gamma_{2,5}$, $\gamma_{5,3} = \gamma_{3,5}$, $\gamma_{5,4} = \gamma_{4,5}$,			
$\gamma_{6,1} = \gamma_{1,6}$, $\gamma_{6,2} = \gamma_{2,6}$, $\gamma_{6,3} = \gamma_{3,6}$, $\gamma_{6,4} = \gamma_{4,6}$, $\gamma_{6,5} = \gamma_{5,6}$,			
R^2: ω_1	0.77	R^2: ω_2	0.77
R^2: ω_3	0.90	R^2: ω_4	0.87
R^2: ω_5	0.91		
Number of observations	302,783,433.00		

Source: IMF staff estimates.

Note: Robustness standard errors in parentheses. QUAIDS = quadratic almost ideal demand system.

*** denotes significance at the 1 percent level; ** at the 5 percent level.

[1] Subscripts denote the following food categories: 1 = milk and milk products; 2 = egg, fish, and meat; 3 = cereals and cereal products; 4 = pulses and pulse products; 5 = vegetables and fruits; 6 = other (oils and fats, sugar, condiments, and spices).

REFERENCES

Anand, Rahul, Ding Ding, and Volodymyr Tulin. 2014. "Food Inflation in India: The Role for Monetary Policy." IMF Working Paper 14/178, International Monetary Fund, Washington.

Anand, Rahul, Naresh Kumar, and Volodymyr Tulin. 2016. "Understanding India's Food Inflation: The Role of Demand and Supply Factors." IMF Working Paper 16/2, International Monetary Fund, Washington.

Basu, Deepankar, and Debarshi Das. 2014. "Social Hierarchies and Public Distribution of Food in Rural India." Working Paper 2014–05, University of Massachusetts Amherst, Massachusetts.

Banks, James, Richard Blundell, and Arthur Lewbel. 1997. "Quadratic Engel Curves and Consumer Demand." *Review of Economics and Statistics* 69 (4): 527–39.

Beatty, Timothy, and Erling Larsen. 2005. "Using Engel Curves to Estimate Bias in the Canadian CPI as a Cost of Living Index." *Canadian Journal of Economics*, 38 (2): 482–99.

Blanciforti, Laura, and Richard Green. 1983. "An Almost Ideal Demand System Incorporating Habits: An Analysis of Expenditures on Food and Aggregate Community Groups." *Review of Economics and Statistics* 65 (3): 511–15.

Blundell, Richard, Alan Duncan, and Krishna Pendakur. 1998. "Semiparametric Estimation and Consumer Demand." *Journal of Applied Econometrics* 13 (5): 435–61.

Commission for Agricultural Costs and Prices (CACP), Government of India. 2013. "Price Policy for Kharif Crops. The Marketing Season 2013–14." Kharif Price Policy Reports. March.

Deaton, Angus S., and John Muellbauer. 1980. "An Almost Ideal Demand System." *American Economic Review* 70 (3): 312–26.

Ganesh-Kumar A., Rajesh Mehta, Hemant Pullabhotla, Sanjay K. Prasad, Kavery Ganguly, and Ashok Gulati. 2012. "Demand and Supply of Cereals in India, 2010–2025." Discussion Paper 01158, International Food Policy Research Institute, Washington.

Gokarn, Subir. 2011. "Food Inflation—This Time It's Different." Kale Memorial Lecture, Gokhale Institute of Politics and Economics, Pune, December 9.

Government of India. 2015. "Reorienting the Role and Restructuring of Food Corporation of India." Report of the High Level Committee, New Delhi.

Gulati, Ashok, Jyoti Gujral, and T. Nandakumar. 2012. "National Food Security Bill, Challenges and Options." Discussion Paper 2, Commission on Agricultural Costs and Prices, New Delhi.

Himani. 2014. "An Analysis of Agricultural Sector in Indian Economy." *Journal of Humanities and Social Science*, 19 (1): 47–57.

Kozicka, Marta, Matthiaș Kalkuhl, Shweta Saini, and Jan Brockhaus. 2014. "Modeling Indian Wheat and Rice Sector Policies." Paper presented at the Agricultural and Applied Economics Association annual meeting, Minneapolis, July 27–29.

Kumar, Praduman, P. Shinoj, S. S. Raju, Anjani Kumar, Karl M. Rich, and Siwa Msangi. 2010. "Factor Demand, Output Supply Elasticities and Supply Projections for Major Crops in India." *Agricultural Economics Research Review* 23 (January–June): 1–14.

International Monetary Fund (IMF). 2011. "India: 2010 Article IV Consultation." IMF Country Report 11/50, Washington.

———. 2012. "India: 2012 Article IV Consultation." IMF Country Report 12/96, Washington.

———. 2013. "India: 2013 Article IV Consultation." IMF Country Report 13/37, Washington.

———. 2014a. "India: 2014 Article IV Consultation." IMF Country Report 14/57, Washington.

———. 2014b. "India: Selected Issues." IMF Country Report 14/58, Washington.

Leser, Conrad. 1963. "Forms of Engel Functions." *Econometrica* 31: 694–703.

Mittal, Surabhi. 2010. "Application of the QUAIDS Model to the Food Sector in India." *Journal of Quantitative Economics* 8(1): 42–54.

Mohan, Rakesh, and Muneesh Kapur. 2015. "Pressing the Indian Growth Accelerator: Policy Imperatives." IMF Working Paper 15/53, International Monetary Fund, Washington.

Organisation for Economic Co-operation and Development (OECD). 2009. *Agricultural Policies in Emerging Economies 2009: Monitoring and Evaluation.* Paris: OECD.

Poi, Brian P. 2002. "From the Help Desk: Demand System Estimation." *Stata Journal* 2 (4): 403–10.

———. 2008, "Demand-System Estimation: Update." *Stata Journal* 8 (4): 554–56.

Rajan, Raghuram. 2014. "Fighting Inflation." Speech at the FIMMDA-PDAI annual conference, Mumbai, February 26.

Reserve Bank of India (RBI). 2014a. *Report of the Expert Committee to Revise and Strengthen the Monetary Policy Framework.* Mumbai: RBI. http://rbidocs.rbi.org.in/rdocs/PublicationReport/Pdfs/ECOMRF210114_F.pdf.

———. 2014b. *Reserve Bank of India Annual Report 2013–14.* Mumbai: RBI.

Saini, Shweta, and Marta Kozicka. 2014. "Evolution and Critique of Buffer Stocking Policy of India." ICRIER Working Paper 283, Indian Council for Research on International Economic Relations, New Delhi.

Sonna, Thangzason, Himanshu Joshi, Alice Sebastian, and Upasana Sharma. 2014. "Analytics of Food Inflation in India." RBI Working Paper Series 10, Reserve Bank of India, Mumbai.

Walsh, James P. 2011. "Reconsidering the Role of Food Prices in Inflation." IMF Working Paper 11/71, International Monetary Fund, Washington.

Yatchew, Adonis. 2003. *Semiparametric Regression for the Applied Econometrician.* Cambridge: Cambridge University Press.

PART II

Consequences of Inflation

CHAPTER 5

Does Inflation Slow Long-Term Growth in India?

KAMIAR MOHADDES AND MEHDI RAISSI

The inflation-growth trade-off and the role of monetary policy in India have received renewed interest among policymakers and academics in recent years as persistently high inflation and weak growth happened to coexist.[1] The conventional view is that inflation at low levels greases the wheels of an economy, while at high levels it negatively affects allocative efficiency and growth. In other words, while the short-term Phillips curve postulates that inflation tolerance could be associated with higher growth, persistently high inflation by itself, and especially beyond a certain threshold, could be a drag on economic growth in the long term.

This chapter revisits the nonlinear effects of inflation on growth in India, and investigates whether a persistently elevated inflation rate (particularly above a certain threshold) could slow economic growth in the long term. Given that estimating the inflation threshold in a cross-country framework runs the risk of being distorted because of cross-country heterogeneity,[2] we instead rely on Indian state-level GDP growth and inflation data, and a heterogeneous panel technique, to estimate the inflation threshold for India. This allows for a more accurate and efficient inference of model parameters than from time-series regressions using all-India consumer price index (CPI) data or from cross-country panel data models.

Specifically, we adopt the cross-sectionally augmented distributed lag (CS-DL) approach of Chudik and others (2013, 2015) for estimation, and contrast this with the panel autoregressive distributed lag (ARDL) approach. We estimate the long-term effects of inflation on economic growth in India using a panel of 14 Indian states over 1989–2013. In contrast with the literature surveyed later in the

We are grateful to Rahul Anand, Paul Cashin, Chetan Ghate, Muneesh Kapur, Siddharth Kothari, and Rakesh Mohan, as well as seminar participants at the IMF Asia and Pacific Department Discussion Forum (November 2014) and the Third Indian Statistical Institute Delhi Macroeconomics Workshop (October 2014), for constructive comments and suggestions.

[1] Consumer price index for industrial workers (CPI-IW) inflation in India declined from 8.8 percent during India's so-called monetary targeting regime (1985/86 to 1997/98) to 5.6 percent during the first decade of the country's "multiple indicator regime" (1998/99 to 2008/09). Since 2008 retail inflation has trended up and persisted at double-digit levels.

[2] Countries with extremely low levels of inflation and those with hyperinflation are included in the same sample.

chapter, the CS-DL estimation strategy takes into account three key features of the panel data (dynamics, heterogeneity, and cross-sectional dependence), with the ARDL approach also being robust to feedback effects. Furthermore, the panel techniques adopted in this chapter allow for states to be affected differently by common factors (monetary policy, oil price spikes, or weather-related shocks),[3] as slope coefficients differ across states and cross-state averages (and their lags) proxy for unobserved common factors. The relationship between growth and inflation is also state-dependent, because high inflation can magnify the effects of supply bottlenecks in different states to varying degrees.

Our findings suggest that, on average, there is a statistically significant negative long-term relationship between inflation and economic growth in India. We also find statistically significant inflation-growth threshold effects in the case of states and periods with inflation rates above 5.5 percent. Specifically: (1) at low enough levels of inflation (below 3 percent) we do not observe any statistically significant effects of inflation on output growth; (2) average growth is higher for those states and periods that experienced inflation below 5.5 percent; and (3) when inflation is greater than 3 percent, we observe a negative and statistically significant effect of inflation on long-term growth (with this negative effect being much larger when inflation is above 5.5 percent). This result is in line with most of the estimates found in the literature on India. Mohanty and others (2011) find evidence of an inflation threshold for India in the order of 5.5 percent. Ahluwalia (2011) notes that inflation above 6 percent is "regressive and also distortionary, damaging both inclusion and growth." Using quarterly data from 1996–2011, IMF (2012) also finds evidence of an inflation threshold of about 5–6 percent in India. A distinguishing feature of this study, compared with most Indian-based writings, is its focus on CPI inflation rather than wholesale price index (WPI) inflation, as well as its use of state-level data rather than national data. And in contrast to earlier studies, we show that inflation does not have to reach the minimum "threshold" before its growth effects turn negative.[4]

Turning to policy implications, inflation is one of the most important problems facing India's economy even though inflation is driven by both supply- and demand-side factors (including the National Rural Employment Guarantee Act, supply bottlenecks, food and energy price pressures, and elevated inflation expectations). Therefore, the authorities—via supply-side reforms as well as monetary policy—should strengthen their anti-inflation efforts to avoid any negative long-term effects of excessive inflation on growth.

[3] See Cashin and others (2014) for the impact of oil-demand and oil-supply shocks on the world economy and Cashin, Mohaddes, and Raissi (2015) for the short-term effects of El Niño weather shocks on output growth and inflation on the global economy, including in India.

[4] Note that, on average, WPI inflation has been lower than CPI-IW inflation over our sample period, with the divergence between the two being more pronounced during 2005–15. Therefore, if we were to replicate the analysis using WPI inflation, we would most likely have estimated a lower WPI inflation threshold.

In the rest of this chapter, we review the literature on long-term effects of inflation on economic growth, and present the findings on the nonlinear long-term effects of inflation on growth in India. We conclude by offering some policy implications.

WHY STUDY THE INFLATION–LONG-TERM GROWTH RELATIONSHIP?

Economic theory provides mixed predictions on the effects of inflation on economic growth. Depending on how money is introduced into the model and the assumptions about its functions, inflation can have either positive or negative effects on real variables such as output and investment. Within a money-in-the-utility-function model, Sidrauski (1967) presents a superneutrality result in which changes in the rate of money growth and inflation have no effect on steady-state capital and output. The same result is obtained by Ireland (1994) within a cash-in-advance model in which money is needed in advance to finance investment expenditures and, at the same time, capital accumulation affects the role of money in the payments system. Tobin (1965) regards money as a substitute for capital, and shows that higher inflation enhances investment and causes a higher level of output. Bayoumi and Gagnon (1996) show that a positive relationship between inflation and investment can also arise if there are distortions in the tax system. Stockman (1981) examines the implications of a cash-in-advance constraint applying to investment, and argues that higher inflation decreases steady-state real-money balances and capital stock; and hence produces a reverse Tobin effect. Dornbusch and Frenkel (1973) show that the effects of inflation on real variables are ambiguous if money is introduced into the model through a transaction-cost function. However, this ambiguity disappears when money is introduced as a transaction device through a shopping-time technology, as in Saving (1971) and Kimbrough (1986).

Gillman and Kejak (2005) survey the theoretical literature on inflation and endogenous growth, and show that a broad range of models can generate a negative association between inflation and growth (see Gomme 1993, De Gregorio 1993, among others). They also analyze whether the inflation-growth relationship is nonlinear (that is, it becomes weaker as the inflation rate rises). In such models, the inflation rate affects growth because it changes the marginal product of capital, either that of physical capital (AK models) or human capital (AH models), or both in combined capital models. In AK and AH models, inflation acts as a tax on physical or human capital, which decreases the marginal product of capital and lowers growth. The nonlinearity property of the inflation-growth relationship can be explained through models that explicitly account for unemployment (see Akerlof, Dickens, and Perry 2000). According to these models, low inflation favors both employment and productivity, resulting in higher capacity utilization, a lower output gap, and, as a consequence, higher growth.

Therefore, the relationship between inflation and output growth may be positive for low levels of the inflation rate.

A large body of empirical literature exists on the relationship between inflation and growth, and we now briefly summarize three main points of these empirical findings. First, inflation could reduce growth by lowering investment and productivity. Barro (2001) provides evidence for a strongly significant negative effect of inflation on growth, while Bruno and Easterly (1998) show the inflation-growth correlation is present only when they base their cross-section regressions on annual observations, with the correlation weakening as longer-term time averages are used. There is also a strong inflation-growth relation with pooled annual data.

Second, the relationship between inflation and growth is highly nonlinear. Khan and Senhadji (2001) find a "threshold" rate of inflation above which the effect on growth is strongly significant and negative, but below which the effect is insignificant and positive. Gylfason and Hebertsson (2001) list 17 studies in which all but one find a significant decrease in the growth rate from increasing the inflation rate from 5 percent to 50 percent. Chari, Jones, and Manuelli (1996) review the empirical results from increasing the inflation rate from 10 percent to 20 percent, and report a significant fall in the growth rate within the interval 0.2 percent to 0.7 percent. Roubini and Sala-i-Martin (1992) study the relationship between inflation and growth in a panel of 98 countries over 1960–85, and find that an increase in the annual rate of inflation from 5 percent to 50 percent reduces growth per capita, all else being equal, by 2.2 percent per year. Rousseau and Wachtel (2001) report a smaller but still significant negative effect of inflation on growth in their panel study of 84 countries over 1960–95. The negative and highly nonlinear inflation-growth effect is also supported in Judson and Orphanides (1999), Ghosh and Phillips (1998), and López-Villavicencio and Mignon (2011). And third, inflation volatility is found to negatively affect production decisions and, hence, growth (see Judson and Orphanides 1999).

The inflation-growth relationship, however, is not always found to be robust. This is often owing to sample selection bias, temporal aggregation, and the omission of consequential variables in levels. Trying to address these misspecifications, Ericsson, Irons, and Tryon (2001), using 40 years of data (1953–92), show that output and inflation are positively related. They find that for most Group of Seven countries, annual time series of inflation and the log-level of output are cointegrated, thus rejecting the existence of a long-term relation between output growth and inflation. Following a different econometric approach, Bullard and Keating (1995), using a large sample of countries, find that a permanent shock to inflation is not associated with a long-term change in real output for high-inflation economies. Using instrumental variables to account for inflation-growth endogeneity bias, Gillman and Nakov (2004) show that the negative nonlinear effect is reinstated at all positive inflation levels for both developed and developing economies.

EMPIRICAL RESULTS

This section examines the long-term effects of inflation on economic growth in India, using both ARDL and CS-DL empirical specifications. We also look at the effects of inflation thresholds on long-term growth. We obtain real gross state domestic product (GSDP) and CPI data from the CEIC database and calculate growth and inflation based on these series. GSDP data is available for 32 states and union territories from 1980/81 (with the exception of Chandigarh, Chattisgarh, Jharkhand, and Uttarakhand, for which data are available only from 1993/94). Excluding the most recent measure of CPI-Combined for which official data are only available from January 2011, there are three CPI measures at the state level that we could potentially use: CPI for industrial workers (CPI-IW), CPI for agricultural laborers (CPI-AL), and CPI for rural laborers (CPI-RL). We collect monthly data on these measures for as many states as possible. CPI-AL and CPI-RL data are available for 20 states from January 1995 to December 2013, thus the number of annual observations on inflation per state is 18, which gives $N_{max} = 20$ and $T_{max} = 18$. CPI-IW data are available for 24 states, with the first observation in January 1988 for most states (except Bihar, Goa, Himachal Pradesh, Kerala, Orissa, Pondicherry, and Tripura, for which we only have data from January 1994). This gives $N_{max} = 24$ and $T_{max} = 25$.

Because our analysis allows for slope heterogeneity across states, we need a sufficient number of time periods to estimate state-specific coefficients. We therefore use CPI-IW as our preferred measure for the CPI, given that the total number of observations will be significantly larger than using either CPI-AL or CPI-RL (both N and T are larger). Moreover, we include only states in our sample for which we have at least 20 consecutive annual observations on inflation and real GDP.[5] Overall, we have an unbalanced panel covering the sample period 1989–2013, with $T_{min} = 21$, and $N = 14$ across all time periods. Figure 5.1 illustrates a simple bivariate relationship between real GSDP growth and inflation for the 14 states over the sample period. It is clear that there is a negative correlation between the two variables. In fact, plotting the two series for each of the states separately, we observe that this negative relationship exists in all states except for Madhya Pradesh and Rajasthan, for which there is a mild positive association between the two variables (Figure 5.2).

Long-Term Estimates

We first investigate the long-term effects of inflation on output growth, using the traditional panel ARDL approach, in which the long-term effects are calculated

[5]We include 14 states, which together cover more than 90 percent of India's current GDP: Andhra Pradesh, Assam, Delhi, Gujarat, Haryana, Jammu and Kashmir, Karnataka, Madhya Pradesh, Maharashtra, Punjab, Rajasthan, Tamil Nadu, Uttar Pradesh, and West Bengal.

Figure 5.1. All Indian States: Real GDP Growth and Inflation, 1989–2013
(Percent)

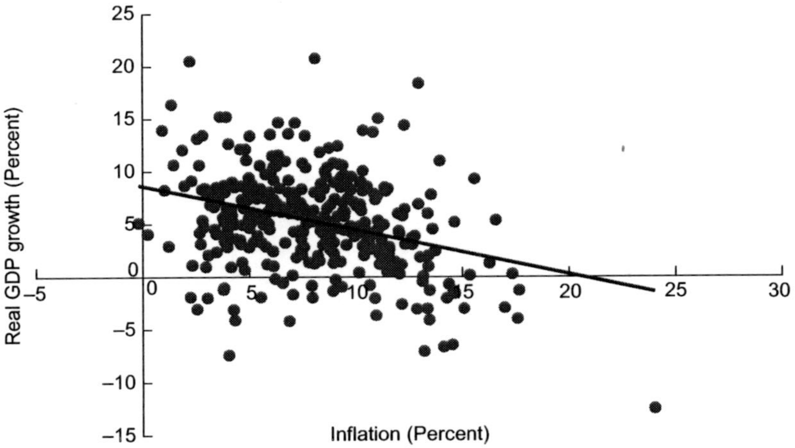

Source: Authors' calculations using data from the CEIC database.
Note: Inflation based on the consumer price index for industrial workers. See the text for a list of the 14 states in the sample.

from ordinary least squares estimates of the short-term coefficients in the following equation:

$$\Delta y_{it} = c_i + \sum_{\ell=1}^{p} \phi_{i\ell} \Delta y_{i,t-\ell} + \sum_{\ell=0}^{p} \beta_{i\ell} \pi_{i,t-\ell} + u_{it}, \tag{5.1}$$

where Δy_{it} is the growth rate of real GSDP for state i in year t, and π_{it} is the inflation rate. The coefficient on the error correction term (λ_i) and the long-term effects (θ_i) are calculated from $\phi_{i\ell}$ and $\beta_{i\ell}$, more specifically: $\lambda_i = 1 - \Sigma_{\ell=1}^{p} \phi_{i\ell}$ and $\theta_i = \lambda_i^{-1} \Sigma_{\ell=0}^{p} \beta_{i\ell}$, respectively.

We use the same lag order, p, for all variables and states, but consider different values of p in the range of 1 to 3. Given that we are working with growth rates that are only moderately persistent, a lag order of 3 should be sufficient to fully account for the short-term dynamics and hence feedback effects. Equation 5.1 allows for a significant degree of cross-sectional heterogeneity and accounts for the fact that the effect of inflation on growth could vary across states (particularly in the short term).

In a series of papers, Pesaran and Smith (1995), Pesaran (1997), and Pesaran and Shin (1999) show that the ARDL approach can be used for long-term analysis; and that it is valid regardless of whether the regressors are exogenous or endogenous, and irrespective of whether the underlying variables are $I(0)$ or $I(1)$. These features of the panel ARDL approach are both appealing and could be very

Figure 5.2. Real GDP Growth and Inflation in 14 States, 1989–2013
(Percent)

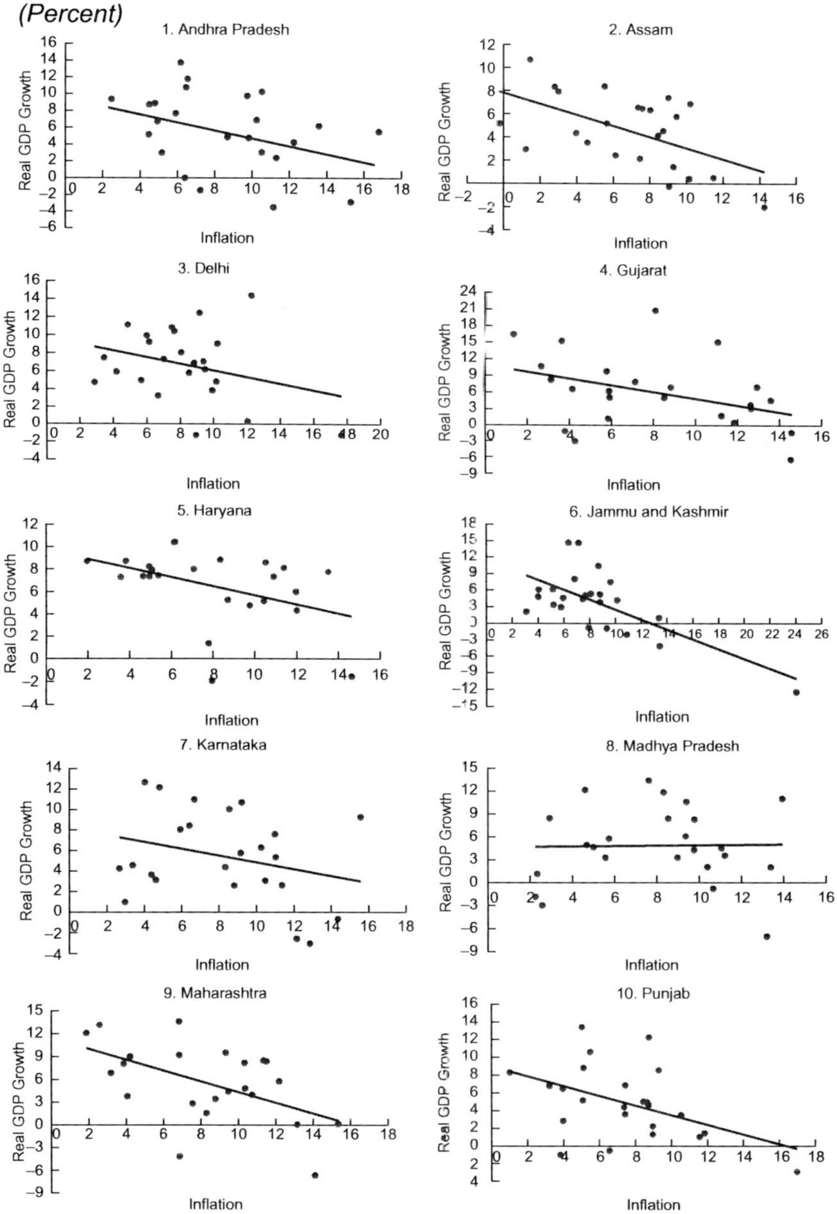

(*Continued*)

Figure 5.2 (*continued*)

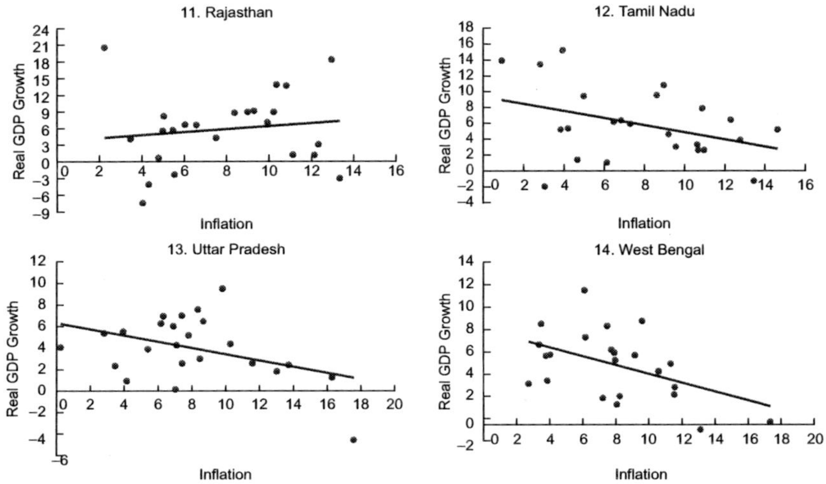

Source: Authors' calculations using data from the CEIC database.
Note: Inflation based on the consumer price index for industrial workers.

important in our empirical application. Note that we do not include any control variables in our specification, following Pesaran and Smith (2014), who argue in favor of parsimonious models when the object of interest is not the "all else equal" impact of a regressor.

The individual estimates of the long-term effects of inflation on growth, $\hat{\theta}i$, can be averaged across i to obtain a consistent estimate of the average long-term effects, given by $\hat{\theta} = N^{-1}\Sigma_i^N \hat{\theta}_i$.

These estimates, together with the mean estimate of the coefficients of the error correction term, denoted by $\hat{\lambda}$, based on the panel ARDL specification in equation 5.1, are reported in Table 5.1. For each lag order p = 1, 2, and 3, it is clear that the fixed-effects estimates, assuming slope homogeneity, suggest an inverse relationship between inflation and economic growth, with this negative effect being significant at the 1 percent level in all cases. The results from the mean group estimates, allowing for slope coefficients to vary across the Indian states, are generally supportive of this negative relationship. $\hat{\theta}$ is negative and significant at the 1 percent level when p = 1 and 2, but not for the ARDL(3,3) case. Overall, the long-term estimates based on the ARDL approach suggest that a 1 percent increase in average CPI inflation can reduce growth in India by 0.35 percent to 0.55 percent in the long term. These estimates, being between –0.05 and –0.10, are much larger than those obtained by, for instance, Chudik and others (2013) using the same ARDL specification as in equation 5.1, but for a panel of 40 countries. Our results therefore suggest that sustained high inflation levels are particularly detrimental for long-term growth in India, compared to the

TABLE 5.1

Fixed Effects and Mean Group Estimates of the Long-Term Effects Based on the ARDL Approach, 1989–2013

	ARDL(1,1)		ARDL(2,2)		ARDL(3,3)	
	FE	MG	FE	MG	FE	MG
$\hat{\theta}$	–0.375***	–0.348***	–0.465***	–0.548***	–0.448***	–0.391
	(0.075)	(0.060)	(0.112)	(0.172)	(0.120)	(0.270)
$\hat{\lambda}$	–1.066***	–0.993***	–0.850***	–0.861***	–0.885***	–0.865***
	(0.057)	(0.074)	(0.088)	(0.094)	(0.108)	(0.162)
CD test statistics	2.33	2.72	6.01	6.61	5.85	4.74
$N \times T$	320	320	306	306	292	292

Source: Authors' estimates.

Note: The autoregressive distributed lag specification is given by:

$$\Delta y_{it} = c_i + \Sigma_{\ell=1}^{p} \phi_{i\ell} \Delta y_{i,t-\ell} + \Sigma_{\ell=0}^{p} \beta_{i\ell} \pi_{i,t-\ell} + u_{it},$$

where Δy_{it} is the growth rate of real gross state domestic product, π_{it} is the inflation rate, and p = 1, 2, and 3.

$$\lambda_i = 1 - \Sigma_{\ell=1}^{p} \phi_{i\ell} \text{ and } \theta_i = \lambda_i^{-1} \Sigma_{\ell=0}^{p} \beta_{i\ell}.$$

Standard errors are reported below the estimates in parentheses. ARDL = autoregressive distributed lag; CD = cross-section dependence test of Pesaran (2004); FE = fixed effect; MG = mean group.

*** denotes significance at the 1 percent level.

average of other advanced, emerging market, and developing economies; and that the authorities should strengthen their anti-inflation efforts through appropriate monetary policies as well as through supply-side reforms. Note also that the speed of adjustment to equilibrium is very quick in all regressions, which is to be expected, given the low persistence of output growth (Table 5.1).

Table 5.1 reports the cross-section dependence (CD) test of Pesaran (2004, 2015), which is based on the average of the pair-wise correlations of the ordinary least squares residuals from the individual state regressions, and which under the null of cross-section independence is distributed as standard normal. For each p = 1, 2, and 3, we observe that the error terms across states in our model exhibit a considerable degree of cross-sectional dependence as the reported CD statistics are highly significant with very large test statistics. The presence of cross-sectional dependence implies that estimates obtained using standard panel ARDL models might be biased. To overcome this problem, one could augment the ARDL regressions with cross-sectional averages of the regressors, the dependant variable, and a sufficient number of their lags. However, as discussed in Chudik and others (2013, 2015), even when including cross-sectional averages in equation 5.1, the panel ARDL approach still has drawbacks. In particular, sampling uncertainty could be large when the time dimension is moderate (as is the case here), and the performance of the estimators also depends on a correct specification of the lag orders of the underlying ARDL specifications. The direct approach to estimating the long-term relationships proposed in Chudik and others (2013, 2015)—the CS-DL method—overcomes these issues and only requires that a truncation lag order be selected. Also, this direct method has better small-sample performance for moderate values of T, which is the case here with $T_{\min} = 20$. Furthermore, it is robust to a number of departures from the baseline specification such as residual serial correlation, and possible breaks in the error processes.

Given the advantages of the direct approach over the ARDL method, we estimate the long-term effects of inflation on the output growth of Indian states based on the CS-DL approach for different truncation lag orders, $p = 1, 2$, and 3. We therefore run the following regressions:[6]

$$\Delta y_{it} = c_i + \theta_i \pi_{it} + \sum_{\ell=0}^{p-1} \delta_{i\ell} \Delta\pi_{i,t-\ell} + \omega_{iy} \overline{\Delta y}_t + \sum_{\ell=0}^{3} \omega_{i,\pi\ell} \bar{\pi}_{t-\ell} + e_{it}, \tag{5.2}$$

where the regressors are defined as in equation 5.1. We always include three lags of the cross-sectional averages of the regressors,

$$\bar{\pi}_t = N^{-1} \Sigma_{j=1}^{N} \pi_{jt},$$

in all specifications together with the cross-sectional average of the dependent variable, $\overline{\Delta y}_t = N^{-1} \Sigma_{j=1}^{N} \Delta y_{jt}$.

The mean group estimates based on the CS-DL regressions in equation 5.2 are summarized in Table 5.2. Specifically, the mean group estimates, $\hat{\theta}$, are negative and statistically significant (in most cases at the 1 percent level). The estimated coefficients fall between –0.65 and –0.91, being much larger than those obtained based on panel ARDL regressions (see Table 5.1). Note also that the CD test statistics are now very small and we therefore cannot reject the null of cross-sectional independence. Overall, both the ARDL and the CS-DL results suggest that if inflation rises permanently and stays elevated, then it will negatively affect India's economic growth in the long term, with potential growth losses being very large. However, if the increase in inflation is temporary (perhaps due to expansionary monetary policy to stimulate the economy or when the Reserve Bank of India sees through transitory exogenous shocks), then there is no long-term adverse effect on economic growth. This requires a credible monetary policy framework that only temporarily tolerates higher inflation.

To check the robustness of our results, we did the same analysis as in equations 5.1 and 5.2 but calculating inflation using CPI-AL and CPI-RL. No matter what the measure of inflation, our results consistently show that inflation has a negative and statistically significant long-term adverse effect on growth in India. The results based on CPI-AL and CPI-RL are not reported here, but are available on request. However, as discussed earlier, note that both the time dimension, T, and the cross-sectional dimension, N, are smaller when using CPI-AL and CPI-RL. Because of this we consider the estimates based on CPI-IW inflation as more reliable.

---

[6] For the MATLAB® codes for the CS-DL mean group and pooled estimators developed in Chudik and others (2013, 2015), see http://people.ds.cam.ac.uk/km418.

TABLE 5.2

Mean Group Estimates of the Long-Term Effects Based on the CS-DL Approach, 1989–2013

	CS-DL(1)	CS-DL(2)	CS-DL(3)
$\hat{\theta}$	−0.906***	−0.835***	−0.649**
	(0.144)	(0.214)	(0.271)
CD test statistics	−0.26	0.11	−0.64
$N \times T$	306	306	306

Source: Authors' estimates.

Note: The cross-sectionally augmented distributed lag (CS-DL) regressions include the cross-sectional average of the dependent variable and three lags for the cross-sectional averages of the regressor. The CS-DL estimates are based on the following specification:

$$\Delta y_{it} = c_i + \theta_i \pi_{it} + \Sigma_{\ell=0}^{p-1} \delta_{i\ell} \Delta \pi_{i,t-\ell} + \omega_{iy} \overline{\Delta y}_t + \Sigma_{\ell=0}^{3} \omega_{i,\pi\ell} \bar{\pi}_{t-\ell} + e_{it},$$

where Δy_{it} is the growth rate of real gross state domestic product, π_{it} is the inflation rate, and p = 1, 2, and 3. Standard errors are reported below the estimates in parentheses. CD = cross-section dependence test of Pesaran (2004); FE = fixed effect; MG = mean group.

*** denotes significance at the 1 percent level, ** at the 5 percent level.

Inflation Threshold Effects on Growth

As discussed in the literature review, there is some evidence in the empirical literature that the relationship between inflation and growth (using cross-country data) is highly nonlinear. To investigate whether there is any threshold effect in the relationship between inflation and output growth for Indian states, we run a modified version of the CS-DL regression in equation 5.2 setting $p = 3$, namely:

$$\Delta y_{it} = c_{i\tau} + \gamma_{i\tau} I_{it}(\tau) + \theta_{i\tau}\pi_{it} + \sum_{\ell=0}^{2} \delta_{i\ell,\tau} \Delta\pi_{i,t-\ell} + \omega_{iy,\tau}\overline{\Delta y}_t + \sum_{\ell=0}^{3} \omega_{i,x\ell,\tau} \bar{\pi}_{t-\ell} + e_{it}, \quad (5.3)$$

where $I_{it}(\tau)$ is a "threshold dummy" defined by the indicator variable $I_{it}(\tau) = I(\pi_{it} < \tau)$ for τ = 3, ..., 6 percent and $I_{it}(\tau) = I(\pi_{it} \geq \tau)$ for τ = 7 and 8 percent, which takes the value of 1 if inflation is below or above the given threshold value of τ, and zero otherwise. All other variables are as defined in equations 5.1 and 5.2.

The results of the inflation-threshold effects on growth are reported in Table 5.3. Interestingly, when $\tau < 3$ percent, the coefficient of the threshold dummy, $\hat{\gamma}_\tau$, is positive and significant, but $\hat{\theta}_\tau$ is negative and insignificant; therefore implying that when inflation is below 3 percent not only is inflation not detrimental for long-term growth, but also that average growth is 3.4 percent greater than when $\pi_t \geq 3$ percent.[7] For all other values of τ, we observe that the long-term effects of inflation on output growth (as denoted by $\hat{\theta}_\tau$ estimates) is significant and negative, with this effect being amplified with rising inflation (the

[7] The dummy variable $I_{it}(\tau)$ divides the sample into two groups (states and periods when inflation is below τ and states and periods when inflation is above τ), and compares the average growth rates of the two groups.

TABLE 5.3

Estimates of the Average Threshold Effects on Output Growth Based on the CS-DL Approach with Three Lags, 1989–2013

τ	–	< 3%	< 4%	< 5%	< 5.5%	< 6%	≥ 7%	≥ 8%
$\hat{\gamma}_\tau$	–	3.356*	2.346*	2.185**	1.899**	−0.955	1.270	3.638
		(1.730)	(1.367)	(0.876)	(0.859)	(1.603)	(1.668)	(2.352)
$\hat{\theta}_\tau$	−0.649**	−0.475	−0.592*	−0.609*	−0.594*	−0.598*	−0.750*	−1.089**
	(0.271)	(0.551)	(0.323)	(0.319)	(0.339)	(0.357)	(0.391)	(0.459)
$N \times T$	306	306	306	306	306	306	306	306

Source: Authors' estimates.

Note: The estimates are based on the following specification:

$$\Delta y_{it} = c_{i\tau} + \gamma_{i\tau} I_{it}(\tau) + \theta_{i\tau}\pi_{it} + \Sigma_{\ell=0}^{2}\delta_{i\ell,\tau}\Delta\pi_{i,t-\ell} + \omega_{iy,\tau}\overline{\Delta y}_t + \Sigma_{\ell=0}^{3}\omega_{i,\pi\ell,\tau}\bar{\pi}_{t-\ell} + e_{it},$$

where $I_{it}(\tau) = I(\pi_{it} < \tau)$ for $\tau < 6$ percent and $I_{it}(\tau) = I(\pi_{it} \geq \tau)$ for $\tau \geq 7$ percent, Δy_{it} is the growth rate of real gross state domestic product, and π_{it} is the inflation rate. The cross-sectionally augmented distributed lag (CS-DL) regressions include the cross-sectional average of the dependent variable and three lags for the cross-sectional averages of the regressors. Standard errors are reported below the estimates in parentheses. CD = cross-section dependence test of Pesaran (2004); FE = fixed effect; MG = mean group.

** denotes significance at the 5 percent level, * at the 10 percent level.

higher the τ threshold is). More importantly, $\hat{\gamma}_\tau$ is positive and significant for all $\tau < 5.5$ percent, suggesting average growth is higher when inflation remains at low levels. More specifically, our estimates suggest that average growth was 1.9 percent higher when $\pi_t < 5.5$ percent. In other words, at lower inflation rates (less than 5.5 percent) some of the negative growth effects of inflation (as represented by $\hat{\theta}_\tau$) are offset, given that the coefficient of the threshold dummy, $\hat{\gamma}_\tau$ is positive and statistically significant. On the other hand, for inflation rates above 5.5 percent we show that the negative growth effect of inflation is larger, while at the same time the coefficient on the threshold dummy ($\hat{\gamma}_\tau$) is no longer statistically significant.

The results in Tables 5.1 and 5.3 consistently show that the effect of inflation on long-term growth in India is negative, but we now also have some evidence for a threshold effect at an inflation rate of 5.5 percent and above, where the detrimental growth effect of inflation is more severe (see Table 5.3). This means that monetary policy would need to balance any short-term growth-inflation trade-off (that is, the short-term Phillips curve) against the long-term negative effects of persistently high inflation on growth, and maintain the allocative efficiency of the Indian economy by keeping inflation below the threshold.[8]

Our results are generally supported by other studies on India, which to the best of our knowledge use time series national data exclusively rather than cross-state data and the WPI (rather than the CPI-IW measure).[9] More specifically, the literature indicates that the Indian inflation threshold is typically 6–7 percent (see for instance Kannan and Joshi 1998, Rangarajan 1998, and Samantaraya and

[8] This chapter does not suggest that the optimal inflation rate for India is 5.5 percent. Instead, it shows that the negative effects of inflation on output growth are substantially larger once the inflation rate is above 5.5 percent.

[9] See RBI (2014) for a summary of the estimates of inflation threshold effects on growth from earlier time-series studies.

Prasad 2001), while Vasudevan, Bhoi, and Dhal (1998) suggest a lower threshold of 5–7 percent. More recent work by Singh (2010) and Pattanaik and Nadhanael (2013), using data from 1970 to 2009 and 2011, respectively, also indicate that the inflation threshold is about 6 percent. In addition, based on quarterly data from 1996–2012, IMF (2012) finds evidence for an inflation threshold of about 5–6 percent in India, while Mohanty and others (2011) estimate the inflation threshold effect at 4.0–5.5 percent.

CONCLUSIONS

Based on annual data on 14 Indian states during 1989–2013, we examined the growth-inflation relationship in the country using the CS-DL approach of Chudik and others (2013, 2015), as well as the standard panel ARDL methodology. We also tested empirically for the existence of a threshold level of inflation beyond which growth is severely undermined. Our results indicate that the negative growth effects of inflation are more pronounced above an inflation threshold of about 5.5 percent. We recognize that inflation in India is a result of a number of factors, including supply-driven food inflation feeding quickly into wages and core inflation; entrenched inflation expectations; binding sector-specific supply constraints (particularly in agriculture, energy, and transportation); and fuel price increases (Anand, Ding, and Tulin 2014). Nevertheless, high and persistent inflation, no matter how it is created, is a key vulnerability, and the Reserve Bank of India should strengthen its anti-inflation efforts to avoid any negative long-term effects of excessive inflation on growth.

REFERENCES

Ahluwalia, M. S. 2011. "Prospects and Policy Challenges in the Twelfth Plan." *Economic and Political Weekly* 46 (21): 88–105.

Akerlof, G. A., W. T. Dickens, and G. L. Perry. 2000. "Near-Rational Wage and Price Setting and the Long-Term Phillips Curve." *Brookings Papers on Economic Activity* (1): 1–44.

Anand, R., D. Ding, and V. Tulin. 2014. "Food Inflation in India: The Role for Monetary Policy." IMF Working Paper 14/178, International Monetary Fund, Washington.

Barro, R. J. 2001. "Human Capital and Growth." *American Economic Review* 91 (2): 12–17.

Bayoumi, T., and J. Gagnon. 1996. "Taxation and Inflation: A New Explanation for Capital Flows." *Journal of Monetary Economics* 38 (2): 303–30.

Bruno, M., and W. Easterly. 1998. "Inflation Crises and Long-Term Growth." *Journal of Monetary Economics* 41 (1): 3–26.

Bullard, J., and J. W. Keating. 1995. "The Long-Term Relationship between Inflation and Output in Postwar Economies." *Journal of Monetary Economics* 36 (3): 477–96.

Cashin, P., K. Mohaddes, and M. Raissi. 2015. "Fair Weather or Foul? The Macroeconomic Effects of El Niño." IMF Working Paper 15/89, International Monetary Fund, Washington.

Cashin, P., K. Mohaddes, M. Raissi, and M. Raissi. 2014. "The Differential Effects of Oil Demand and Suppl-y Shocks on the Global Economy." *Energy Economics* 44 (July): 113–34.

Chari, V. V., L. E. Jones, and R. E. Manuelli. 1996. "Inflation, Growth, and Financial Intermediation." *Federal Reserve Bank of St. Louis Review* (May/June): 41–58.

Chudik, A., K. Mohaddes, M. H. Pesaran, and M. Raissi. 2013. "Debt, Inflation and Growth: Robust Estimation of Long-Term Effects in Dynamic Panel Data Models." CESifo Working Paper 4508, CESifo Group, Munich.

———. 2015. "Long-Term Effects in Large Heterogeneous Panel Data Models with Cross-Sectionally Correlated Errors." Working Paper 223, Federal Reserve Bank of Dallas.

De Gregorio, J. 1993. "Inflation, Taxation, and Long-Term Growth." *Journal of Monetary Economics* 31 (3): 271–98.

Dornbusch, R., and J. A. Frenkel. 1973. "Inflation and Growth: Alternative Approaches." *Journal of Money, Credit and Banking* 5 (1): 141–56.

Ericsson, N. R., J. S. Irons, and R. W. Tryon. 2001. "Output and Inflation in the Long Run." *Journal of Applied Econometrics* 16 (3): 241–53.

Ghosh, A., and S. Phillips. 1998. "Warning: Inflation May Be Harmful to Your Growth." *IMF Staff Papers* 45 (4): 672–710.

Gillman, M., and M. Kejak. 2005. "Contrasting Models of the Effect of Inflation on Growth." *Journal of Economic Surveys* 19 (1): 113–36.

Gillman, M., and A. Nakov. 2004. "Granger Causality of the Inflation-Growth Mirror in Accession Countries." *Economics of Transition* 12 (4): 653–81.

Gomme, P. 1993. "Money and Growth Revisited: Measuring the Costs of Inflation in an Endogenous Growth Model." *Journal of Monetary Economics* 32 (1): 51–77.

Gylfason, T., and T. T. Herbertsson. 2001. "Does Inflation Matter for Growth?" *Japan and the World Economy* 13 (4): 405–28.

International Monetary Fund (IMF). 2012. "The Output-Inflation Trade-Off in India: Implications for Disinflation." Box 5 in "India: Article IV Consultation Report." IMF Country Report 12/96, Washington.

Ireland, P. N. 1994. "Money and Growth: An Alternative Approach." *American Economic Review* 84 (1): 47–65.

Judson, R., and A. Orphanides. 1999. "Inflation, Volatility and Growth." *International Finance* 2 (1): 117–38.

Kannan, R., and H. Joshi. 1998. "Growth-Inflation Trade-Off: Empirical Estimation of Threshold Rate of Inflation for India." *Economic and Political Weekly* 33 (42/43): 2724–28.

Khan, M. S., and A. S. Senhadji. 2001. "Threshold Effects in the Relationship between Inflation and Growth." *IMF Staff Papers* 48 (1): 1–21.

Kimbrough, K. P. 1986. "The Optimum Quantity of Money Rule in the Theory of Public Finance." *Journal of Monetary Economics* 18 (3): 277–84.

López-Villavicencio, A., and V. Mignon. 2011. "On the Impact of Inflation on Output Growth: Does the Level of Inflation Matter?" *Journal of Macroeconomics* 33 (3): 455–64.

Mohanty, D., A. B. Chakraborty, A. Das, and J. John. 2011. "Inflation Threshold in India: An Empirical Investigation." RBI Working Paper Series 18/2011, Reserve Bank of India, Mumbai.

Pattanaik, S., and G. Nadhanael. 2013. "Why Persistent High Inflation Impedes Growth: An Empirical Assessment of Threshold Level of Inflation for India." *Macroeconomics and Finance in Emerging Market Economies* 6 (2): 204–20.

Pesaran, M. H., 1997. "The Role of Economic Theory in Modelling the Long Run." *Economic Journal* 107: 178–191.

———. 2004. "General Diagnostic Tests for Cross Section Dependence in Panels." Discussion Paper 1240, Institute for the Study of Labor, Bonn.

———. 2015. "Testing Weak Cross-Sectional Dependence in Large Panels." *Econometric Reviews* 34 (6–10): 1089–117.

Pesaran, M. H., and Y. Shin. 1999. "An Autoregressive Distributed Lag Modelling Approach to Cointegration Analysis." In *Econometrics and Economic Theory in the 20th Century: The Ragnar Frisch Centennial Symposium*, edited by S. Strom. Cambridge: Cambridge University Press.

Pesaran, M. H., and R. Smith. 1995. "Estimating Long-Term Relationships from Dynamic Heterogeneous Panels." *Journal of Econometrics* 68 (1): 79–113.

———. 2014. "Signs of Impact Effects in Time Series Regression Models." *Economics Letters* 122 (2): 150–53.

Rangarajan, C. 1998. "Development, Inflation and Monetary Policy." In *India's Economic Reforms and Development*, edited by I. S. Ahluwalia and I. M. D. Little. Oxford: Oxford University Press.

Reserve Bank of India (RBI). 2014. *Report of the Expert Committee to Revise and Strengthen the Monetary Policy Framework*. Mumbai: RBI.

Roubini, N., and X. Sala-i-Martin. 1992. "Financial Repression and Economic Growth." *Journal of Development Economics* 39 (1): 5–30.

Rousseau, P. L., and P. Wachtel. 2001. "Inflation, Financial Development and Growth." In *Economic Theory Dynamics and Markets: Essays in Honor of Ryuzo Sato*. Berlin: Springer.

Samantaraya, A., and A. Prasad. 2001. "Growth and Inflation in India: Detecting the Threshold." *Asian Economic Review* 43: 414–20.

Saving, T. R. 1971. "Transactions Costs and the Demand for Money." *American Economic Review* 61 (3): 407–20.

Sidrauski, M. 1967. "Rational Choice and Patterns of Growth in a Monetary Economy." *American Economic Review* 57 (2): 534–44.

Singh, P. 2010. "Searching Threshold Inflation for India." *Economics Bulletin* 30 (4): 3209–20.

Stockman, A. C. 1981. "Anticipated Inflation and the Capital Stock in a Cash-in-Advance Economy." *Journal of Monetary Economics* 8 (3): 387–93.

Tobin, J. 1965. "Money and Economic Growth." *Econometrica* 33 (4): 671–84.

Vasudevan, A., B. K. Bhoi, and S. C. Dhal. 1998. "Inflation Rate and Optimal Growth: Is There a Gateway to Nirvana?" In *Fifty Years of Developmental Economics: Essays in Honour of Professor P. R. Brahmananda*, edited by A. Vasudevan. Mumbai: Himalaya Publishing House.

CHAPTER 6

Inflation and Income Inequality in China and India: Is Food Inflation Different?

JAMES P. WALSH AND JIANGYAN YU

Rapid growth in developing economies has led to an important decline in poverty both at the national level and, owing to the large size of China and India where growth has been especially rapid, globally. However, in many emerging markets, income inequality has risen as more open and market-oriented economies increased profits and potential wages, particularly for skilled labor. At the same time, rapid growth has pushed up commodity prices around the globe, raising questions about whether a seemingly inexorable rise in food prices is aggravating the problems faced by the world's poor.

Although inflation is often seen as aggravating poverty and worsening income distribution, the distinction between food and nonfood inflation bears examining. Higher food prices can hurt the well-being of many poor people, particularly in urban areas, but may benefit producers, thereby reducing poverty among some in rural areas. Based on datasets of food and nonfood prices available at the global level (described in Annex 6.1), as well as subnationally for Chinese provinces and Indian states, the analysis in this chapter attempts to distinguish between the effect of food and nonfood inflation on changes in income inequality.

INFLATION AND POVERTY

The relationship between inflation on the one hand, and poverty and income inequality on the other, remains unsettled in the literature, though many find that inflation generally worsens inequality. Romer and Romer (1999) look at the incomes of the poor and show that both in the United States and globally, higher inflation when accompanying economic growth can support the incomes of the poor in the short term. But in the long term, by adding to economic uncertainty, it can depress both average incomes and the incomes of the poor. Easterly and Fischer (2000) looked at a very large sample of household survey data across a wide range of countries and found that the poor were more likely than the rich to cite inflation as a problem, and that inflation tended to worsen the assessment of their own well-being more than it did for the rich. Various household-level studies on countries including Brazil, India, and the Philippines also found that higher inflation leads to a lower share of income held by the poorest share of the population.

How Does Inflation Hurt the Poor?

Various channels are posited through which inflation might hurt incomes of the poor more than the rich, such as their ability to borrow and smooth consumption, deposit cash in banks or buy bonds with a return that can exceed inflation, or their greater likelihood of owning a house and being insulated from rents. These channels might exist in any country, but some are likely to be more prevalent in developed economies, and others, such as the inadequate indexation of social benefits, are unlikely to be significant in developing economies. There are various channels by which inflation might disproportionately affect the poor. Economies of scale and barriers to entry in financial services can reduce the access of the poor to inflation hedges that the rich can access; the relatively competitive labor market for unskilled labor in developing economies reduces the bargaining power of poor workers; and storage technology (home storage for buying quantities of goods for later use and the ability to freeze perishable foods, for example) can help lock in prices for goods consumed later. Households can also hedge by allocating their portfolios between cash, which rapidly loses value, and consumption goods, which may lose value less quickly. Middle-income households confronted with rising inflation might therefore bring forward purchases of clothing, appliances, houseware, or other products in their consumption basket. But the consumption basket of poor households is disproportionately focused on food, which cannot really be brought forward because of its perishability. This same dependence on cash balances can also hurt the power of poor households in negotiating prices or wages, compared to rich households.

Another strand of the literature looks specifically at food prices and the poor. Rising food prices are likely to raise the incomes of food producers. This could compensate for lower incomes that would accrue to artisans or other households in rural areas, but only if rural households that do not own land or are net purchasers of food are relatively few. Deaton (1989) uses a nonparametric analysis of the effect of higher rice prices across different regions of Thailand, and shows that higher food prices can benefit many groups in society, though middle-class food producers benefit the most overall. Ravallion (2000) looks at the interrelationship over more than 30 years between food prices, poverty, and wages in India to analyze whether agricultural reform helps or hurts the poor. While corroborating other work that shows inflation reduces rural expenditure, he notes that once agricultural output and overall inflation are taken into account, food prices do not appear to have an independent effect on real wages. So although households may take an immediate hit when food prices rise, rising rural productivity will, in the longer term, affect both food producers and the wages of rural laborers, which would reduce rural income inequality. The effect of higher food prices on income distribution can thus be neutral if wages for laborers adjust sufficiently.

Other studies suggest that wages may not be so flexible. Numerous studies present evidence suggesting that wages may not fully adjust to higher food prices, in which case the poor suffer more, given the higher share of food in their consumption basket. Overall, the distributional impact will depend on the extent to which households are net producers or consumers of food. And both first- and second-round effects can matter. Incomes for nonfood-producing households could rise if the greater income accruing to food-producing households trickles down to other households via greater economic activity.

Urban and Rural Differences

In countries with significant rural-urban migration, such as China or India, higher rural wages (from higher food prices) relative to urban ones (also from higher food prices) affect household migration decisions. A shift in relative prices toward food, which constitutes a very large share of the consumption basket for the very poor, could have large effects on these decisions by discouraging marginal households in rural areas from sending workers to cities, or encouraging newly impoverished urban workers to return to the countryside. As these urban workers move home to rural areas, they remove the poorest segment of urban society from the cities, and, all else being equal, reduce income inequality in cities there. This movement mitigates the effect of higher food prices on income distribution (though obviously not mitigating its effect on individual households). Conversely, if higher food prices encourage the landless or other net food purchasers in rural areas to take advantage of the better wage opportunities cities afford, the net effect on rural areas could be the opposite. That is, those with relatively high and stable incomes are unlikely to leave, meaning that the rural poor who migrate are likely to be poorer and that their movement to the cities can thus reduce income inequality there.[1]

Given the evidence that headline inflation in many cases exacerbates income inequality, while rising food prices may have a more moderate or even benign impact, the likely upshot is that nonfood inflation must be particularly damaging to the poor. If higher food prices in rural areas pass through to wages, (that is, if wages in rural areas are elastic to food price increases), then food inflation should be less harmful, or possibly beneficial, in its effect on income inequality in rural areas. The relationship could also hold in urban areas, but given that more rural inhabitants are likely to be involved in agriculture, the relationship is likely to be stronger in rural areas. Nonfood inflation, on the other hand, should widen income inequality in both urban and rural areas.

---

[1] They are unlikely to be the very poorest among rural households, however, because the lowest-income rural households, including the elderly, disadvantaged groups, and extremely small households, are unlikely to have the assets to leave home.

HOW DO OTHER FACTORS MATTER?

Nonfood inflation could thus be strongly correlated with worsening income inequality once other factors known to mitigate worsening income inequality, such as education and average income growth, have been taken into account. For food inflation, the relationship is less clear.

At the international level, food inflation should immiserate the poor in food-importing countries, while it could reduce inequality in food-exporting countries. Because most countries both import and export some food, and because the incomes of producers of different types of food can differ greatly, the aggregate relationship may not be clear just from the balance of trade. If food inflation adds to income inequality at the international level, by raising inequality in some countries by more than it reduces it elsewhere, then, on average, it is likely that wages in general are not particularly responsive to food prices. A link between higher food inflation and declining income inequality would most likely imply that the wages for the rural poor across the world are elastic to food prices. On the other hand, if food prices have little effect in aggregate, or if food inflation tends to reduce income inequality, then these wage effects must be present and could be quite large. As a first pass at this question, the following section uses a large dataset of food and nonfood inflation across a wide range of countries to assess how these price changes affect income inequality across countries and across time. The analysis is then extended to Chinese provinces, for which appropriate data are available, to see whether these effects are also visible at a national level.

At the domestic level, if wages in rural areas are relatively elastic to food prices, then higher food inflation will improve or at least not worsen income inequality in rural areas, while its effect in urban areas is likely to be negative, as with non-food inflation. These effects can be studied more closely in the case of India, where richer subnational data are available. India estimates income inequality for both urban and rural areas across the various states. Consumer price index (CPI) data are estimated at the state level of rural areas within each state, and proxies can be calculated for urban areas. Using these data, we can separately assess the impact of food and nonfood inflation on both rural and urban income inequality. Nonfood inflation should lead to worsening income inequality in both regions, and food inflation in urban areas should also result in worsening income inequality. But if wages in rural areas react elastically to increases in food prices, then higher food inflation should lead to a decline in income inequality in rural areas.

STYLIZED FACTS

Global Inequality

Figure 6.1 shows how Gini coefficients have changed over time for the countries in the sample, compared to GDP per capita. On average, Gini coefficients have not changed drastically across countries in the sample, except in richer countries,

Figure 6.1. Cross-Country GDP per Capita and Gini Change, 2000–10

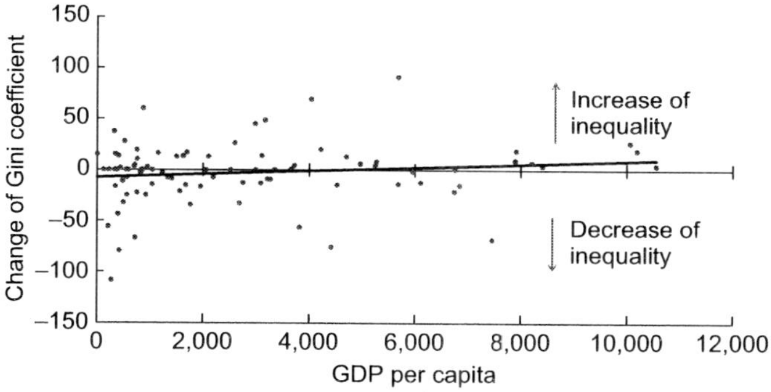

Source: World Bank, World Development Indicators.

Figure 6.2. Cross-Country Food Inflation and Gini Change, 2000–10

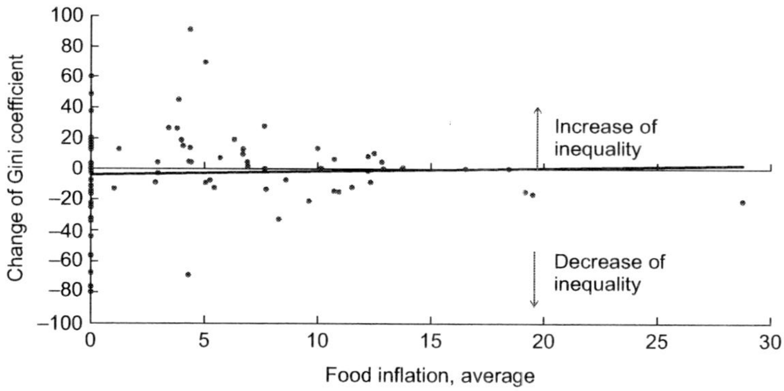

Sources: World Bank, World Development Indicators; and IMF staff calculations.

where they have risen slightly since 2000. Figures 6.2 and 6.3 show Gini coefficients related to food and nonfood inflation. In general, during 2000–10, income inequality actually declined in countries with higher inflation, both food and nonfood; and the relationship between inequality and food inflation does not appear significantly different than that between inequality and nonfood inflation, though in these charts other control factors, such as GDP growth, are not yet taken into account.

China

China's rapid economic growth over the past few decades has coincided with a noticeable deterioration in income distribution. The country's Gini coefficient is estimated to have reached 0.42–0.47 in the late 2000s, from below 0.3 in the early

Figure 6.3. Cross-Country Nonfood Inflation and Gini Change, 2000–10

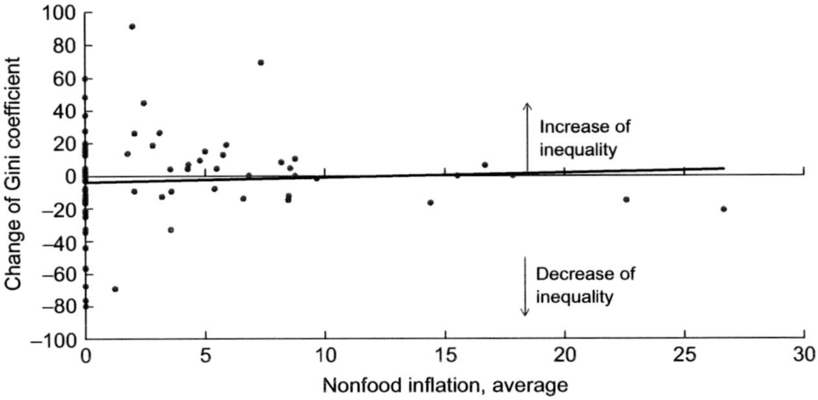

Sources: World Bank, World Development Indicators; and IMF staff calculations.

Figure 6.4. China: Provincial GDP per Capita and Inequality Change, 2000–05

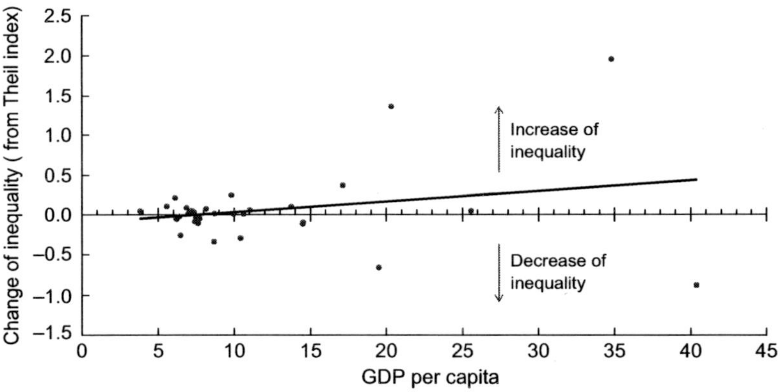

Sources: Data from the University of Texas Inequality Project; and World Bank, World Development Indicators.

1980s.[2] Since 1992 the urban income disparity has replaced the rural one to become the most important driver of overall income inequality.

Figure 6.4 shows that GDP per capita grew very rapidly across all Chinese provinces in the first half of the 2000s, but most provinces also saw an increase in inequality, with the fastest-growing ones seeing slightly larger increases. Figures 6.5

[2] Estimates of the Gini coefficient by international institutions range from 0.42 to 0.47 in 2005–07. Cheng (2007) estimates the Gini coefficient at 0.29 in 1981.

Figure 6.5. China: Food Inflation and Theil Index Change, 2000–05

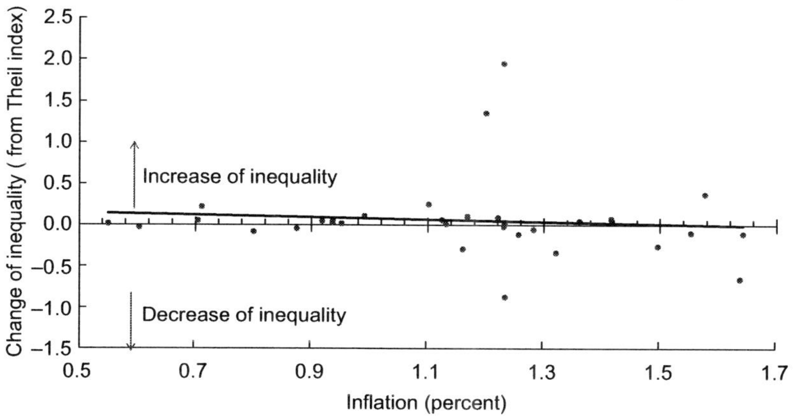

Source: IMF staff calculations.

Figure 6.6. China: Nonfood Inflation and Theil Index Change, 2000–05

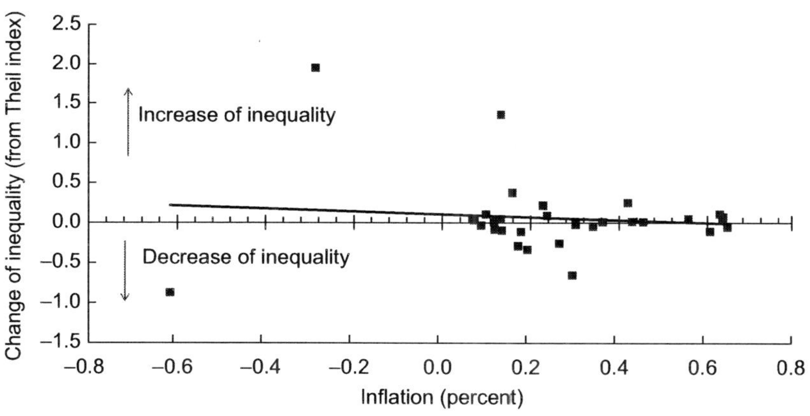

Source: IMF staff calculations.

and 6.6 show that the change in the Theil index is only slightly correlated with food and nonfood inflation. However, these simple correlations do not account for (very rapid) growth in income or other significant macroeconomic and structural factors.

India

Figure 6.7 shows the pattern of urban and rural inequality across the largest Indian states. Rural inequality is higher than urban inequality in every state, and

Figure 6.7. India: Inequality and GDP per Capita by State

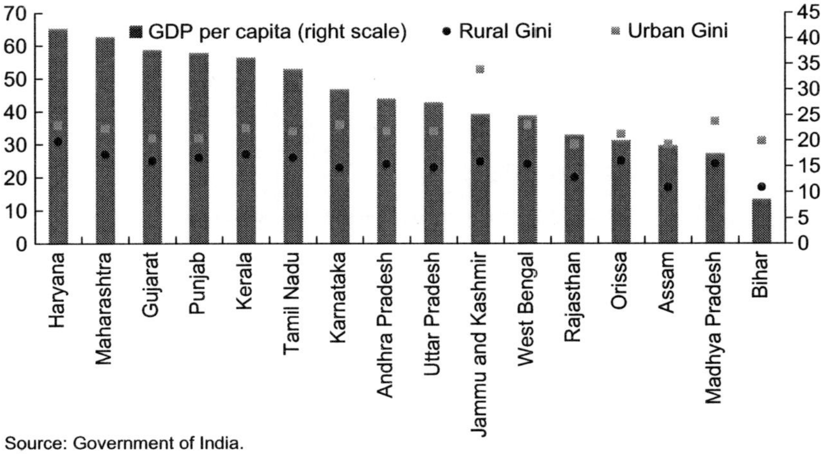

Source: Government of India.

Figure 6.8. India: GDP Per Capita Growth and Gini Change in 16 States, 1994–2004

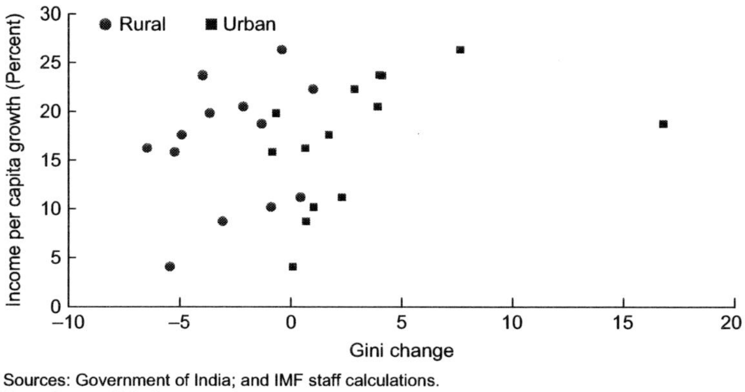

Sources: Government of India; and IMF staff calculations.
Note: Covers 16 Indian states.

while the former tends not to vary much across states, urban inequality tends to be greater in the richer states than poorer ones. Figure 6.8 shows how income per capita growth between 1994 and 2004 related to changes in income inequality. In general, as in China, inequality rose more in the faster-growing states, and with the breakdown between rural and urban data available, it can be seen that this effect was stronger in urban areas.

RESULTS

International Sample

In this sample and analysis, headline inflation does not appear to have a strong relationship with income inequality under most specifications (Annex Table 6.2.1). Once simultaneity is taken into account (under the Arellano-Bond specification in column 4 of the table), higher GDP growth is associated with higher income inequality, while higher GDP per capita is associated with slightly lower income inequality. Higher rates of enrollment in primary education are associated with decreases in income inequality. Secondary school enrollment has a less consistent effect, but when significant is also associated with falling inequality. Breaking inflation down into food and nonfood inflation produces somewhat different results, as shown in Annex Table 6.2.2. The relationship between changes in income inequality and food and nonfood inflation is significant only when simultaneity is taken into account under specification (4), and is not consistent across specifications. Nonfood inflation is associated with rising income inequality, the expected result, only under the Arellano-Bond specification. Food inflation is only significant under this specification and is associated with falling income inequality. Income, as measured by GDP per capita, is not significant under any specification, while average real GDP growth is associated with slightly lower income inequality in the fixed- and random-effects specifications, but not when simultaneity is taken into account. The counterintuitive results about education are no longer present, with secondary school enrollment now intuitively associated with somewhat lower income inequality under the Arellano-Bond specification.[3]

China

The results from Chinese provinces, once endogeneity is taken into account via the Arellano-Bond specification, show that higher headline inflation is associated with more rapid widening of inequality, as measured by a Theil coefficient (Annex Table 6.2.3). Higher GDP growth is associated with a slower pace of deterioration in income inequality, while richer provinces tend to have bigger increases.

When inflation is divided into food and nonfood inflation, the picture is somewhat different (Annex Table 6.2.4). The coefficient on nonfood inflation has the expected positive sign in three of the four specifications, but is only significant under the Arellano-Bond generalized method of moments specification. Food inflation is associated with less income inequality under each specification, but this is not significant. As in the headline CPI regressions, faster GDP growth is associated with declining inequality, while this effect is mitigated in richer provinces, where inequality tends to rise more rapidly.

---

[3]This in itself may be surprising, because access to primary education might be expected to be a more important driver of reducing income inequality than secondary or tertiary education.

India

Indian income inequality data are available not only on a state level, but also broken down between urban and rural areas, allowing for some distinction between food-producing and food-importing regions.

Annex Tables 6.2.5 and 6.2.6 show the relationship between headline CPI and income inequality (as measured with Gini coefficients) across rural and urban areas in Indian states. In rural areas (Annex Table 6.2.5) headline inflation shows little relation to income inequality, with the coefficient very close to zero, except under the Arellano-Bond specification. Higher income per capita is associated with higher inequality under three specifications, however. In urban areas (Annex Table 6.2.6), the results are more intuitive: the coefficient on headline inflation is positive and significant under two specifications, including when accounting for simultaneity, while higher levels of income per capita are also associated with rising income inequality. Literacy and real GDP growth are not generally significant.

When the CPI is divided into food and nonfood inflation, the results are stronger. In rural areas (Annex Table 6.2.7), food inflation is strongly linked to lower income inequality, while nonfood inflation, intuitively, is linked to higher income inequality. Again, states with higher levels of income per capita are associated with rising income inequality, though real GDP growth itself, as well as literacy, are not.

In urban areas, as expected, higher nonfood inflation is strongly tied to higher income inequality (Annex Table 6.2.8). Food inflation, on the other hand, is more ambiguous. The coefficient on food inflation is negative in all specifications, implying that wages are flexible and respond to higher food prices, though the result is significant only in two specifications and not under Arellano-Bond. As with rural inflation, states with higher income appear to have rising income inequality, while GDP growth and literacy have little effect.

CONCLUSION

The results presented in this chapter are relatively agnostic about whether headline inflation is detrimental to income inequality, but they are able to extend the analysis beyond this broad measure of inflation. Higher nonfood inflation is associated with worsening income inequality in all three samples (international, China, India), supporting the results from previous work suggesting that income inequality is aggravated by higher levels of inflation. This is intuitive, given that an individual household's income can benefit from higher prices only for the goods or services that it produces, and no individual household is likely to be a producer of a sufficiently wide share of the country's nonfood consumption basket.

However, this detrimental impact is smaller for food inflation. In the international sample, and once the endogeneity of inflation, inequality, and growth are taken into account, higher food inflation is associated with declining income inequality—and the same is true for the Chinese data. These results suggest that food inflation may not be bad for all lower-income people, or at least that the hit to income taken by some groups may be balanced or even exceeded by increased income accruing to other groups, such as low-income food producers.

The Indian data allow some finer conclusions to be drawn. By differentiating between urban and rural inequality, they provide further support to the view that nonfood inflation widens income inequality in both urban and rural areas. Food inflation has different effects, however. The effect on urban inequality is ambiguous, but in rural areas it is strongly associated with lower inequality. This is somewhat counterintuitive. Because few urban dwellers are likely to be food producers, it seems reasonable to expect that higher food prices have a negative effect on households that are most exposed to food prices; that is, the poor. But here the effect of rising food prices on urban inequality does not appear to be particularly strong. And in rural areas, the effect appears to be strongly positive (in the sense of lower inequality).

These results should also be taken with a number of caveats. China and India are relatively closed economies for staple foods. Countries that import a large share of their staple crops, such as wheat or corn, may have very different dynamics of food prices and income inequality than countries where some important staple crops (rice in both countries, and also pulses in India) are not as susceptible to global commodity shocks. Unlike corn or wheat, the global market for rice and pulses is small and relatively unimportant; beyond that, even differing provinces in China or states in India have limited substitutability of crops. Thus, self-sufficiency means that China and India are as likely to have a higher share of households producing staple crops as countries that either export or are reasonably self-sufficient in staples. Even within China and India, the effect of food inflation is likely to be greatest in food-importing states and provinces, though this would have to be studied using household data across states or provinces.

India and particularly China, as high-growth economies, may have a different relationship between food production and rural wages. With relatively good opportunities for labor in urban areas and, especially in China, rising agricultural productivity, the ease with which unskilled workers are able to shift from the rural to the urban labor force may be greater than in other countries. This process mutes increases in income inequality in rural areas and provides more of a safety valve for rural workers than would exist in countries with slower growth. With more limited employment opportunities in urban areas, food inflation could be significantly more immiserating for rural consumers in slower-growing economies.

ANNEX 6.1. DATA SOURCES

International data on food and nonfood inflation are compiled from public country sources and were used in Walsh (2010). GDP per capita, as well as real economic growth, are from the IMF's World Economic Outlook database. Macroeconomic data for China and India come from CEIC. For China, provincial-level food and nonfood price indices were derived from consumer price index (CPI) data, with weights estimated by IMF staff. For India, state-level food and nonfood inflation were also estimated based on CPI data. CPI for agricultural workers is calculated on a state-by-state basis; this is used as the rural price index. CPI for industrial workers is calculated on a municipal basis. For each state, CPI for industrial worker indices for each city in the state were averaged and weighed by the urban area's 2001 population to arrive at a proxy for urban CPI indices for each state.

Inequality data come from a variety of sources. For the global regression, the data for inequality are measured by annual Gini coefficients from the World Bank's World Development Indicators database estimated from 1990 to 2010 for 75 advanced, transition, and developing economies. Because there is no official publication of Gini coefficients for Chinese provinces, this chapter uses provincial Theil indices estimated by the University of Texas to measure inequality. The data cover 31 provinces, municipalities, and autonomous regions over 1994–2006. Indian inequality data come from various government sources and are based on the government's National Sample Survey Rounds covering 1990–2004, when India began to open to reforms. However, there are not yet income inequality data for the high-growth period of the mid-2000s.

The following sources were used for other data. For the international sample, education level is presented as the levels of primary and secondary school enrollment rates from the World Bank's World Development Indicators database. For China, the picture is more complicated. According to data published by the Ministry of Education, the primary enrollment ratio changed by a small margin from 108¾ percent in 1994 to 106¼ percent in 2006, meaning there is little variation over time that can be used in estimation. However, although provincial-level data are not published in a comprehensive way, it is believed that western provinces tend to have lower enrollment than the more developed provinces in the middle and coastal provinces. For tertiary education, there is some difference: during the period under study, enrollment in higher education rose significantly. However, the dramatic mobility of educated workers makes it difficult to gauge the relationship of well-educated workers with inequality. Therefore in this model, education level is treated as a province-specific and time-invariant factor. In India, educational attainment differs more across states than it does in China, and both urban and rural literacy rates are available by state. These data are used in the analysis.

ANNEX 6.2. REGRESSION RESULTS

ANNEX TABLE 6.2.1

International Sample: Headline Inflation

	(1) OLS Δ Gini Coefficient	(2) Fixed Effects Δ Gini Coefficient	(3) Random Effects Δ Gini Coefficient	(4) Arellano-Bond Δ Gini Coefficient
CPI Inflation	0.00698	−0.0455	−0.0136	0.0433
	−0.32	(−1.77)	(−0.59)	−1.73
Nominal GDP	−0.00159	0.00291	−0.000738	0.00705**
	(−1.74)	−1.23	(−0.59)	−3.12
Real GDP Growth	−0.000164	−0.0174	−0.0102	0.0133
	(−0.01)	(−0.89)	(−0.58)	−0.82
GDP per Capita	0.000150*	0.0000264	0.000126	−0.000246*
	−2.09	−0.2	−1.4	(−1.98)
Primary School Enrollment	−0.0244*	−0.0753*	−0.0341*	−0.00453
	−2	−2.24	−2.25	−0.12
Secondary School Enrollment	0.00545	−0.116***	0.000887	−0.0273
	−0.65	(−3.78)	−0.08	(−0.87)
Lag of Dependent Variable				0.433***
				−8.71
Constant	−3.206*	1.121	−3.741*	
	(−2.58)	−0.31	(−2.56)	
R^2	0.029	0.05		
Adjusted R^2	0.016	−0.162		
N	446	446	446	242

Source: IMF staff calculations.
Note: t-statistics in parentheses. CPI = consumer price index; OLS = ordinary least squares.
* $p < 0.05$; ** $p < 0.01$; *** $p < 0.001$.

ANNEX TABLE 6.2.2

International Sample: Food and Nonfood CPI

	(1) OLS Δ Gini Coefficient	(2) Fixed Effects Δ Gini Coefficient	(3) Random Effects Δ Gini Coefficient	(4) Arellano-Bond Δ Gini Coefficient
Food Inflation	−0.0338	0.208	0.0377	−0.233*
	(−0.27)	−1.26	−0.3	(−2.59)
Nonfood Inflation	−0.0549	−0.325*	−0.171	0.318**
	(−0.45)	(−2.08)	(−1.34)	−2.86
Nominal GDP	−0.00387	0.00625	−0.00232	0.00346
	(−1.30)	−0.62	(−0.57)	−0.71
Real GDP Growth	−0.0924	−0.153*	−0.145*	0.0372
	(−1.58)	(−2.17)	(−2.42)	−1.06
GDP per Capita	0.0000428	−0.0000498	0.0000931	0.0000068
	−0.33	(−0.21)	−0.63	−0.06
Primary School Enrollment	−0.0944*	−0.116	−0.0991	−0.101
	(−1.99)	(−0.67)	(−1.57)	(−1.22)
Secondary School Enrollment	0.00534	−0.129	0.000702	−0.139*
	−0.17	(−1.20)	−0.02	(−2.17)
Lag of Dependent Variable				0.342***
				−3.67
Constant	11.52*	25.65	12.55*	
	−2.36	−1.32	−1.97	
R^2	0.086	0.132		
Adjusted R^2	0.016	−0.15		
N	99	99	99	59

Source: IMF staff calculations.
Note: t-statistics in parentheses. OLS = ordinary least squares.
* $p < 0.05$; ** $p < 0.01$; *** $p < 0.001$.

ANNEX TABLE 6.2.3

China: Headline Inflation

	(1) OLS Δ Theil Coefficient	(2) Fixed Effects Δ Theil Coefficient	(3) Random Effects Δ Theil Coefficient	(4) Arellano-Bond Δ Theil Coefficient
CPI Inflation	−0.518	0.165	0.0930	0.732***
	(−0.76)	(0.36)	(0.21)	(11.03)
Real GDP Growth	0.391	−0.184	−0.114	−0.660***
	(0.79)	(−0.47)	(−0.30)	(−8.03)
GDP per Capita	−0.00888	0.0162	0.0139	0.00330**
	(−0.75)	(1.90)	(1.65)	(2.83)
Constant	5.728	6.438	6.014	6.677***
	(0.87)	(1.37)	(1.02)	(5.98)
Lag of Dependent Variable				0.859***
				−279.67
R^2	0.005	0.015		
Adjusted R^2	−0.006	−0.122		
N	271	271	271	270

Source: IMF staff calculations.

Note: *t*-statistics in parentheses. CPI = consumer price index; OLS = ordinary least squares.

** $p < 0.01$; *** $p < 0.001$.

ANNEX TABLE 6.2.4

China: Food and Nonfood CPI

	(1) OLS Δ Theil Coefficient	(2) Fixed Effects Δ Theil Coefficient	(3) Random Effects Δ Theil Coefficient	(4) Arellano-Bond Δ Theil Coefficient
Nonfood Inflation	−1.641	2.020	1.664	0.995***
	(−0.82)	(1.61)	(1.31)	(8.06)
Food Inflation	0.458	−0.877	−0.764	−0.0978
	(0.47)	(−1.45)	(−1.24)	(−1.81)
GDP per Capita	−0.00946	0.0179*	0.0146	0.00307*
	(−0.79)	(2.09)	(1.70)	(2.06)
Real GDP Growth	0.379	−0.153	−0.0695	−0.609***
	(0.76)	(−0.39)	(−0.18)	(−7.35)
Lag of Dependent Variable				0.860***
				(152.74)
Constant	5.097	7.029	6.466	6.348***
	(0.77)	(1.49)	(1.13)	(5.33)
R^2	0.007	0.026		
Adjusted R^2	−0.008	−0.115		
N	271	271	271	270

Source: IMF staff calculations.

Note: *t*-statistics in parentheses. CPI = consumer price index; OLS = ordinary least squares.

* $p < 0.05$; *** $p < 0.001$.

ANNEX TABLE 6.2.5

India: Headline CPI, Rural Areas

	(1) OLS Δ Gini Coefficient	(2) Fixed Effects Δ Gini Coefficient	(3) Random Effects Δ Gini Coefficient	(4) Arellano-Bond Δ Gini Coefficient
CPI Inflation	0.00200	0.0215	0.00200	−0.0341
	(0.11)	(0.98)	(0.11)	(−1.41)
Real GDP Growth	−0.0231	−0.0104	−0.0231	0.00936
	(−1.00)	(−0.39)	(−1.00)	(0.39)
GDP per Capita	0.0604*	0.111*	0.0604*	−0.0288
	(2.21)	(2.60)	(2.21)	(−0.48)
Literacy Rate	−0.00000212		−0.00000212	
	(−0.00)		(−0.00)	
Lag of Dependent Variable				0.162*
				(2.04)
Constant	−1.276	−2.953*	−1.276	
	(−1.27)	(−2.11)	(−1.27)	
R^2	0.045	0.053		
Adjusted R^2	0.024	−0.033		
N	194	194	194	132

Source: IMF staff calculations.
Note: t-statistics in parentheses. CPI = consumer price index; OLS = ordinary least squares.
* $p < 0.05$.

ANNEX TABLE 6.2.6

India: Headline CPI, Urban Areas

	(1) OLS Δ Gini Coefficient	(2) Fixed Effects Δ Gini Coefficient	(3) Random Effects Δ Gini Coefficient	(4) Arellano-Bond Δ Gini Coefficient
CPI Inflation	−0.00995	0.111*	−0.00995	0.114**
	(−0.34)	(2.58)	(−0.34)	(2.69)
Real GDP Growth	−0.0133	−0.0132	−0.0133	−0.0308
	(−0.39)	(−0.35)	(−0.39)	(−0.85)
GDP per Capita	0.0908*	0.344***	0.0908*	0.345***
	(2.38)	(4.75)	(2.38)	(4.22)
Literacy Rate	−0.0305		−0.0305	
	(−0.90)		(−0.90)	
Lag of Dependent Variable				−0.124
				(−1.41)
Constant	3.550	−7.336**	3.550	
	(1.28)	(−2.99)	(1.28)	
R^2	0.065	0.176		
Adjusted R^2	0.040	0.078		
N	152	152	152	127

Source: IMF staff calculations.
Note: t-statistics in parentheses. CPI = consumer price index; OLS = ordinary least squares.
* $p < 0.05$; ** $p < 0.01$; *** $p < 0.001$.

ANNEX TABLE 6.2.7

India: Food and Nonfood CPI, Rural Areas

	(1) OLS Δ Gini Coefficient	(2) Fixed Effects Δ Gini Coefficient	(3) Random Effects Δ Gini Coefficient	(4) Arellano-Bond Δ Gini Coefficient
Food Inflation	−0.0497*	−0.0366	−0.0497*	−0.0790***
	(−2.31)	(−1.55)	(−2.31)	(−3.44)
Nonfood Inflation	0.247**	0.273**	0.247**	0.256**
	(2.83)	(2.96)	(2.83)	(2.97)
Real GDP Growth	−0.0180	−0.00676	−0.0180	0.0154
	(−0.80)	(−0.26)	(−0.80)	(0.64)
GDP per Capita	0.0691*	0.122**	0.0691*	−0.00686
	(2.56)	(2.89)	(2.56)	(−0.11)
Literacy Rate	−0.00493		−0.00493	
	(−0.40)		(−0.40)	
Lag of Dependent Variable				0.145
				(1.83)
Constant	−2.115*	−4.112**	−2.115*	
	(−2.06)	(−2.87)	(−2.06)	
R^2	0.084	0.094		
Adjusted R^2	0.060	0.006		
N	194	194	194	132

Source: IMF staff calculations.
Note: *t*-statistics in parentheses. CPI = consumer price index; OLS = ordinary least squares.
* $p < 0.05$; ** $p < 0.01$; *** $p < 0.001$.

ANNEX TABLE 6.2.8

India: Food and Nonfood CPI, Urban Areas

	(1) OLS Δ Gini Coefficient	(2) Fixed Effects Δ Gini Coefficient	(3) Random Effects Δ Gini Coefficient	(4) Arellano-Bond Δ Gini Coefficient
Food Inflation	−0.131***	−0.0484	−0.131***	−0.0636
	(−4.33)	(−1.14)	(−4.33)	(−1.61)
Nonfood Inflation	0.314***	0.303***	0.314***	0.344***
	(4.16)	(3.63)	(4.16)	(4.31)
Real GDP Growth	0.0189	0.0144	0.0189	−0.00232
	(0.57)	(0.38)	(0.57)	(−0.07)
GDP per Capita	0.0422	0.250**	0.0422	0.253**
	(1.13)	(3.15)	(1.13)	(3.08)
Literacy Rate	0.00111		0.00111	
	(0.03)		(0.03)	
Lag of Dependent Variable				−0.174*
				(−2.06)
Constant	−0.646	−6.572**	−0.646	
	(−0.23)	(−2.72)	(−0.23)	
R^2	0.184	0.217		
Adjusted R^2	0.156	0.118		
N	152	152	152	127

Source: IMF staff calculations.
Note: *t*-statistics in parentheses. CPI = consumer price index; OLS = ordinary least squares.
* $p < 0.05$; ** $p < 0.01$; *** $p < 0.001$.

REFERENCES

Cheng, Y. 2007. "Evolution of Gini Coefficient Since the Start of the Reform and Its Urban-Rural Decomposition." *Social Sciences in China* 2007/04.

Deaton, A. 1989. "Rice Prices and Income Distribution in Thailand: A Non-Parametric Analysis." *The Economic Journal* 99 (395): 1–37.

Easterly, W., and S. Fischer. 2000. "Inflation and the Poor." NBER Working Paper 2335, National Bureau of Economic Research, Cambridge, Massachusetts.

Ravallion, M. 2000. "Prices, Wages and Poverty in Rural India: What Lessons Do the Time Series Data Hold for Policy?" *Food Policy* 25 (3): 351–64.

Romer, C. D., and D. H. Romer. 1998. "Monetary Policy and the Well-Being of the Poor." NBER Working Paper 6793, National Bureau of Economic Research, Cambridge, Massachusetts.

Walsh, J. P. 2010. "Reconsidering the Role of Food Prices in Inflation." IMF Working Paper 11/71, International Monetary Fund, Washington.

CHAPTER 7

Transmission of India's Inflation to Neighboring Countries

SONALI DAS, ADIL MOHOMMAD, AND YASUHISA OJIMA

Inflation dynamics in Nepal and Bhutan are closely linked to inflation dynamics in India. Both countries have an open border with India, facilitating the free movement of goods, and a hard peg to the Indian rupee.[1] Thus, inflation shocks from India are transmitted to its two Himalayan neighbors through trade and exchange rate channels. Even though Nepal and Bhutan try to retain domestic monetary control to some extent at the expense of financial openness (Figure 7.1), having a hard peg and an open border (likely undermining closed capital accounts) limits the ability of their monetary policy to respond to inflationary pressures.[2]

Both Nepal and Bhutan have a relatively narrow and weak domestic production base, and thus rely heavily on imports. Nepal's import-to-GDP ratio is about 25–30 percent and Bhutan's about 50–60 percent (Table 7.1). India's share in Bhutan's total imports ranged from 70–90 percent over the past decade,[3] and has remained steady in Nepal, accounting for about two-thirds of total goods imports.

Food and petroleum products are key imports from India to Nepal and Bhutan. Food imports are estimated at about 13 percent of total goods imports from India in Nepal (2013) and Bhutan (2012). Given the high share of food in the consumer price index (CPI) basket in Nepal (47 percent) and Bhutan (40 percent), imports are an important source of spillover from Indian food inflation to these countries. In addition, both countries rely entirely on India for fuel. Bhutan subsidizes kerosene, and both countries subsidize cooking gas. Aviation fuel, diesel, and petrol prices are adjusted frequently—though not automatically—in line with import price changes. Fuel imports

---

[1]The Nepalese rupee (Nr) is pegged at Nrs 1.6 to 1.0 Indian rupee (Re), while the Bhutanese ngultrum (Nu) is pegged at Nu 1.0 to Re 1.0. Nepal has maintained this rate since 1993, and Bhutan since 1974.

[2]The trilemma index reflects the well-known "impossible trinity," which posits a trade-off between two of the following three policy dimensions: monetary independence (or domestic monetary control), exchange rate stability, and financial openness (Aizenman, Chinn, and Ito 2008).

[3]Imports from India related to the jointly developed hydropower projects in Bhutan are shown separately because they tend to be high during the construction phase, but decline once electricity generation begins.

Figure 7.1. Trilemma Index for Nepal and Bhutan, 1996–2009

1. Nepal

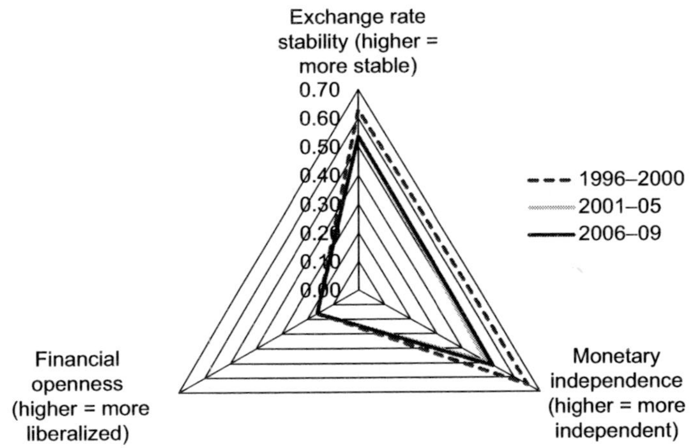

2. Bhutan

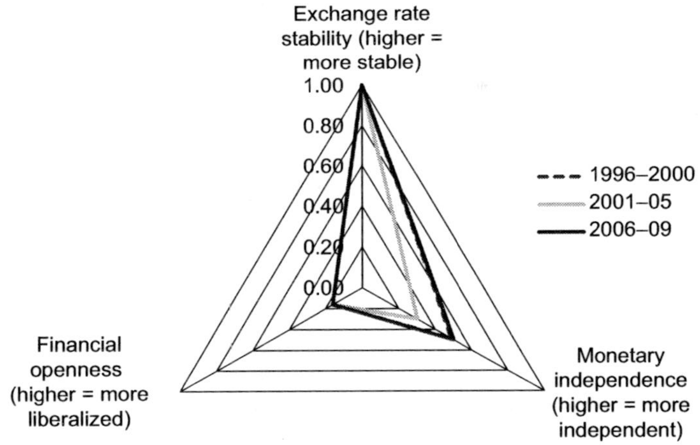

Source: Updated database based on Aizenman, Chinn, and Ito (2008).

constitute more than 20 percent of imports from India to Nepal, and imports of high-speed diesel, gasoline, and aviation fuel are about 12 percent of imports from India to Bhutan. The high share of food and fuel imports provides a link between inflation and inflation volatility in these countries and in India.

Against this backdrop, this chapter looks at the transmission of prices from India to Nepal and Bhutan, quantifies its impact on both these countries, and discusses the policy implications.

TABLE 7.1

Imports from India and Other Countries *(Percent of GDP)*

	2003/04	2004/05	2005/06	2006/07	2007/08	2008/09	2009/10	2010/11	2011/12	2012/13
Bhutan										
India	34.8	36.1	35.9	36.5	41.7	40.6	42.3	51.3	43.5	42.2
of which: hydropower	6.8	4.9	3.5	0.1	0.2	4.0	6.3	10.4	7.9	13.9
Other countries	4.4	24.4	14.8	12.0	8.2	7.5	13.1	13.1	11.4	6.8
Total imports	39.2	60.5	50.7	48.5	49.9	48.1	55.4	64.4	54.9	49.0
Nepal										
India	14.9	15.3	16.6	16.1	17.7	16.8	18.3	19.3	19.9	22.0
Other countries	9.9	9.4	9.6	10.0	9.1	11.5	12.5	9.1	9.9	10.4
Total imports	24.8	24.7	26.2	26.2	26.7	28.3	30.7	28.4	29.8	32.3

Sources: Annual Report of the Royal Monetary Authority of Bhutan; and Nepal Rastra Bank.

THE CASE OF NEPAL

Headline inflation in Nepal has been broadly stable over the last decade, but remains stubbornly high—hovering around the low double digits. The persistence of high inflation, including nonfood inflation (Figure 7.2, panel 1), is a continuing concern, particularly given the impact of high prices on the poor. As expected, historical data suggest that Nepal's headline and food inflation rates appear to be closely linked to India's (Figure 7.2, panel 2).

Nepal's inflation rate has been around the median of low-income countries since the early 2000s. The mean value of its headline inflation rate was almost the same as other low-income countries' from 2002 to 2014 (Table 7.2). Nepal's inflation rate has been less volatile than most other South Asian countries, as indicated by the lower coefficient of variation. A dynamic inflation rate path during that period, however, indicates that Nepal's inflation appears to have leveled off at a higher rate compared with world inflation (Figure 7.3, panels 1 and 3). Since 2008, however, inflation in Nepal has been structurally higher, primarily driven by food price inflation. During 2003–15 food price inflation was higher and more volatile than headline CPI inflation (Table 7.3). Especially since 2008, food price inflation in Nepal has risen, suggesting that food prices drive up headline CPI inflation (Figure 7.3, panel 3). Put differently, food prices in Nepal have been structurally higher and less stable than nonfood prices. Thus, food price inflation has become a key driver of headline inflation in Nepal.

Food price inflation in Nepal is highly correlated with food price changes in India and also, to some extent, with monetary aggregates and the exchange rate. The correlation matrix (Table 7.4) displays contemporaneous relationships among key variables. On year-over-year inflation rates, India's food CPI is highly correlated with Nepal's food CPI. Nepal's inflation is also correlated with key macroeconomic variables such as monetary aggregates, the nominal

Figure 7.2. Inflation Trend in Nepal

1. Consumer price inflation (2005/06 = 100)

2. India vs. Nepal: consumer price inflation rate (2005/06 = 100)

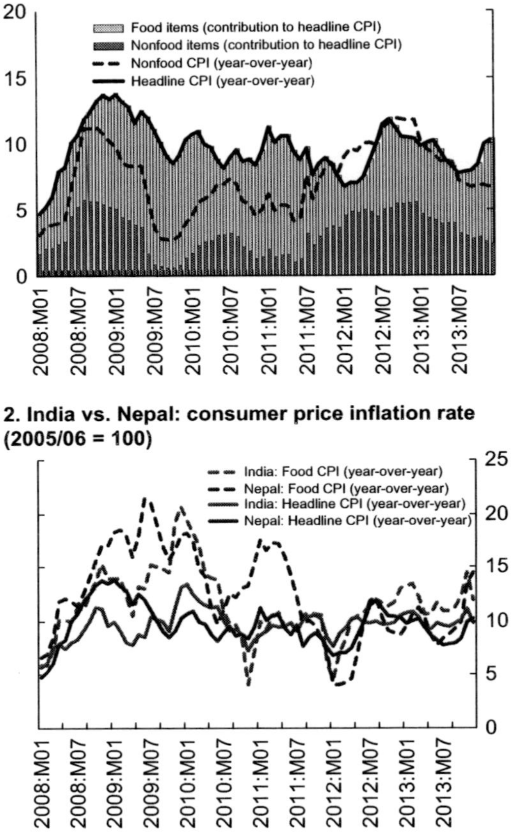

Sources: Haver Analytics; Nepalese authorities; and IMF staff estimates.
Note: CPI = consumer price index.

effective exchange rate, and workers' remittances, albeit less so than with Indian inflation.

The currency peg and close trade relations with India imply that Nepal imports India's inflation. To better understand the determinants of inflation in Nepal, an empirical exercise was carried out using data on prices, exchange rates, and broad money from March 2001 to December 2013. The following equation was estimated:

$$\Delta \ln(CPI) = \alpha + \beta_1 \Delta \ln(CPI(-1)) + \beta_2 \Delta \ln(CPI\_India) + \beta_3 \Delta \ln(Broad\ Money(-1)) + \beta_4 \Delta \ln(NEER(-1))$$

TABLE 7.2

Descriptive Statistics of Overall CPI inflation (2001–13)

Country/Group	Mean	Standard Deviation	Coefficient of Variation
Nepal	7.5	3.0	0.40
India	6.8	3.1	0.46
Bangladesh	6.8	2.7	0.39
Maldives	8.4	5.6	0.66
Sri Lanka	10.3	5.9	0.57
Pakistan	9.3	5.4	0.58
FD Asia median[1]	7.9	6.1	0.70
LICs median[2]	7.0	4.2	0.75
World median	4.6	3.2	0.64

Source: Authors' calculation based on IMF, International Financial Statistics database.

Note: FD Asia = frontier and developing Asia; LICs = low-income countries.

[1]FD Asia comprises 11 countries: Bangladesh, Bhutan, Cambodia, Lao People's Democratic Republic, Maldives, Mongolia, Myanmar, Nepal, Papua New Guinea, Timor-Leste, and Vietnam. Data not available for Bhutan, Papua New Guinea, and Timor-Leste.

[2]LICs comprise the Poverty Reduction and Growth Trust-eligible countries.

Figure 7.3. Inflation: Nepal versus the World and versus India

1. CPI Inflation: Nepal vs. World
(Percent, year-over-year)

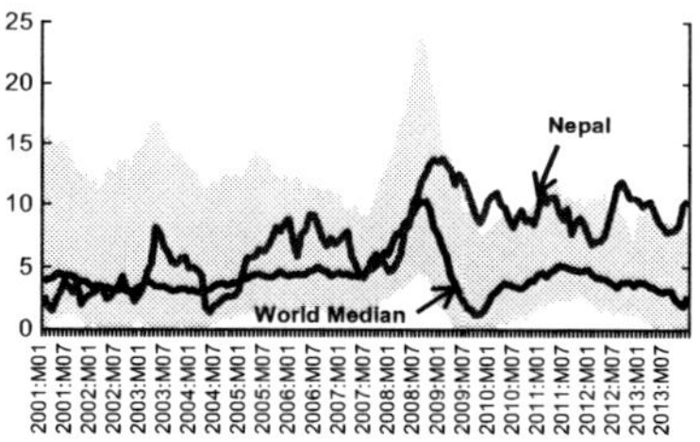

Note: Shaded area represents world's 90th and 10th percentiles.

2. CPI Inflation: Nepal vs. India
(Percent, year-over-year)

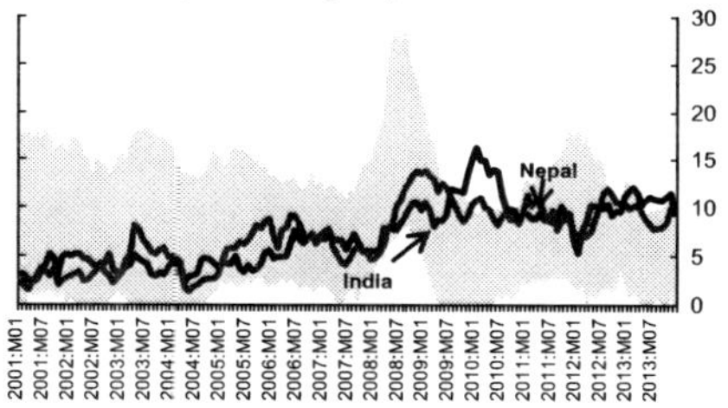

Note: Shaded area represents low-income countries' (LICs) 90th and 10th percentiles. LICs are Poverty Reduction and Growth Trust-eligible countries.

3. Food CPI Inflation: Nepal vs. World
(Percent, year-over-year)

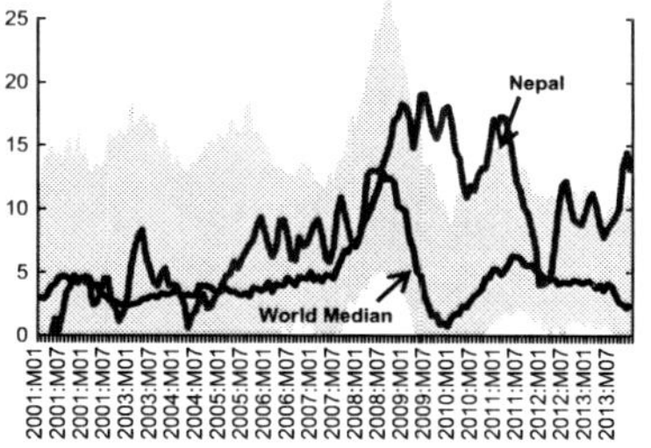

Note: Shaded area represents world's 90th and 10th percentiles.

4. Food CPI Inflation: Nepal vs. India
(Percent, year-over-year)

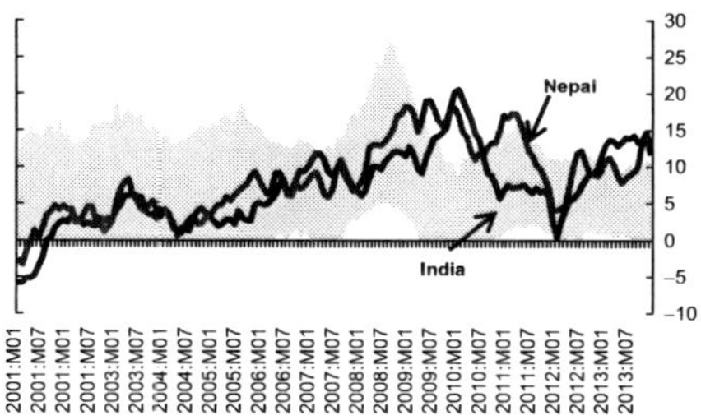

Note: Shaded area represents world's 90th and 10th percentiles.

Sources: FAOSTAT database for panels 3 and 4; IMF, International Financial Statistics database for panels 1 and 2; and IMF staff calculations.

TABLE 7.3

Descriptive Statistics of the Nepali CPI with Food Subcomponents

	Weights	Mean	Median	Maximum	Minimum	Standard Deviation	Coefficient of Variation[1]
Overall CPI	100.00	**7.47**	**7.66**	**13.77**	**1.31**	**2.95**	**0.40**
Food prices	46.82	9.17	8.14	21.47	0.62	5.19	0.57
Cereals, grains and their products	14.81	9.02	8.60	24.16	−3.66	6.13	0.68
Vegetables	5.65	13.47	8.47	73.19	−22.15	20.70	1.54
Meat and fish	5.70	9.83	6.83	32.65	−1.23	7.57	0.77
Milk products and egg	5.01	7.71	6.98	19.03	−0.46	5.73	0.74
Ghee and oil	2.70	8.43	6.41	36.97	−7.71	11.59	1.37
Fruits	2.23	9.89	7.67	38.41	−10.94	10.75	1.09
Sugar and sweets	1.36	12.94	7.74	77.20	−18.45	22.29	1.72
Spices	1.46	8.40	5.09	45.36	−14.10	14.16	1.69
Soft drinks	0.96	6.67	4.37	29.81	−3.03	7.75	1.16
Hard drinks	1.72	6.29	6.27	16.16	−2.26	5.23	0.83
Tobacco products	0.85	8.04	6.54	18.92	−0.07	5.42	0.67
Restaurant and hotel	2.35	10.14	8.08	26.69	1.07	7.30	0.72
Nonfood and services	53.18	6.46	6.14	11.79	2.60	2.68	0.41

Source: Nepalese authorities; and author's calculations.
Note: Sample period December 2001–December 2013.
[1]Standard deviation divided by the mean.

TABLE 7.4

Nepal: Correlation Matrix, December 2001–December 2013

	1	2	3	4	5	6	7	8	9	10
Headline CPI	1.00									
Food CPI	0.86	1.00								
Nonfood CPI	0.65	0.18	1.00							
India headline CPI	0.73	0.75	0.29	1.00						
India food CPI	0.70	0.76	0.23	0.83	1.00					
India UP food CPI	0.37	0.37	0.16	0.49	0.66	1.00				
Broad money	0.59	0.56	0.30	0.61	0.69	0.35	1.00			
Exchange rate (NEER)	−0.37	−0.17	−0.45	−0.16	−0.04	0.07	−0.39	1.00		
Fiscal spending	0.11	0.17	−0.03	0.11	0.11	−0.02	0.25	−0.04	1.00	
Worker's remittances	0.30	0.20	0.29	0.06	0.08	−0.05	0.27	−0.24	0.10	1.00

Source: Nepalese authorties; and author's calculations.
Note: CPI = consumer price index; NEER = nominal effective exchange rate.

The explanatory variables include the lagged dependent variable (because of adaptive inflation expectations), India's inflation (because of the currency peg), and the first lag of changes in the nominal effective exchange rate. Broad money growth was included to test whether there is a statistically significant relationship between monetary aggregates and inflation in Nepal.

TABLE 7.5

Determinants of Nepalese Inflation

Dependent Variable: Δln(CPI)t	Coefficient/(SE)
$\Delta\ln(\text{CPI})_{t-1}$	0.373***
	(0.06)
$\Delta\ln(\text{CPI\_India})_t$	0.452***
	(0.08)
$\Delta\ln(\text{Broad Money}_{t-1})$	0.110**
	(0.05)
$\Delta\ln(\text{NEER}_{t-1})$	–0.06
	–0.019
Constant	0.000
	(0.00)
Observations	152
R^2	0.41

Source: Authors' calculations.

Note: Sample period March 2001–December 2013. CPI = consumer price index; NEER = nominal effective exchange rate; SE = standard error. Standard errors in parentheses.

*** $p < 0.01$, ** $p < 0.05$.

Estimation results show that inflation in India has a significant pass-through to prices in Nepal (Table 7.5). A 1 percent increase in India's inflation corresponds to a 0.45 percent increase in Nepal's inflation. The result is significant at a 1 percent confidence level. As expected, lagged inflation rate plays a significant role. Lagged broad money growth is significant at about the 5 percent confidence level. While monetary aggregates also play a role and should not be dismissed in formulating policies, Indian inflation has the biggest explanatory power.

Vector autoregression (VAR) analysis also illustrates that both Indian inflation and food price shocks are significantly propagated into inflation in Nepal. A VAR is estimated on the seasonally adjusted, month-over-month inflation rate in Nepal and India. Unit root tests (Augmented Dickey Fuller and Phillips-Perron) confirm that both inflation series are stationary. The lag length selection criteria suggest using one lag. The estimated impulse response functions suggest that India's CPI inflation transmits to Nepal's (Figure 7.4, panel 1), and India's food CPI shocks (such as weather-related shocks to agriculture) affect food inflation in Nepal (panel 2). This food price transmission from India to Nepal could be partly explained as coming through Uttar Pradesh (panel 3). Specifically, a one standard deviation shock in food price in India pushed Nepal's food price inflation up by 0.2–0.3 percentage points with a one-month lag. This is also similar to the impact from food price shocks in Uttar Pradesh to Nepal.

Transmission from food prices to nonfood prices appears weak. Impulse response functions illustrate that in Nepal, food price shocks do not show

Figure 7.4. Impulse Response Functions: Response to Cholesky One Standard Deviation Innovations

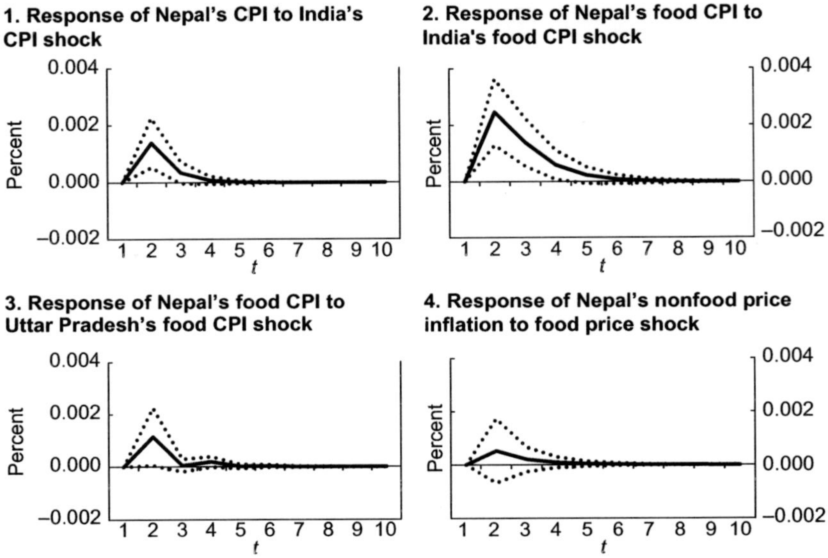

Source: Authors' calculations.
Note: Dotted lines show a band of ±2 standard deviations around the impulse response.

statistically significant propagation into nonfood inflation, but exhibit some weak responses with lags (Figure 7.4, panel 4). Hence, if supply-side shocks affecting food prices are transmitted to nonfood inflation, policymakers should remain vigilant in the presence of rising food prices (Walsh 2011; Barnett, Bersch, and Ojima 2012).

Transmission of price pressures from India could intensify in the near term. Nepal's food prices on the border with India have been structurally higher for major food items such as maize, coarse paddy, and coarse rice (Figure 7.5). Lower prices in India may stem in part from various policy supports to farmers in India, including fertilizer subsidies, irrigation fee subsidies, discounted electricity tariffs, and directed lending to agriculture. These price differentials could intensify an incentive for India's traders and farmers to export more to Nepal. Ginger exhibits a somewhat different picture: Nepal's ginger price was sometimes lower than India's (Figure 7.5, panel 4). For the period when ginger prices were lower in Nepal, the country tended to export ginger to India, driving up the domestic ginger price with lags. Given this price arbitrage and that trade data show a sharp increase in food imports from India since 2012, particularly for rice and vegetables (Figure 7.6), transmission lines between Nepal and India could intensify.

Figure 7.5. Border Price Differentials: Nepal versus India

1. Maize
(Nepalese rupees per 100 kg)

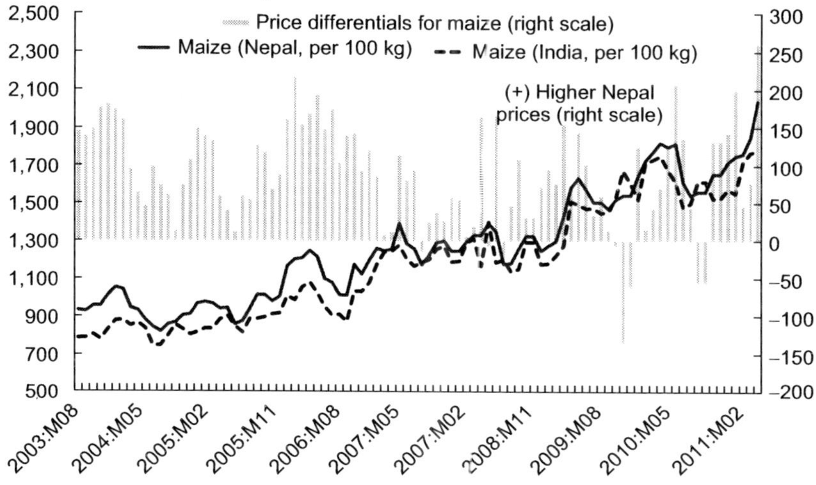

2. Coarse paddy
(Nepalese rupees per 100 kg)

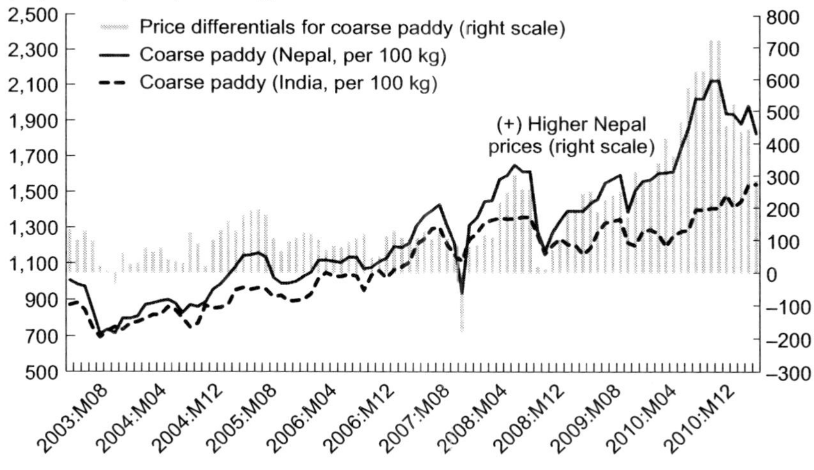

(continued)

THE CASE OF BHUTAN

Inflation in Bhutan has increased over the past decade on account of increases in both food and nonfood inflation. Headline inflation in 2004–08 rose from an average of just under 6 percent to 8 percent in 2009–13, with a sharp increase in average food inflation from just below 7 percent to 10 percent in the same period,

Figure 7.5. *(continued)*

3. Coarse rice

(Nepalese rupees per kg)

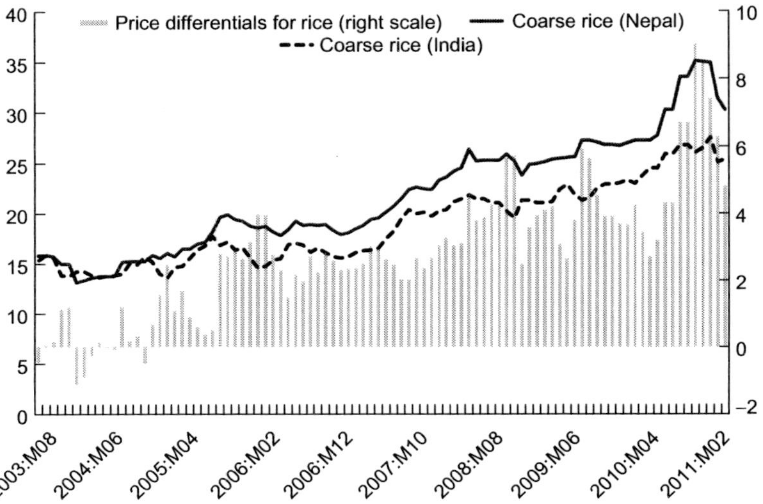

4. Ginger

(Nepalese rupees per 250 g)

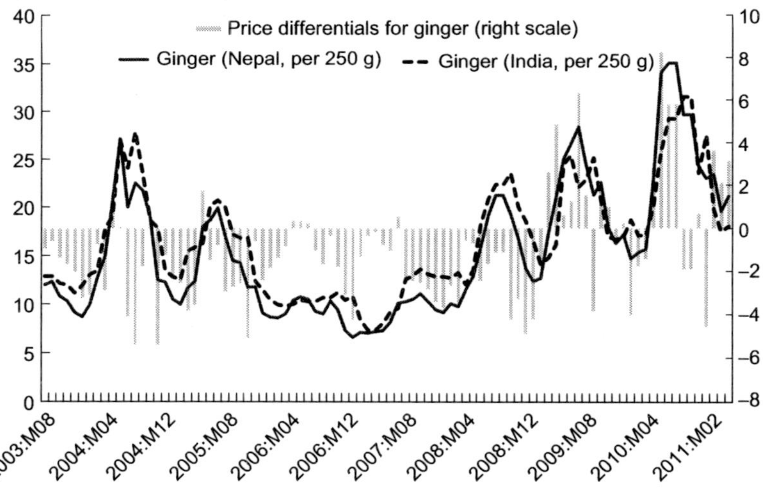

Sources: Nepalese authorities; and IMF staff estimates.

Note: g = gram; kg = kilogram.

Figure 7.6. Nepal: Rice and Vegetable Imports from India
(Millions of Nepalese rupees)

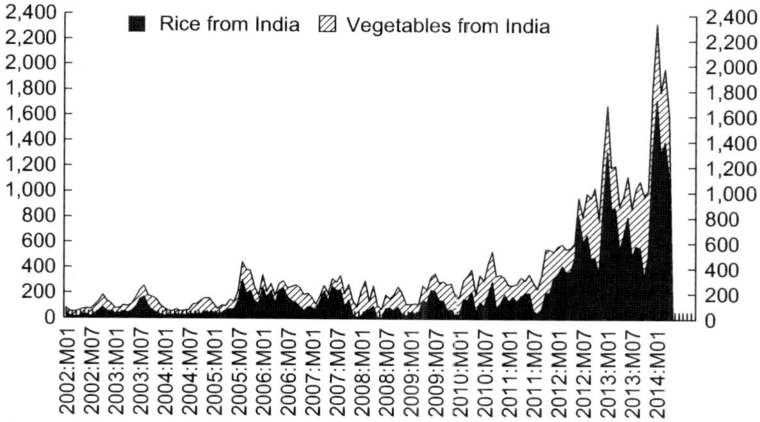

Sources: Nepalese authorities; and IMF staff estimates

TABLE 7.6

Bhutan: Inflation Trends *(Percent)*

Average Inflation	2004–08	2009–2014
Headline	5.7	8.0
Food	6.8	10.2
Nonfood	5.2	6.8
Contribution to Inflation (share)		
Food	0.38	0.46
Nonfood	0.62	0.53

Source: National Statistics Bureau; and IMF staff estimates.

and a smaller increase in nonfood inflation (Table 7.6). Food inflation has contributed a rising share of headline inflation,[4] but the contribution from nonfood inflation remains sizeable.

Bhutan's headline inflation tracked the median inflation of low-income countries closely in the first half of the past decade, but has diverged since 2009–10 (Figure 7.7). Headline inflation has remained at or above the 90th percentile of world inflation since mid-2009, resembling inflationary developments in India. Compared to the median standard deviation and coefficient of variation of headline inflation in the low-income country group, inflation in Bhutan is less volatile. Compared to its South Asian neighbors, average headline inflation over the past decade appears to be in the middle of the pack (Table 7.7), though volatility has been lower.

[4] This may also be partly owing to the upward revision of the weight of food in the CPI basket from 31½ percent to nearly 40 percent from the second quarter of 2013.

Figure 7.7. Inflation: Bhutan versus the World and versus India

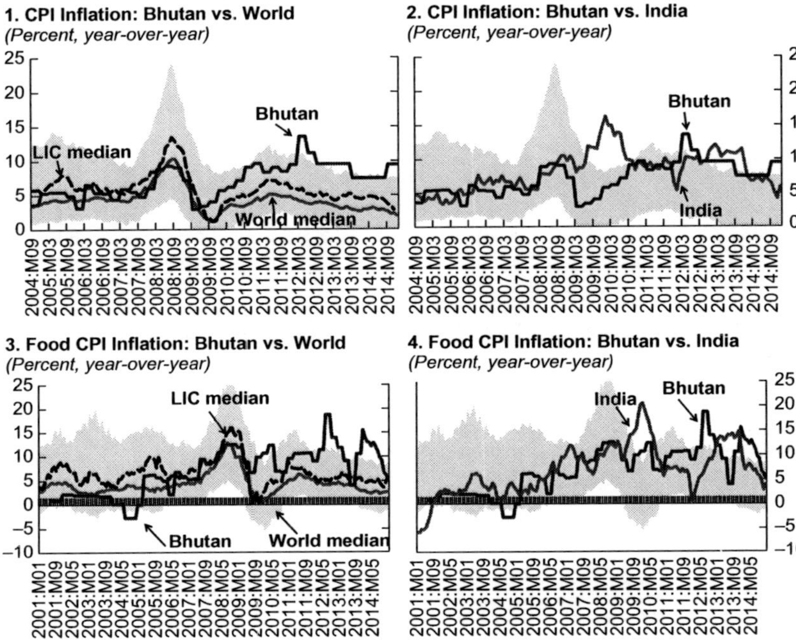

Source: IMF, International Financial Statistics database; and IMF staff estimates.
Note: Shaded area represents world's 90th and 10th percentiles. LIC = low-income country.

TABLE 7.7

Descriptive Statistics of Overall CPI Inflation, 2004–14

Country/Group	Mean	Standard Deviation	Coefficient of Variation
Bhutan	7.0	2.5	0.36
Nepal	8.4	2.4	0.28
India	8.4	2.9	0.35
Bangladesh	7.7	1.9	0.25
Maldives	6.8	5.2	0.77
Sri Lanka	10.3	6.0	0.58
Pakistan	11.2	4.6	0.41
LICs median[1]	6.6	4.0	0.69
World median	4.8	2.7	0.58

Source: Authors' calculation based on IMF, International Financial Statistics database.
Note: CPI = consumer price index; LICs = low-income countries.
[1]Median of the average for all countries in the LIC group.

Food inflation in Bhutan has on average been higher and more volatile than headline inflation. It was lower than the world (and low-income countries) median food inflation in the early part of the previous decade, and subsequently tracked the rising world and low-income-country median up to mid-2009. Even though world and low-income-country food inflation rates have generally fallen since 2009, they remained elevated in Bhutan, possibly driven by the sharp rise in food inflation in India around this time (Figure 7.7). Food inflation has continued on a higher trajectory than the world and low-income-country medians. Although Bhutan's food inflation generally appears to follow trends in India's food inflation, there have been large observable divergences in the rate and pattern in the past five years. Compared to other South Asian countries (Table 7.8), food inflation was at the higher end, and higher than CPI for agricultural workers inflation in India (a proxy for food inflation). Also, food inflation in Bhutan has been less volatile than regional comparators except Bangladesh.

India is Bhutan's main trading partner and its currency, the ngultrum, is pegged one-for-one to the Indian rupee. More than 80 percent of Bhutan's imports come from India, of which nonfood items account for about 80 percent, the remainder being food imports. Figure 7.8 shows the correlations between inflation in headline, food, and nonfood inflation in the two countries. Because of the nascent state of price statistics in Bhutan, we are able to consider a long time-series for headline inflation from 1980 onward (semiannually), but only a shorter series for food and nonfood components, from 2003 onward (quarterly).

- Headline inflation shows a tendency to comove with India's headline CPI rate, though there are notable yet short-lived deviations at various points. The correlation between the level of year-over-year inflation during 1980–2013 is positive and high.
- For food inflation, we use Food and Agriculture Organization data, which employ a proxy for India (CPI for agricultural laborers) and give us a longer time series for Bhutan than the official quarterly series. We observe that the two series tended to comove in the past, though the relationship appears to have weakened since about 2009, with wide gaps between the level and movements of food inflation in the two countries. For the period as a whole, the correlation appears to be quite strong and positive.

TABLE 7.8

Descriptive Statistics of the Food CPI Inflation, 2004–14

Country/Group	Mean	Standard Deviation	Coefficient of Variation
Bhutan	**9.0**	**3.9**	**0.4**
Nepal	10.1	4.4	0.4
India (agricultural worker)	8.3	4.4	0.5
Bangladesh	8.6	2.6	0.3
Maldives	8.9	11.6	1.3
Sri Lanka	8.1	10.8	1.3
Pakistan	12.4	6.5	0.5
LIC median[1]	6.2	7.7	1.2
World median	4.3	4.4	0.9

Source: Authors' calculations based on FAOSTAT database.
Note: CPI = consumer price index; LIC = low-income country.
[1]Median of the average for all countries in the LIC group.

Figure 7.8. Inflation Trends in India and Bhutan

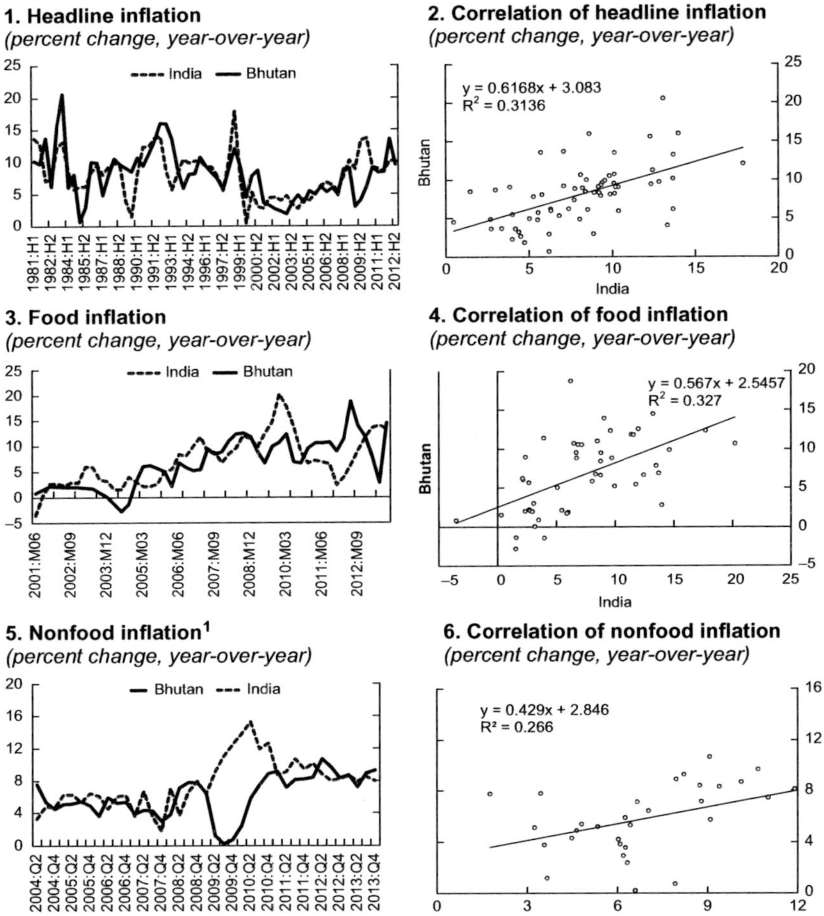

Sources: FAOSTAT database; Haver Analytics; IMF, International Finance Statistics database, and India desk data; Royal Monetary Authority of Bhutan; and authors' calculations.
[1]Core inflation is used for India to proxy nonfood inflation.

- For nonfood items, we use Indian core inflation as a proxy. Only a short sample is available for Bhutan's nonfood inflation. Although there appears to be little contemporaneous correlation between the two series, with a two-quarter lag of Indian core inflation, the correlation is positive, though weaker than in food and headline inflation. This is possibly because of the short sample and because core inflation is an imperfect proxy for nonfood inflation in India.

Given the economic relationship between the two countries, it is expected that the main driver of inflation in Bhutan is inflation in India. This is supported by

TABLE 7.9

Vector Error Correction Model Estimates Cointegrating Equation

	Change in Bhutan CPI Inflation	Change in India CPI Inflation
DLOG_BTN_CPI(−1)	1.000	
DLOG_IND_CPI(−1)	−0.99919	
	(−14.557)	
Error Correction	D(DLOG_BTN_CPI)	D(DLOG_IND_CPI)
CointEq1	−0.93936	0.285818
	(−4.247)	(1.371)
D(DLOG_BTN_CPI(−1))	−0.343532	−0.054343
	(−2.747)	(−0.461)
D(DLOG_IND_CPI(−1))	−0.299941	−0.588479
	(−2.048)	(−4.265)
R^2	0.762968	0.609538

Source: Authors' calculations.
Note: *t*-statistics in parentheses.

Granger causality tests that indicate (1) the hypothesis that lagged changes in India's headline inflation do not Granger-cause changes in headline inflation in Bhutan can be rejected at the 5 percent confidence level; and (2) the reverse hypothesis, that lagged changes in Bhutan's inflation do not Granger-cause Indian inflation cannot be rejected. This relationship can be established for headline inflation, but Granger causality tests do not offer conclusive results for food and nonfood inflation, not finding Granger causality in either direction. This is the likely effect of data constraints; only a shorter sample is available for the food and nonfood series than for the headline series. However, the headline CPI data can be used to show that Bhutan's inflation converges to India's level over the long term. To establish this, we show that there is a cointegrating relationship between inflation in India and in Bhutan, and that Bhutan's inflation follows an error correction process with respect to India's inflation.

First, augmented Dickey-Fuller unit root tests[5] indicate that inflation (log differences of the headline index) is I(1) for both India and Bhutan. Second, the Johansen cointegration test rejects the hypothesis of no cointegrating relationship between headline inflation in Bhutan and in India, and fails to reject the hypothesis of at most 1 cointegrating relationship. Table 7.9 shows the results of the estimated error correction model.[6] The estimated coefficients show that Bhutan's inflation adjusts in response to a deviation from the long-term relationship, while India's does not. If Bhutan's inflation exceeds India's, the coefficient on the lag

[5] Modified Akaike, Shwarz, and Hannan-Quinn information criteria with the inclusion of a trend and intercept term in the augmented Dickey-Fuller equation.

[6] Results are qualitatively similar with the introduction of an intercept term in both the cointegrating equation and the VAR; they turn out to be not significant. The coefficient on India's inflation in the cointegrating equation remains close to 1, and the short-term dynamics show Bhutan's CPI adjusts to errors.

change in Bhutan's inflation shows that inflation adjusts downward, which is consistent with the equilibrium relationship.

Hence, Indian inflation appears to be the key driver of inflation in Bhutan. Studies on drivers of Bhutan's inflation are very few. But an extant research paper published by the National Statistics Bureau (Nidup 2012) also finds a strong relationship between inflation in the two countries in an autoregressive distributed lag model, and does not find conclusive evidence of domestic drivers (money supply) having an impact on inflation.

CONCLUSIONS

Given both countries' exchange rate regimes and close trade ties with India, it is unlikely that inflation in Nepal and Bhutan can be delinked from India in the near term. In the case of Bhutan, imported goods have more than a 52.6 percent weight in the CPI, of which imported food has a 22.8 percent share and nonfood 29.8 percent. Nepal's imports of food from India have also been growing. Key near-term policy implications can be drawn from the analysis:

- *Data surveillance*—Efforts to collect data should be stepped up, including border price information, as a part of efforts to improve food price forecasts. Historical data suggest that food price data in India played a significant role in its neighbors' food inflation.
- *Transmission from India*—Given the high and increasing volume of food trade, the price transmission from India, especially for food prices, could intensify. As neither Nepal nor Bhutan is self-sufficient, fear of food price inflation in India could amplify food inflation in Nepal and Bhutan.
- *Transmission to nonfood price inflation*—There could be some propagation from food price inflation to nonfood price inflation (albeit weak), suggesting that policymakers should remain vigilant against food price inflation as a sign of the near-term pressures on core inflation.

Over the medium term, however, both countries can gradually shield themselves from Indian inflation. On food inflation, they can make efforts to become self-sufficient, with fewer imports from India. Given the small domestic manufacturing base, both are likely to continue importing nonfood inflation from their trading partners. Nonetheless, they may be well placed to take advantage of abundant hydropower to minimize dependence on hydrocarbons (imported from India) and reduce energy price pressures, because fuel imports are a significant share of total imports and could contribute to high inflation and increased volatility. As both economies mature (for example, through financial deepening, institutional setups, and economic diversification), they may also revisit their exchange rate and monetary policy frameworks in order to insulate them from price shocks in India.

REFERENCES

Aizenman, J., Chinn, D. Menzie, and H. Ito. 2008. "Assessing the Emerging Global Financial Architecture: Measuring the Trilemma's Configurations over Time." NBER Working Paper 14533, National Bureau of Economic Research, Cambridge, Massachusetts.

Barnett, Steve, Julia Bersch, and Yasuhisa Ojima. 2012. "Inflation Dynamics in Mongolia: Understanding the Roller Coaster." IMF Working Paper 12/192, International Monetary Fund, Washington.

Nidup, Jigme. 2012. "Money and Price in Bhutan: Relationship Augmented with Indian Inflation." Monograph 3, National Statistics Bureau, Thimphu.

Walsh, James P. 2011. "Reconsidering the Role of Food Prices in Inflation." IMF Working Paper 11/79, International Monetary Fund, Washington.

PART III

Policies to Affect Inflation

CHAPTER 8

Monetary Policy Transmission in India

SONALI DAS

Inflation management requires a clear understanding of the channels through which monetary policy affects the economy. As a demand management policy, the effectiveness of monetary policy in combating inflation depends on the strength of its effects on aggregate demand; that is, on the strength of monetary policy transmission. This chapter provides new evidence on monetary policy transmission in India since 2002.

The monetary policy framework of India's central bank has been evolving since the mid-1990s, and the Patel Committee Report to the Reserve Bank of India (RBI 2014) laid out a path for a strengthened framework. Of the potential channels through which monetary policy can affect output—through interest rates, the credit channel, asset prices, and exchange rates—this chapter focuses on the first part of the credit channel, namely pass-through from the policy rate to bank deposit and lending rates. Mishra and Montiel (2012) review the reasons why the credit (bank lending) channel is likely to be the dominant one for developing economies, and previous studies of the potential channels in India have found this to be the case (for example, Sengupta 2014).

The questions this chapter seeks to shed light on are: (1) what are the extent and speed of pass-through from monetary policy to the deposit and lending rates of Indian banks; (2) is pass-through symmetric or do episodes of monetary tightening and loosening have different effects on bank interest rates; and (3) has pass-through changed over time, with changes to the monetary policy operating framework? To answer these questions, we estimate the pass-through from monetary policy changes to bank interest rates in two steps (Figure 8.1): from the monetary policy rate to the interbank market rate that is targeted by the framework, and then from the target rate to bank interest rates (deposit and lending rates).

There are two advantages to this stepwise estimation. The results from the first step indicate how well the framework is set up to control its target market rate.[1] And the interpretation of relationships is clearer than it would be in a vector error cointegration model with multiple (three) cointegrating relationships.

[1] Many studies on transmission in India and in other countries assume a correspondence between the policy stance and the target rate, and use the target rate as a starting point in the analysis of transmission.

Figure 8.1. Stepwise Estimation of Error Correction Models

Source: Author.
Note: VECM = vector error correction model.

In each step, an error correction model is used, which allows for the estimation of the long-run relationship between policy and bank rates, as well as the speed of adjustment to this long-run pass-through. The method also allows for the estimation of asymmetric adjustment parameters to study whether there are differential responses to policy rate increases and decreases.

STUDIES OF MONETARY POLICY TRANSMISSION IN INDIA

Concerns about transmission are not unique to India; the strength of monetary policy transmission in developing economies as a whole has come into question (Mishra and Montiel 2012; Mishra and others 2014).[2] Sengupta (2014) uses a vector autoregression (VAR) to study the various channels of monetary transmission in India from 1993 to 2012. She finds a structural break in transmission corresponding to the introduction of the Liquidity Adjustment Facility (LAF) in 2000, with the bank lending channel remaining important since the facility's introduction, but with the interest rate and asset price channels becoming stronger. Singh (2011) uses a VAR model from March 2001 to June 2012 to estimate pass-through from the policy rate to a variety of short- and long-run market interest rates.[3] He finds significant contemporaneous pass-through under deficit liquidity conditions, as well as significant lagged effects.[4] A drawback of this estimation method is that while it gives an idea of the effect of changes in the policy rate on other interest rates, it does not give a sense of the speed of transmission, which is a factor that policymakers must consider when making policy rate decisions. Mohanty (2012) also narrows in on the interest rate channel, studying policy rate changes through to their effects on output and inflation. Estimating a quarterly structural VAR model, he finds that policy rate increases have a negative

[2] The literature studying the effects of monetary policy is vast. See Christiano, Eichenbaum, and Evans (2000) for a review of the literature on monetary policy transmission; and Beck, Colciago, and Pfajfar (2014) for a review of the role of financial intermediaries in monetary policy transmission.

[3] The study includes 11 interest rates, the exchange rate, a stock index return, the LAF balance, and the wholesale price index to measure inflation.

[4] For example, a 1 percentage point change in the repo rate leads to a 75–80 basis point change in several short-run rates, and to a 50 basis point change in medium- and long-run rates.

effect on output growth with a lag of two quarters and a moderating impact on inflation with a lag of three quarters, with both effects persisting for eight to 10 quarters.

BRIEF DESCRIPTION OF INDIA'S MONETARY POLICY FRAMEWORK

India's monetary policy framework has undergone several changes in recent years.[5] An interim LAF was introduced in April 1999 and then transitioned toward a full-fledged LAF through periodic modifications. The LAF has helped in developing policy interest rates as the main monetary policy instrument, and, since November 2004, has operated using overnight fixed-rate repos and reverse repos with banks. The LAF is the key element in the RBI's operating framework and is meant to operate in a deficit liquidity mode, with liquidity contained around ±1 percent of all banks' net demand and time liabilities. Banks pledge government securities as collateral, most of which should be over and above the securities they must hold to comply with liquidity regulations (the standard liquidity ratio).[6] In May 2011 the LAF was enhanced along several dimensions, a key point of which was the explicit recognition of the weighted-average overnight call money rate (WACMR) as the operating target of monetary policy. Chapter 4 of RBI (2014) discusses likely impediments to monetary transmission and provides exploratory evidence[7] of an asymmetric effect of the policy rate on deposit and lending rates in India. It groups likely impediments to transmission into three broad categories: fiscal dominance, the large informal sector, and financial and credit market frictions.

Because some banks were pricing loans under their advertised prime lending rates, the transparency of lending rates became a concern. The RBI instituted a "base rate" system, which became effective in July 2010, with the aim of enhancing transparency in the lending rates of banks and enabling better assessment of the transmission of monetary policy (RBI 2010). Under this system, a bank's base rate is the minimum rate at which it can lend, as loans are priced from the base rate with the addition of borrower-specific charges. Banks are free to use their own formula to calculate their base rate, as long as it is calculated in a consistent manner and made available for supervisory review. Banks are expected to calculate their base rate taking their costs of funds, costs of complying with certain regulations (cash reserve ratio and standard liquidity ratio), overhead costs, and profits into account. Although banks now price loans from the base rate, they still report prime lending rates. In practice, the prime lending

[5] See Mohanty (2011) for a history of the framework up to 2011.

[6] Banks in India are subject to a statutory liquidity ratio—a certain share of net total demand and time liabilities that they must invest in gold and/or government-approved securities. This ratio was 25 percent in 2002, and was decreased from 22 percent to 21.5 percent in February 2015.

[7] Summary statistics of the policy rate, and deposit and lending rates over periods of monetary tightening and loosening.

Figure 8.2. Bank Base Rates and Prime Lending Rates

1. State Bank of India

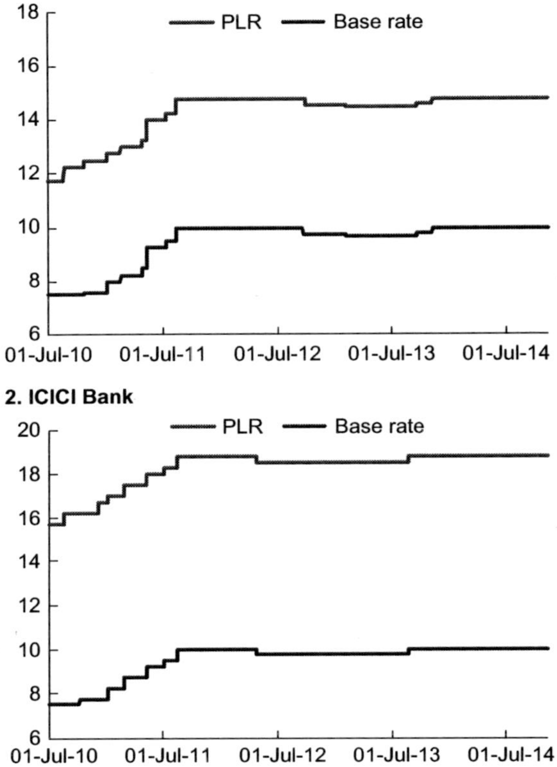

Source: CEIC.
Note: PLR = prime lending rate.

and base rates move together. Figure 8.2 shows both rates at the State Bank of India, the country's largest publicly owned bank, and ICICI Bank, the largest privately owned bank.

DATA AND DESCRIPTIVE STATISTICS

The data come from CEIC[8] and Thomson Reuters Datastream and are made up of two groups of variables: those capturing the monetary policy stance, and information on bank interest rates and balance sheets (Figures 8.3 and 8.4). The sample runs from the end of March 2002 to the end of October 2014; each observation is a two-week period. Daily data on interest rates and LAF transactions are averaged over two-week periods; the bank balance-sheet data are

[8] CEIC sources these data series from the RBI.

Figure 8.3. Monetary Policy Rates

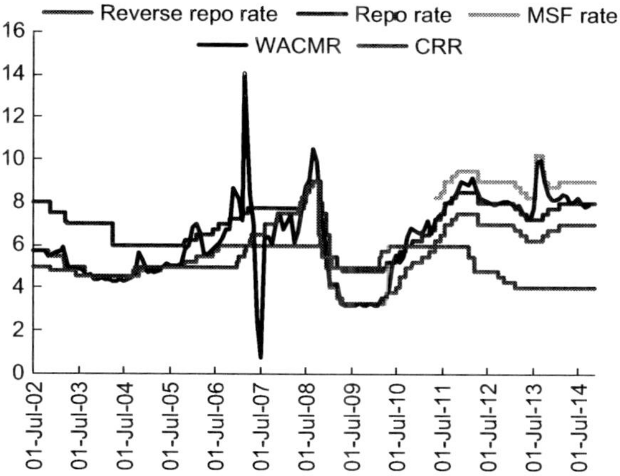

Source: CEIC.
Note: CRR = cash reserve ratio; WACMR = weighted-average call money rate; MSF = marginal standing facility.

Figure 8.4. Interest Rates and the Aggregate Ratio of Bank Loans to Assets

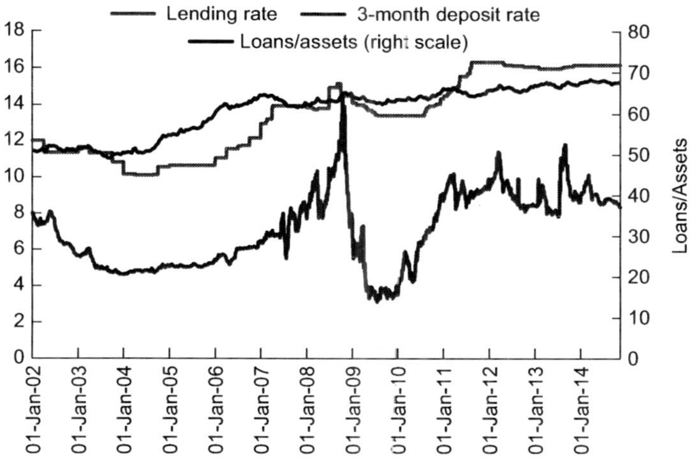

Sources: CEIC; and Thomson Reuters Datastream.
Note: WACMR = weighted-average call money rate.

available on a biweekly basis (see Box 8.1). The monetary policy rates considered are the reverse repo rate and the repo rate. The daily net injection by the RBI to banks through the LAF is equal to the amount lent through the overnight repo facility (amount outstanding on a given day), plus the amount lent through the term repo facility, less the amount borrowed through the reverse repo facility. The

Box 8.1 Empirical Method

The variables used in this chapter are I(1) with the exception of the Liquidity Adjustment Facility net injection, which is I(0). A lag length of four two-week periods is used in both steps of the estimation, based on the Hannan-Quinn information criterion.

Step 1: Pass-Through to the Target Rate from Monetary Policy

An error correction model that has two stages, corresponding to the long-run pass-through and short-run dynamics, is estimated as follows:

$$(LR) = WACMR_t = \beta_0 + \beta_1 \text{RepoRate}_t + \varepsilon_t$$

$$(SR)\ \Delta WACMR_t = \alpha ECT_t + \sum_{k=1}^{K} \delta_{2k} \Delta WACMR_{t-k} + \delta_{3k} \Delta(LAFnetinj / NTDL)_{t-k} + v_t$$

where the error correction term:

$$ECT_t = WACMR_{t-1} - \hat{\beta}_0 - \hat{\beta}_1 \text{RepoRate}_{t-1}$$

is the residual from the LR equation, which measures period $t-1$ deviations from the long-run stationary relationship.

The identifying assumption that underlies this step of the empirical method is that the repo rate is weakly exogeneous to the WACMR. That is, there is no feedback to the repo rate from the WACMR. This is a reasonable assumption, in that the repo rate is a policy rate decided by the central bank.

The average elasticity of WACMR with respect to the repo rate is:

$$\eta = \beta_1 \frac{mean(\text{RepoRate})}{mean(\text{WACMR})}$$

and the α coefficient is the share of the deviation from the LR equilibrium that decays each month, representing the speed of adjustment.

Alternate specification: in principle, the repo rate is the one policy rate that signals the stance of monetary policy, with the reverse repo rate being a fixed distance under the repo rate and the marginal standing facility rate being a fixed distance above the repo rate. However, before implementation of the Liquidity Adjustment Facility, there were considered to be two effective policy rates, depending on the liquidity situation:

- Reverse repo rate when in a liquidity surplus ($LAFnetinj < 0$)
- Repo rate when in a liquidity deficit ($LAFnetinj > 0$)

To account for the effective policy rate depending on the liquidity situation, a specification is estimated where both the reverse repo rate and repo rate are included in the long-run stage:

$$(LR1)\ WACMR_t = \beta_0 + \beta_{11}\text{RevRepoRate}_t \times LiqDef_t + \beta_{12}\text{RepoRate}_t \times LiqDef_t + \varepsilon_t$$

$$\text{where } LiqDef_t = \begin{cases} 0 & \text{if } LAFnetinj < 0 \\ 1 & \text{if } LAFnetinj > 0 \end{cases}$$

Step 2: Pass-Through to Bank Interest Rates from the Target Rate

As Johansen's trace statistic method suggests the presence of two cointegrating relationships between the WACMR, the deposit rate, and the lending rate, a vector error correction model is estimated with the following cointegrating relationships:

Box 8.1 (continued)

$$(LRl)\ LendingRate_t = \theta_0^l + \theta_1^l WACMR_t + \varepsilon_{1t}$$

$$(LR2)\ DepositRate_t = \theta_0^d + \theta_1^d WACMR_t + \varepsilon_{2t}$$

The key short-run equations of interest in the vector error correction model are represented as follows:

$$(SRl)\ \Delta LendingRate_t = \alpha_1^l ECT1_t + \alpha_2^l ECT2_t + \sum_{k=1}^{K} \delta_{3k}\Delta Rate_{lt-k} + \delta_{4k}\Delta WACMR_{t-k} + \delta_{5k}\Delta Loans/Assets_{t-k} + v_{lt}$$

$$(SRd)\ \Delta DepositRate_t = \alpha_1^d ECT1_t + \alpha_2^d ECT2_t + \sum_{k=1}^{K} \delta_{3k}\Delta Rate_{lt-k} + \delta_{4k}\Delta WACMR_{t-k} + \delta_{5k}\Delta Loans/Assets_{t-k} + v_{dt}$$

where the error correction terms are:

$$ECT1_t = \hat{\varepsilon}_{1t} \text{ and } ECT2_t = \hat{\varepsilon}_{2t}$$

The identifying assumptions that underlie this step of the empirical method are that the lending rate is weakly exogenous to the WACMR, and that the deposit rate is weakly exogenous to the WACMR. The first assumption is reasonable because changes in interest rates on bank loans, which will be of longer maturity, are unlikely to have feedback effects on overnight call money transactions. The second assumption is perhaps more difficult in that an increase in the cost of deposits could make raising funds in the overnight market more attractive. This funding strategy would not be viable for an extended period, however, so any feedback effects are likely to be small.

The coefficient on the first error correction term, *ECT1*, in (*SRl*) represents the speed of adjustment of the lending rate to a deviation in the relationship between the lending rate and the WACMR. The coefficient on the second error correction term, *ECT2*, in (*SRl*) represents the speed of adjustment of the lending rate to a deviation in the relationship between the deposit rate and the WACMR. Similarly, the coefficient on the first error correction term, *ECT1*, in (*SRd*) represents the speed of adjustment of the deposit rate to a deviation in the relationship between the lending rate and the WACMR. The coefficient on the second error correction term, *ECT2*, in (*SRd*) represents the speed of adjustment of the deposit rate to a deviation in the relationship between the deposit rate and the WACMR.

Asymmetric Speed of Adjustment

The error correction terms in the step 2 estimation, *ECT1* and *ECT2*, are then split into their positive and negative components (corresponding to a decrease in the WACMR and an increase in the WACMR, respectively) to test whether the adjustment parameters are the same for instances of monetary loosening and tightening.

market interest rate targeted by the monetary policy framework is the WACMR, and the two main bank interest rates considered are the rate on three-month certificates of deposits and the average prime lending rate of five major banks. All quantity series are deflated using the consumer price index. See Table 8.1 for descriptive statistics.

TABLE 8.1

Descriptive Statistics

	Mean	Standard Deviation	Minimum	Maximum
Reverse repo rate	5.56	1.14	3.25	7.5
Repo rate	6.99	1.09	4.75	9
LAF net injection/NDTL (%)	0.22	1.26	−3.21	2.93
Cash reserve requirement	5.26	1.06	4	9
Statutory liquidity ratio	24.4	0.83	22	25
WACMR	6.30	1.82	2.42	10.5
Deposit rate, 3-month	7.03	2.05	3.4	11.5
Prime lending rate	13.4	2.12	10.1	16.3
Bank securities/loans	52.0	15.6	36.9	85.7
Bank loans/assets	61.0	6.0	49.0	68.3

Source: Author's calculations.
Note: 328 observations. LAF = Liquidity Adjustment Facility; NDTL = net demand and time liabilities; WACMR = weighted-average call money rate.

RESULTS

The vector error correction model (VECM) estimation method is used because of the presence of cointegrating vectors in the variables. In the first step, trace statistics suggest the presence of a cointegrating vector between the repo rate and the WACMR. In the second step, no cointegrating vector between the deposit rate and the lending rate is found, but test results indicate two cointegrating vectors between the WACMR, the deposit rate, and the lending rate.

Deposit rates are expected to have an effect on lending rates, as deposit rates make up part of a bank's cost of funds, which should in turn affect the cost at which a bank lends out funds. The relationship between the rate on deposits of a particular maturity and the lending rate could be weak, however, when the deposit instrument under consideration does not make up an important part of the bank's borrowed funds, and because lending rate decisions are determined only in part by the bank's cost of funds. Although this chapter shows no cointegrating vector between the deposit rate and lending rate, this does not indicate that there is no empirical relationship between these two variables, but only that there is no long-run relationship over the sample period (see Table 8.2).

Step 1: Pass-Through to the Target Rate from Monetary Policy

Results from the first step of estimation show there is a cointegrating vector between the monetary policy rate and the operating target rate. The coefficient

TABLE 8.2

Summary of Cointegration Test Results

Variables	Maximum Rank
WACMR, repo rate	1
Lending rate, deposit rate	0
Lending rate, deposit rate, WACMR	2

Source: Results from Johansen tests for cointegration, at 95 percent confidence level.
Note: WACMR = weighted-average call money rate.

on the repo rate in column 1 of Annex Table 8.1.1 of 1.287 indicates a long-run elasticity between the repo rate and the WACMR of 1.43. Another aspect of monetary policy, the cash reserve ratio, was not found to have a significant relationship with the WACMR.[9] From the estimates of the alternate specification, where the effective policy rate is the reverse repo rate when there is a liquidity surplus and the repo rate when there is a liquidity deficit, we see that both rates are part of a cointegrating relationship with the WACMR. The long-run elasticity of the WACMR for the reverse repo rate is 0.48 and the elasticity for the repo rate is 0.99, shown in column 2 of Annex Table 8.1.1, which together come to about the same elasticity with the WACMR as the repo rate does in the first specification. The repo rate appears to sufficiently capture the monetary policy stance of the RBI.

Turning to the estimates of the adjustment parameters and short-run coefficients, in Annex Table 8.1.2, we find an estimate of α equal to –0.06. This indicates that, when there is deviation from the equilibrium between the WACMR and the repo rate, the WACMR adjusts by 6 percent per time period toward the repo rate to reestablish equilibrium. At this rate, it would take 5.6 months (11.2 two-week periods) to achieve 50 percent of the pass-through from an increase in the repo rate.

Step 2: Pass-Through to Bank Interest Rates from the Target Rate

The long-term results of the VECM estimated in the second step are shown in Annex Table 8.1.3. The top part shows the cointegrating vector between the lending rate, the WACMR, and the share of loans in assets. The elasticity of the lending rate with respect to the WACMR is 0.30, meaning that, on average, only 30 percent of a change in the WACMR gets passed on to the lending rate. The coefficients in the lower panel indicate an elasticity of the three-month deposit rate with respect to the WACMR is 1.11.

The estimates of the (symmetric) adjustment parameters and short-run coefficients, in Annex Table 8.1.4, show that the speed of adjustment has also increased in recent years. The adjustment coefficients are as expected: with a negative and statistically significant coefficient in the differenced lending (deposit) rate equation on the lending (deposit) error correction model and the other adjustment parameter coefficients being mainly statistically insignificant. The coefficient of –0.042 indicates that the lending rate adjusts by 4 percent per time period toward the WACMR after a deviation from equilibrium, resulting in 8.1 months to achieve 50 percent of the pass-through from a change in the WACMR. This estimate does not allow us to distinguish between instances of monetary tightening and loosening, which are explored in a later section with estimates of asymmetric adjustment parameters. The deposit rate adjusts to

[9]The cash reserve ratio was not found to have a cointegrating vector with the WAMCR; nor was it found to Granger-cause WACMR after a simple VAR with both variables.

deviations between the deposit rate and the WACMR more quickly, with the coefficient of –0.081 indicating 4.1 months to achieve 50 percent of pass-through.

Cumulative Pass-Through and Adjustment

This section combines the results of the two steps of estimation to give an overall picture of the transmission of monetary policy to deposit and lending rates. Over the two steps of the analysis, the cumulative long-run elasticity of the deposit rate with respect to the repo rate is 1.58. This indicates that a 1 percentage point increase in the repo rate is associated with a 1.58 percentage point increase in the deposit rate over time. Pass-through to the lending rate is partial—the cumulative long-run elasticity of the lending rate with respect to the repo rate is 0.43. A larger pass-through to the deposit rate than to the lending rate is as expected, because the deposit rate in the analysis is a three-month rate, while loans tend to have longer maturities. This is also consistent with previous studies that find greater pass-through to interest rates with shorter maturities.

Next, we consider the speed of adjustment under the assumption that adjustment to a monetary tightening and loosening is symmetric. This assumption is relaxed in the next section to estimate potential asymmetric adjustment speeds. Pass-through to deposit and lending rates is relatively slow and the deposit rate adjusts more quickly to monetary policy changes than the lending rate does (Table 8.3). In the first step of transmission, it takes about 5.6 months for 50 percent of the pass-through from a change in the repo rate to the WACMR. In the second step, 50 percent of the pass-through from a change in WACMR passes through to the deposit rate in four months, while it takes eight months to pass through to the lending rate.

The pass-through is nonlinear, with more of the adjustment taking place in earlier periods than later. It takes considerably longer for a pass-through of, say, 80 percent to occur. Figure 8.5 shows the path of adjustment to the long-run equilibrium over time, where each tick on the x-axis denotes a two-week period.

TABLE 8.3

Speed of Adjustment: Number of Months Required to Complete 50 Percent Pass-Through of Repo Rate Increase

Lending Rate	Repo-WACMR	WACMR-Lending	Total
Adjustment coefficient	–0.06	–0.042	
Number of periods	11.2	16.2	34
Number of months	5.6	8.1	17

Deposit Rate	Repo-WACMR	WACMR-Deposit	Total
Adjustment coefficient	–0.060	–0.081	
Number of periods	11.2	8.2	24
Number of months	5.6	4.1	12

Source: Author's calculations, using Annex Tables 8.1.2 and 8.2.2.
Note: WACMR = weighted-average call money rate.

Figure 8.5. Cumulative Speed of Adjustment

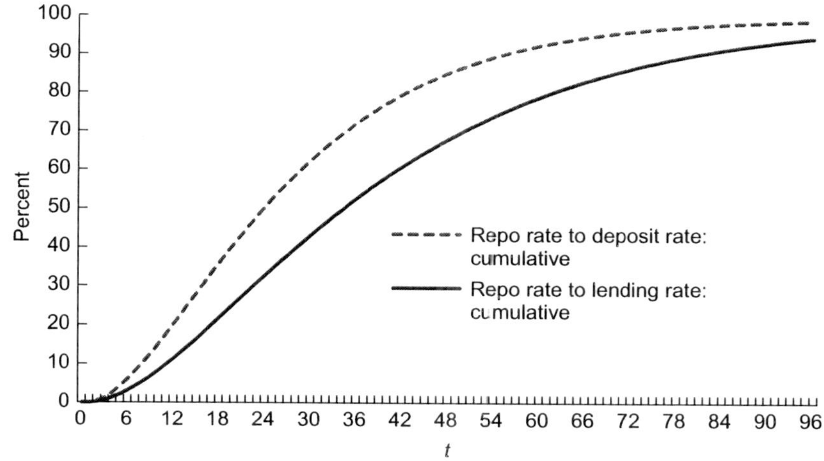

Source: Author's calculations.

Sørensen and Werner (2006) apply a similar method to estimating monetary policy transmission in the euro area. Across euro area countries, they estimate speeds of adjustment of short-run lending rates ranging from –0.027 to –0.925, with an average elasticity of 0.7 with respect to the policy rate. For deposit rates, they estimate adjustment parameters from –.054 to –0.320, with an average elasticity of 0.145. Although the results are not exactly comparable to the estimates in this paper,[10] it is interesting to note that the pass-through to deposit and lending rates in India is within the ranges of pass-through estimates for a variety of maturities of euro area deposits and loans found by Sørensen and Werner (2006).

Asymmetric Speed of Adjustment

There is evidence of asymmetry in the pass-through to bank interest rates. In Table 8.4, the coefficient on ECT1 pos (lending) corresponds to a decrease in the WACMR, and ECT1 neg (lending) to an increase in the WACMR. The estimates of these speed-of-adjustment coefficients indicate that the lending rate adjusts more quickly to an increase in the WACMR than to a decrease. On the right side of Table 8.4, the coefficient on ECT2 pos (deposit) corresponds to a decrease in the WACMR, while ECT1 neg (deposit) corresponds to an increase in the WACMR. The estimated speed-of-adjustment coefficients indicate that the deposit rate adjusts downward when the WACMR falls, but not upward

[10] Instead of focusing on a particular monetary policy indicator, their analysis is on the pass-through from different market interest rates to bank interest rates of comparable maturity. Their paper is focused on studying interest rates of different maturities and heterogeneity in the euro area.

TABLE 8.4

Bank Interest Rates and WACMR: Asymmetric Short-Run VECM Results

	Lending Rate D.Lending Rate Full sample		Deposit Rate D.Deposit Rate Full sample
ECT1 pos (lending)	−0.033 (0.022)	ECT1 (lending)	0.014 (0.025)
ECT1 neg (lending)	−0.042*** (0.009)		
ECT2 (deposit)	0.010 (0.007)	ECT2 pos (deposit)	−0.111*** (0.029)
		ECT2 neg (deposit)	−0.033 (0.032)
Number of observations	324	Observations	324
F-test: lending ECT asymmetry (*p*-value)	0.73	*F*-test: deposit ECT asymmetry (*p*-value)	0.07

Note: Standard errors in parentheses. Constant and lags of differenced WACMR, lending rate, deposit rate, loans/assets also included. ECT = error correction term; VECM = vector error correction model; WACMR = weighted-average call money rate.

*** $p < 0.01$.

to a monetary tightening. The adjustment coefficient on ECT2 pos (deposit) is negative and statistically significant, indicating that the deposit rate adjusts downward in response to a monetary loosening. The insignificant coefficient on ECT2 neg (deposit) indicates, however, that it does not adjust upward after a tightening.

HAS MONETARY POLICY TRANSMISSION IMPROVED?

Since changes have been made to the monetary policy operating framework, and the base rate system was put into place in 2010, it may be the case that monetary policy transmission has strengthened in recent years. In this section, the sample is split into two periods: from the end of March 2002 to the end of August 2010 and from the start of September 2010 to the end of October 2014. The long- and short-run pass-through from monetary policy to the deposit and lending rates is estimated for both periods. The LAF was in deficit for the duration of the second period.[11] The overall result is that the extent of pass-through to the deposit rate decreased somewhat in the later period, but the pass-through to the lending rate has increased. The speed of transmission to both the deposit rate and lending rate has increased.

[11] After alternating between liquidity deficit and surplus since the start of the LAF, liquidity has been in deficit continuously since September 9, 2010.

Annex Table 8.1.5 shows the results of the long-run stage of the VECM estimated over the two periods. The extent of pass-through from the WACMR to the lending rate appears to have risen since 2010, with an elasticity of 0.20 in the first part of the sample and 0.32 in the period since September 2010. The extent of pass-through to the deposit rate appears to have fallen, from an elasticity of 1.33 in the first eight years of the sample to an elasticity of 0.71 in the last four years. Annex Table 8.1.6 shows the results of the short-run stage of the VECM estimated over the two periods. The estimated speeds of adjustment of both the deposit rate to the WACMR and the lending rate to the WACMR are higher in the second period than in the first.

Finally, estimation of separate adjustment parameters for monetary loosening and tightening was also done for both sample periods. Annex Table 8.1.7 shows the results. The asymmetric adjustment of the lending rate to monetary tightening and loosening is present in both periods. For the deposit rate, the asymmetry whereby deposit rates adjust downward to loosening but not upward to tightening is present in the first period, but in the second period the estimated adjustment coefficients suggest that the deposit rate adjusts similarly to both loosening and tightening.

CONCLUSION

This chapter provides new evidence on monetary policy transmission in India from the end of March 2002 to the end of October 2014. A two-step VECM was used to estimate the pass-through from changes in the monetary policy stance to the operating target rate, and from the target rate to bank deposit and lending rates. The results show a significant, albeit slow, pass-through of policy changes to bank interest rates in India. The extent of pass-through to the deposit rate is larger than to the lending rate, and the deposit rate adjusts more quickly to changes in the policy rate. There is evidence of asymmetric adjustment to monetary policy. Throughout most of the sample period, deposit rates do not adjust upward in response to monetary tightening, but they do adjust downward to loosening; and the lending rate adjusts more quickly to monetary tightening than to loosening. The extent of pass-through to the lending rate increased in the latter part of the sample, to a cumulative elasticity of 0.46 with respect to the policy rate. For both the deposit rate and lending rate, the speed of adjustment to changes in the policy rate increased in the latter part of the sample. As changes in bank lending rates are only the first step in the bank lending channel, further research on bank lending behavior is needed to understand the importance of the bank lending channel in India.

ANNEX 8.1

ANNEX TABLE 8.1.1

WACMR and Policy Rate: Long-Run ECM Results

	(1) WACMR Full Sample	(2) WACMR Full Sample
Repo rate	1.287*** (0.213)	
Reverse repo rate * Liq deficit dummy		1.815*** (0.379)
Repo rate * Liq deficit dummy		1.285*** (0.244)
Number of observations	324	324
Pass-through elasticity (reverse repo rate)		0.48
Pass-through elasticity (repo rate)	1.43	0.99
Mean dependent variable	6.30	6.30

Source: Author's calculations.

Note: Standard errors in parentheses. ECM = error correction model; Liq = liquidity; WACMR = weighted-average call money rate.

*** $p < .01$.

ANNEX TABLE 8.1.2

WACMR and Policy Rate: Short-Run ECM Results

	(1)	
	D. WACMR Full Sample	D. Repo Rate Full Sample
Error correction term	−0.060*** (0.015)	0.009 (0.006)
LD.repo rate	0.510*** (0.147)	0.401*** (0.054)
L2D.repo rate	0.080 (0.160)	−0.121** (0.059)
L3D.repo rate	−0.148 (0.144)	0.264*** −0.053
LD.WACMR	0.746*** (0.055)	0.049** (0.020)
L2D.WACMR	−0.305*** (0.066)	−0.029 (0.025)
L3D.WACMR	0.133** (0.058)	0.037* (0.021)
R^2	0.449	0.3288
Number of observations	324	324

Source: Author's calculations.

Note: Standard errors in parentheses. Specification includes constant and lags of differenced LAFnetinj/NDTL (the net injection under the Liquidity Adjustment Facility as a share of net demand and time liabilities). ECM = error correction model; LD = one lag of differenced variable; WACMR = weighted-average call money rate.

*** $p < .01$, ** $p < .05$, * $p < .1$.

ANNEX TABLE 8.1.3

Bank Interest Rates and WACMR: Long-Run VECM Results

Lending Rate	Lending Rate Full Sample
WACMR	0.638***
	(0.100)
Number of observations	324
Pass-through elasticity (WACMR)	0.30
Mean dependent variable	13.44

Deposit Rate	Deposit Rate Full Sample
WACMR	1.235***
	(0.116)
Number of observations	324
Pass-through elasticity (WACMR)	1.11
Mean dependent variable	7.01

Source: Author's calculations.

Note: Standard errors in parentheses. VECM = vecto· error correction model; WACMR = weighted-average call money rate.

*** $p < .01$.

ANNEX TABLE 8.1.4

Bank Interest Rates and WACMR: Short-Run VECM Results

	Lending Rate D.Lending rate Full sample	Deposit Rate D.Deposit rate Full sample
ECT1 (lending)	−0.042***	0.031
	(0.008)	(0.022)
ECT2 (deposit)	0.010	−0.081***
	(0.008)	(0.022)
LD.WACMR	0.007	0.311***
	(0.024)	(0.065)
L2D.WACMR	−0.053*	−0.177**
	(0.030)	(0.081)
L3D.WACMR	0.084***	0.195***
	(0.026)	(0.071)
Number of observations	324	324

Source: Author's calculations.

Note: Standard errors in parentheses. Specifications include constant, and lags of differenced lending rate, deposit rate, and loans/assets. ECT = error correction term; LD = one lag of differenced variable; VECM = vector error correction model; WACMR = weighted-average call money rate.

*** $p < .01$, ** $p < .05$, * $p < .1$.

ANNEX TABLE 8.1.5

Bank Interest Rates and WACMR: Long-Run VECM Results, Split Sample

Lending Rate	Lending Rate April 2002–August 2010	Lending Rate September 2010–October 2014
WACMR	0.442***	0.637***
	(0.123)	(0.095)
Number of observations	216	108
Pass-through elasticity (WACMR)	0.20	0.32
Mean dependent variable	12.2	15.8
Deposit Rate	**Deposit Rate April 2002–August 2010**	**Deposit Rate September 2010–October 2014**
WACMR	1.466***	0.806***
	(0.129)	(0.166)
Number of observations	216	108
Pass-through elasticity (WACMR)	1.33	0.71
Mean dependent variable	6.00	9.03

Source: Author's calculations.
Note: Standard errors in parentheses. VECM = vector error correction model; WACMR = weighted-average call money rate.
*** $p < .01$.

ANNEX TABLE 8.1.6

Bank Interest Rates and WACMR: Short-Run VECM Results, Split Sample

	April 2002–August 2010		September 2010–October 2014	
	Lending Rate D.Lending Rate	Deposit Rate D.Deposit Rate	Lending Rate D.Lending Rate	Deposit Rate D.Deposit Rate
ECT1 (lending)	−0.045***	0.046	−0.063***	−0.160
	(0.015)	(0.033)	(0.016)	(0.102)
ECT2 (deposit)	−0.002	−0.067**	0.025**	−0.153***
	(0.012)	(0.026)	(0.011)	(0.056)
LD.WACMR	−0.002	0.248***	0.025	1.076***
	(0.029)	(0.067)	(0.045)	(0.227)
L2D.WACMR	−0.067*	−0.153*	0.041	−0.575**
	(0.037)	(0.084)	(0.055)	(0.281)
L3D.WACMR	0.089***	0.219***	−0.053	−0.119
	(0.033)	(0.075)	(0.046)	(0.233)
Number of observations	216	216	108	108

Source: Author's calculations.
Note: Standard errors in parentheses. ECT = error correction term; LD = one lag of differenced variable; VECM = vector error correction model; WACMR = weighted-average call money rate. Specifications include constant, and lags of differenced lending rate, deposit rate, and loans/assets.
*** $p < .01$, ** $p < .05$, * $p < .1$.

ANNEX TABLE 8.1.7

Bank Interest Rates and WACMR: Asymmetric ECM Results, Split Sample

Lending Rate	D.Lending Rate April 2002–August 2010	D.Lending Rate September 2010–October 2014
ECT1 pos (lending)	0.009	0.004
	(0.033)	(0.053)
ECT1 neg (lending)	−0.053***	−0.061***
	(0.015)	(0.019)
ECT2 (deposit)	0.000	0.030**
	(0.010)	(0.012)
Number of observations	216	108
F-test: lending ECM asymmetry (*p*-value)	0.08	0.28

Deposit Rate	D.Deposit Rate April 2002–August 2010	D.Deposit Rate September 2010–October 2014
ECT1 (lending)	0.036	−0.215**
	(0.034)	(0.083)
ECT2 pos (deposit)	−0.113***	−0.117*
	(0.033)	(0.091)
ECT2 neg (deposit)	−0.023	−0.221***
	(0.026)	(0.130)
Number of observations	216	108
F-test: deposit ECM asymmetry (*p*-value)	0.01	0.04

Source: Author's calculations.

Note: Standard errors in parentheses. Constant and lags of differenced WACMR, lending rate, deposit rate, loans/assets also included. ECM = error correction model; ECT = error correction term; WACMR = weighted-average call money rate.

*** $p < .01$, ** $p < .05$, * $p < .1$.

REFERENCES

Beck, T., A. Colciago, and D. Pfajfar. 2014. "The Role of Financial Intermediaries in Monetary Policy Transmission." *Journal of Economic Dynamics and Control* 43 (June): 1–11.

Christiano, Laurence, Martin Eichenbaum, and Charles Evans. 2000. "Monetary Policy Shocks: What Have We Learned and to What End?" In *Handbook of Macroeconomics*, edited by J. Taylor and M. Woodford. Amsterdam: North-Holland.

Mishra, Prachi, and Peter Montiel. 2012. "How Effective Is Monetary Transmission in Developing Countries? A Survey of the Empirical Evidence." IMF Working Paper 12/143, International Monetary Fund, Washington.

Mishra, Prachi, Peter Montiel, Paolo Pedroni, and Antonio Spilimbergo. 2014. "Monetary Policy and Bank Lending Rates in Low-Income Countries: Heterogeneous Panel Estimates." *Journal of Development Economics* 111 (November): 117–31.

Mohanty, Deepak. 2011. "How Does the Reserve Bank of India Conduct Its Monetary Policy?" Speech by Shri Deepak Mohanty, Executive Director, Reserve Bank of India, at the Indian Institute of Management, Lucknow, August 12.

———. 2012. "Evidence of Interest Rate Channel of Monetary Policy Transmission in India." RBI Working Paper 6, Reserve Bank of India, Mumbai.

Reserve Bank of India (RBI). 2010. Guidelines on the Base Rate, April 9. www.rbi.org.in/scripts/NotificationUser.aspx?Mode=0&Id=5579.

———. 2014. *Report of the Expert Committee to Revise and Strengthen the Monetary Policy Framework.* https://rbi.org.in/Scripts/PublicationReportDetails.aspx?ID=743.

Sengupta, Nandini. 2014. "Changes in Transmission Channels of Monetary Policy in India." *Economic and Political Weekly* 49 (49): 62–71.

Singh, B. 2011. "How Asymmetric Is the Monetary Policy Transmission to Financial Markets in India?" RBI Occasional Papers 32/2, Reserve Bank of India, Mumbai.

Sørensen, Christoffer Kok, and Thomas Werner. 2006. "Bank Interest Rate Pass-Through in the Euro Area: A Cross Country Comparison." ECB Working Paper 580, European Central Bank, Frankfurt.

CHAPTER 9

Food Inflation in India: What Role for Monetary Policy?

RAHUL ANAND AND VOLODYMYR TULIN

Persistent and elevated food inflation has presented challenges for monetary management in India. While it is a widely held view that central banks should only respond to changes in underlying core inflation and second-round effects on core inflation from commodity price shocks, there is growing evidence that the dynamics of food price inflation are very different in emerging market economies. Ignoring it in monetary policy action may lead to policy mistakes. As former Reserve Bank of India (RBI) governor Duvvuri Subbarao pointed out: "If food inflation is higher, as is typically the case in many low-income countries including India, then we would be underestimating inflationary pressures on a systemic basis. That would mislead policy prescriptions."[1]

India is not unique in the nontrivial role food price shocks play in shaping inflation shocks. Food price inflation shocks in emerging market economies are more volatile and persistent than in advanced economies, and are propagated strongly into nonfood inflation (Walsh 2011). They also tend to have stronger and longer-lasting effects on inflation in economies with high food shares in their consumption baskets and in economies with less firmly anchored expectations (IMF 2011a). Accordingly, excluding commodity-price inflation in economies where food and fuel represent a large share of household expenditure, and where commodity price changes affect core inflation through second-round effects, may not be appropriate (Catão and Chang 2010; Walsh 2011). Anand and Prasad (2010) also conclude that in an environment of credit-constrained consumers, a narrow policy focus on nonfood inflation can lead to suboptimal outcomes.

In this chapter we estimate the second-round effects of food price inflation and investigate their importance for monetary policy formulation in India. To do that, we document why second-round effects may have nontrivial consequences for monetary policy formation in emerging market economies. Then we carry out econometric analysis investigating the importance of these second-round effects in India. Lastly, we develop and estimate a suitable dynamic stochastic general equilibrium model that builds on a stylized gap model in which each variable is expressed in terms of its deviation from equilibrium; in other words in "gap" terms.[2]

[1]Comments made at the meeting of the Central Bank Governance Group in Basel, May 9, 2011.
[2]See for example, Berg, Karam, and Laxton (2006a, 2006b).

This is tailored to India's fundamentals so that various aspects of monetary policy transmission there can be studied.

RECENT INFLATION DYNAMICS IN INDIA: THE ROLE OF FOOD INFLATION

High and persistent inflation remains a key macroeconomic challenge in India. Elevated inflation has coincided with the growth slowdown of recent years, distinguishing India from other major emerging market economies. Among the several factors that contributed to this were food inflation feeding quickly into wages and core inflation; entrenched inflation expectations; cost-push shocks from binding sector-specific supply constraints (particularly in agriculture, energy, and transportation); the pass-through from a weaker rupee; and ongoing energy price increases (Figures 9.1 and 9.2). However, food inflation has played an important role in shaping inflation dynamics in India because of the following factors: (1) the share of food expenditure in total household expenditure is high; (2) inflation expectations are anchored by food inflation; and (3) inflation expectations, anchored by food inflation, feed into wages (Figures 9.1 and 9.2).

In India, as in other emerging markets, the share of food expenditure in total household expenditure is much higher than in advanced economies (Table 9.1). Correspondingly, the weight on food in the consumer price index (CPI) basket is also high. In the CPI-Combined index, the weight on food, beverages, and tobacco is 49.7 percent.

Food inflation also appears to play a pivotal role in informing inflation expectations. The RBI's inflation expectations survey of households suggests that general price expectations are more consistently aligned with food price expectations than with any other product groups. The share of households expecting headline

Figure 9.1. Inflation in India, 2011–14
(Percent, year-over-year)

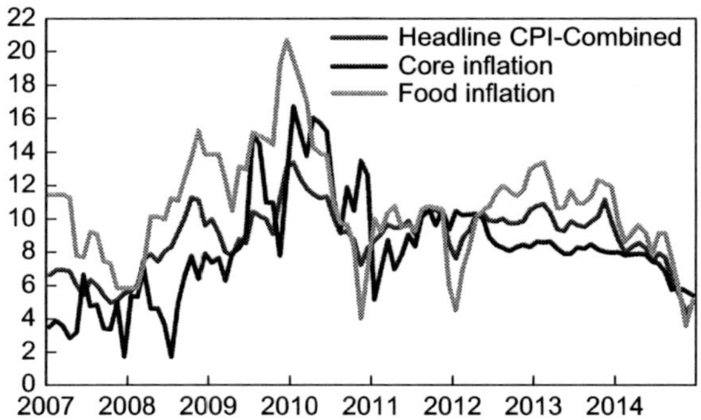

Sources: Haver Analytics; and IMF staff calculations.

Figure 9.2. Role of Food Inflation in India
(Percent, year-over-year)

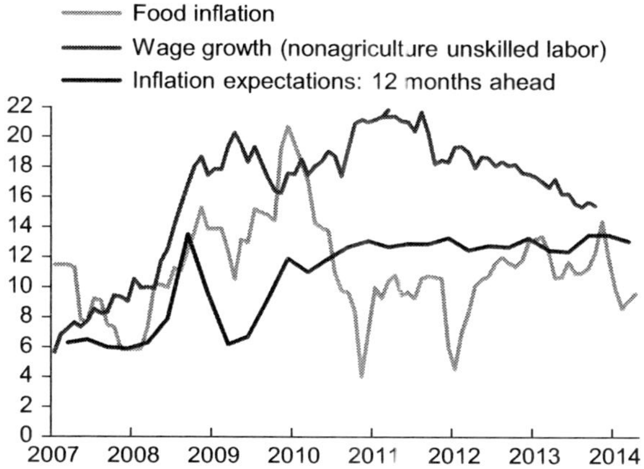

Sources: CEIC; Haver Analytics; and IMF staff calculations.

TABLE 9.1

Share of Food Expenditure in Total Household Expenditure *(Percent)*

Emerging Markets		Advanced Economies	
Indonesia	53.0	Japan	14.7
Vietnam	49.8	Germany	11.5
India	48.8	Australia	10.8
China	36.7	Canada	9.3
Russia	33.2	United Kingdom	8.8
Malaysia	28.0	United States	5.7
Average	41.6	Average	10.1

Sources: CEIC; household surveys; U.S. Department of Agriculture, Economic Research Service, International Food Consumption Patterns Dataset; and authors' calculations.
Note: Data for emerging markets for 2005; data for advanced economies for 2006. Expenditure on food includes expenditure on food consumed at home only and does not include expenditure on beverages and tobacco.

CPI inflation to move in coherence with food inflation has averaged about 90 percent in recent years. In December 2012, for example, more than 95 percent of the respondents appeared to have been influenced by expected changes in food prices for arriving at general price expectations, suggesting that they consider food prices to be very important when they think about price dynamics.

Wage growth accelerated during 2009–13, and both agricultural and nonagricultural wages have been on sustained growth trajectories since about 2005. Real wage growth has also been significantly positive. Admittedly, several factors contributed to this. Of them, the Mahatma Gandhi National Rural Employment Guarantee Act scheme stands out. Although it has undoubtedly benefited inclusiveness and enhanced the socioeconomic position of India's rural population, it also probably buttressed inflation pressures during 2010–13. The scheme has not only set a floor on many rural wages and strengthened the bargaining position of the rural labor force, but has also tied up wage growth indexation to retail inflation, reinforcing the nexus between prices and wages. Furthermore, wage increases buttressing demand further reinforced India's food inflation, underpinned by wage and input cost inflation. As econometric analysis in Mohanty (2014) suggests, both the costs of material inputs and wages have sharp positive impact on food inflation in India. However, wage growth affects food inflation gradually, and is more persistent than the impact of the increase in the costs of material inputs.

FACED WITH FOOD INFLATION, WHAT CAN MONETARY POLICY DO?

The established conventional wisdom for monetary policy is to look through transitory supply shocks, to food and fuel prices in particular. Persistent supply shocks, however, require monetary policy action to mitigate their second-round effects on generalized inflation, and to keep the inflation process in check by anchoring inflation expectations. It is therefore important to ascertain whether second-round effects are important in India, and, if they are, to estimate their size.

Are Second-Round Effects Important in India?

To formalize the relationship between food inflation and its pass-through to core inflation, it is worth assessing the dynamics of headline inflation with respect to core inflation. To do so, we ask the following questions:

- *Does headline inflation revert to core inflation*?—If headline inflation reverts quickly to core inflation, then the impact of food and fuel price shocks is temporary, and second-round effects are probably limited. But if headline inflation does not revert to core, either the shocks are persistent or the second-round effects are large because of higher inflation expectations and accelerating wages.
- *Does core inflation revert to headline inflation?*—If core inflation reverts to headline inflation, it would indicate that shocks to headline inflation, such as those caused by commodity price spikes, feed into inflation expectations and price setting, driving core inflation to catch up with headline inflation.

The empirical results suggest that second-round effects are indeed significant (Box 9.1). It can therefore be concluded that headline does not revert to core, suggesting that either food shocks are persistent or second-round effects are large. This suggests that core inflation catches up with headline inflation and reverts to headline quickly. Thus, large second-round effects are present.[3]

[3]The estimates reported correspond to consumer price index for industrial workers (CPI-IW) inflation. Conclusions remain the same if wholesale price index inflation is used instead.

BOX 9.1 How Important Are Second-Round Effects in India?

We follow Cecchetti and Moessner (2008) and Clark (2001) to estimate the following equations, using monthly inflation data for 1996–2013, to answer these two questions:

Does headline inflation revert to core inflation?

$$\pi_t^{headline} - \pi_{t-12}^{headline} = \alpha + \beta\left(\pi_{t-12}^{headline} - \pi_{t-12}^{core}\right) + \varepsilon_t$$

Does core inflation revert to headline inflation?

$$\pi_t^{core} - \pi_{t-12}^{core} = \delta + \gamma\left(\pi_{t-12}^{core} - \pi_{t-12}^{headline}\right) + \varepsilon_t$$

where $\pi_t^{headline}$ and π_t^{core} denote headline and core year-over-year CPI inflation, respectively.

The empirical results suggest that second-round effects are indeed significant (Table 9.1.1). Specifically, if headline reverts to core, the coefficient β is expected to be negative. The results, however, suggest that the null of $\beta = 0$ cannot be rejected, which implies that headline inflation does not revert to core inflation. At the same time, individually both the hypothesis that $\beta = -1$ and that $\beta = -1$ and $\alpha = 0$, (that is, that headline fully reverts to core within a year) are rejected. Therefore, it can be concluded that headline does not revert to core, suggesting that either food shocks are persistent or second-round effects are large. On the other hand, the estimate of γ is –0.68, which is highly statistically significant, suggests that core inflation reverts to headline inflation. At the same time, the null hypothesis of $\gamma = 0$, which corresponds to a situation where core does not revert to headline, is rejected. Moreover, both the hypothesis that $\gamma = -1$ and that $\gamma = -1$ and $\delta = 0$ cannot be rejected. This suggests that core inflation catches up with headline inflation and reverts to headline quickly. Therefore, large second-round effects are present.

TABLE 9.1.1

Regression Analysis of Noncore Inflation Pass-Through

Dependent Variable	$\pi_t^{headline} - \pi_{t-12}^{headline}$	$\pi_t^{core} - \pi_{t-12}^{core}$
$\pi_{t-12}^{headline} - \pi_{t-12}^{core}$	–0.31	
	(0.27)	
$\pi_{t-12}^{core} - \pi_{t-12}^{headline}$		–0.68***
		(0.21)
Constant	0.136	–0.11
	(0.59)	(0.49)
Sample: 1997–2013		

Source: IMF staff estimates.
Note: Robust standard errors in parenthesis.
*** $p < .001$.

Quantifying the Size of Second-Round Effects

Analysis of inflation dynamics suggest that second-round effects are big, and policymakers need to pay close attention to food price shocks.[4] Incorporating the second-round effects of food price inflation is essential for monetary policy formulation in India, and estimating their size is important for understanding the

[4] We also estimated using 12-month monthly CPI-IW headline and core inflation. The results are similar.

country's inflation dynamics and monetary transmission. We estimate these effects using a variant of the small New Keynesian macroeconomic model with rational expectations developed by Berg, Karam, and Laxton (2006a, 2006b).

We then estimate a New Keynesian Phillips curve in a dynamic small open economy model, and analyze the effect of the output gap, lagged inflation, exchange rate, and inflation expectations on current inflation. To estimate the second-round effects, we modify the model to capture the pass-through from headline to core inflation. Although this model is simple and abstracts from many important features of the economy, such specifications have long been the workhorse of monetary policy analysis at the IMF. In addition to effectively capturing the key channels of monetary policy transmission, this framework has the virtues of clarity and tractability.

The Model

The model features a small open economy, including forward-looking aggregate supply and demand with micro foundations, and with stylized (realistic) lags in the different monetary transmission channels. Output developments in the rest of the world feed directly into the small economy because they characterize foreign demand for Indian products. Changes in foreign inflation or interest rates affect the exchange rate, and, subsequently, demand and inflation in the Indian economy. The model is set up in gap terms (that is, deviation of variables from their respective steady-state value). To estimate the second-round effects, we add an equation to capture the pass-through from headline to core inflation.

The baseline model has five behavioral equations: (1) an aggregate demand curve that relates the level of real activity to expected and past real activity, the real interest rate, the real exchange rate, and the foreign output gap; (2) a price-setting or Phillips curve equation that relates core CPI inflation to past and expected inflation, the output gap, and the exchange rate, as well as the pass-through from the headline to core inflation; (3) a food inflation equation that relates food inflation to past and expected inflation, the output gap, and the exchange rate; (4) an uncovered interest parity condition for the exchange rate, with some allowance for backward-looking expectations; and (5) a rule for setting the policy interest rate as a function of the output gap and expected inflation.

The output gap equation is given by:

$$ygap_t = \beta_{ld}\, ygap_{t+1} + \beta_{lag}\, ygap_{t-1} - \beta_{RRgap} RRgap_{t-1} + \beta_{Zgap} zgap_{t-1} + \beta_{RWygap}\, ygap_t^{RW} + \varepsilon_t^{ygap}$$

in which *ygap* is the output gap, *RRgap* the real interest rate gap, *zgap* the gap of real exchange rate, $ygap^{RW}$ the output gap in the rest of the world, β a series of parameters attached to those variables, and ε^{ygap} an error term, which captures other temporary exogenous effects.[5]

[5] We use the U.S. output gap as the proxy for the output gap of the rest of the world.

The headline inflation equation is given as the aggregation of the core and food and fuel inflation:

$$\pi_t = (1-\vartheta)\pi_t^c + \vartheta\pi_t^{ff} + \varepsilon_t^{\pi}$$

in which π_t^c is core inflation rate, $\pi_{c,t}^{ff}$ is noncore (food and fuel), ϑ is the weight on noncore inflation, and ε_t^{π} an error term. A residual captures other temporary exogenous effects that are not explicitly modeled.

We then have two pricing equations for core inflation and food and fuel inflation, which have a very similar structure except for an additional term in the former to capture the pass-through from headline to core inflation, or the second-round effects.

$$\pi_t^c = \alpha_{c,\pi ld}\pi 4_{t+4}^c + (1-\alpha_{c,\pi ld})\pi 4_{t-1}^c + \alpha_{c,ygap}\, ygap_{t-1} + \alpha_{c,z}(z_t - z_{t-1}) + \alpha_{c,\pi}(\pi 4_{t-1} - \pi 4_{c,t-1}) + \varepsilon_t^{\pi,c}$$

$$\pi_t^{ff} = \alpha_{ff,\pi ld}\pi 4_{t+4}^{ff} + (1-\alpha_{ff,\pi ld})\pi 4_{t-1}^c + \alpha_{ff,ygap}\, ygap_{t-1} + \alpha_{ff,z}(z_t - z_{t-1}) + \varepsilon_t^{\pi,ff}$$

in which $\pi_t^c 4_{t+4}$ and $\pi_t^{ff} 4_{t+4}$ are the four-quarter-ahead year-over-year core and food and fuel inflation rates, respectively,[6] $\pi_t^c 4_{t-1}$ and $\pi_t^{ff} 4_{t-1}$ are their one-quarter lagged year-over-year inflation rates, *ygap* the output gap, $z_t - z_{t-1}$ the real depreciation, α_c a series of parameters, and $\varepsilon_t^{\pi,c}$ and $\varepsilon_t^{\pi,ff}$ are error terms. The additional term $(\pi 4_{t-1} - \pi 4_{c,t-1})$ is added to the core inflation equation to allow for the possibility of relative price and real wage resistance; or more precisely that workers and other price setters may try to partially keep their prices rising in pace with past movements in headline CPI (Berg, Karam, and Laxton 2006b). Expected inflation enters the equation due to the assumption of staggered price-setting (Calvo 1983), while indexation schemes can rationalize the backward-looking inflation component. The real exchange rate z reflects the effect of the prices of imported goods on inflation in an open economy.[7]

The real exchange rate equation is given by:

$$z_t = \delta_z z_{t+1} + (1-\delta_z)z_{t-1} - (RR_t - RR_t^{RW} - \rho^*)/4 + \varepsilon_t^z$$

in which z_t is the real exchange rate (an increase represents a depreciation), RR_t the real interest rate, RR_t^{RW} the real interest rate in the United States, ρ^* the equilibrium risk premium on the domestic currency, δ_z parameters, and ε_t^z an error term. A residual captures other temporary exogenous effects.

Finally, the monetary policy rule is given by:

$$RS_t = \gamma_{RSlag} RS_{t-1} + (1-\gamma_{RSlag}) * [RR_t^* + \pi 4_t + \gamma_{\pi}(\pi 4_{t+4} - \pi_{t+4}^*) + \gamma_{ygap}\, ygap_t] + \varepsilon_t^{RS}$$

in which RS_t is the nominal interest rate, RR^* the equilibrium real interest rate, π^* the inflation objective, γ parameters, and ε_t^{RS} an error term.

---

[6] Core CPI is compiled by stripping out food and energy items from the CPI basket.

[7] An increase in the real exchange rate (z) corresponds here to a real depreciation.

The model is a two-country model where the home country is small and open, whereas the foreign country—the home country's main trading partner—is relatively large and closed; in effect, exogenous to the home country. Thus, the foreign country enters the home country equations through the impact of its activity on the home country demand, and the impact of its real interest rate on the bilateral exchange rate. Conversely, the home country does not affect the foreign country, which implies that the output gap of the foreign country does not depend on the bilateral exchange rate or the home country activity; and foreign country inflation does not depend on the bilateral exchange rate. Hence, the uncovered interest rate parity condition is irrelevant for the foreign country model. So there are three additional behavioral equations that describe the foreign sector: an output-gap equation, an inflation equation, and a policy reaction function, except that no rest-of-the-world (*RW*) variables appear.

Estimation

The parameter values are chosen based on the modeling experience of other country models, but adapted to our knowledge about the characteristics of the Indian economy and policy making. The model is estimated as an open economy, where the United States is treated as the relevant foreign sector for India. For the United States, we use the prior distributions used in Berg, Karam, and Laxton (2006b).

The long-term steady-state values for key parameters—the inflation objective, real exchange rate, and real interest rate—are chosen to match the historical average of these variables. The equilibrium real interest rate for the rest of the world is set at 1.5 percent and the inflation rate at 2.4 percent. We set India's long-term headline CPI inflation rate at 6.5 percent and the equilibrium real interest rate at 1.5 percent. This implies an equilibrium nominal short-term interest rate of about 8 percent. Because we use a detrended real exchange rate series, which removes average real appreciation of about 1 percent a year, we make a technical assumption of zero equilibrium risk premium. All gaps that measure deviations of actual variables from their long-run equilibrium are, by definition, zero.

To estimate the model, we use key macroeconomic variables for India from the first quarter of 1996 to the fourth quarter of 2013. The three-month Treasury bill rate is used as a proxy for nominal interest rate, and real exchange rate (CPI-based) is used as a proxy for real exchange rate. For India's inflation, we use a backcasted CPI-Combined based on the CPI-IW. We use U.S. GDP, inflation, and interest rate data for the rest of the world in the model. Variables are seasonally adjusted using an X12 filter.

Estimated Aggregate Demand Equation

Coefficient estimates for the output gap equation are reported in Table 9.2:

$$ygap_t = \beta_{ld}\, ygap_{t+1} + \beta_{lag}\, ygap_{t-1} - \beta_{RRgap} RRgap_{t-1} + \beta_{Zgap} zgap_{t-1} + \beta_{RWygap}\, ygap_t^{RW} + \varepsilon_t^{ygap}$$

TABLE 9.2

Aggregate Demand Equation		
Parameter	**Prior Mean**	**Posterior Mean**
β_{ld}	0.40	0.19
β_{lag}	0.60	0.59
β_{RRgap}	0.05	0.04
β_{Zgap}	0.05	0.04
β_{RWygap}	0.15	0.10

The β parameters in the output gap equation depend to a large extent on the degree of inertia in the economy, the effectiveness of monetary policy transmission, and the openness of the economy. Drawing on the experience of several applied country modeling efforts, Berg, Karam, and Laxton (2006b) suggest that the value of β_{lag} should lie between 0.5 and 0.9, with a lower value for countries more susceptible to volatility.

The estimated coefficient of 0.6 for β_{lag} is comparable to other emerging markets. The lead of the output gap β_{ld} is typically small, and the estimated value for India is 0.2. The coefficient estimate on the lead of the output gap indicates that expectations on the future level of the output gap are important. This corroborates the importance of confidence effects in promoting economic activity in India (Anand and Tulin 2014). The parameter β_{RRgap} depends on the effectiveness of monetary transmission mechanism, while β_{zgap} and β_{RWygap} depend on the importance of the exchange rate channel and the degree of openness. Significant lags in the transmission of monetary policy imply that the sum of β_{RRgap} and β_{zgap} should be small relative to the parameter on the lagged gap in the equation. A β_{RRgap} coefficient of 0.04 implies that a one percentage point increase in real interest rates would lead a 0.04 percent fall in the output gap the following period. The value for β_{RWygap} of 0.1 implies that a 1 percentage point increase in the foreign output gap leads to a contemporaneous 0.1 percentage point increase in the Indian output gap.

Estimated Philips Curve Equations

Coefficient estimates for the core and headline CPI inflation equations are reported in Tables 9.3 and 9.4:

$$\pi_t^c = \alpha_{c,\pi ld}\pi 4_{t+4}^c + (1-\alpha_{c,\pi ld})\pi 4_{t-1}^c + \alpha_{c,ygap} ygap_{t-1} + \alpha_{c,z}(z_t - z_{t-1}) + \alpha_{c,\pi}(\pi 4_{t-1} - \pi 4_{c,t-1}) + \varepsilon_t^{\pi,c}$$

$$\pi_t^{ff} = \alpha_{ff,\pi ld}\pi 4_{t+4}^{ff} + (1-\alpha_{ff,\pi ld})\pi 4_{t-1}^c + \alpha_{ff,ygap} ygap_{t-1} + \alpha_{ff,z}(z_t - z_{t-1}) + \varepsilon_t^{\pi,ff}$$

The α parameters in the core inflation equations depend on the role of expectations and aggregate demand on inflation, and the degree of pass-through from the exchange rate to prices. The $\alpha_{c,\pi ld}$ parameter in the core inflation equation determines the forward component of inflation (while its inverse, $1-\alpha_{c,\pi ld}$,

TABLE 9.3

Phillips Curve Equation for Core Inflation

Parameter	Prior Mean	Posterior Mean
$\alpha_{c,\pi ld}$	0.20	0.26
$\alpha_{c,ygap}$	0.25	0.25
$\alpha_{c,z}$	0.30	0.15
$\alpha_{c,\pi}$	0.30	0.32

TABLE 9.4

Phillips Curve Equation for Food Inflation

Parameter	Prior Mean	Posterior Mean
$\alpha_{ff,\pi ld}$	0.20	0.22
$\alpha_{ff,ygap}$	0.25	0.28
$\alpha_{ff,z}$	0.30	0.33

determines the backward component). This can be interpreted as depending in part on the credibility of the central bank, and in part on institutional arrangements regarding wage indexation and other price-setting mechanisms. A higher value of $\alpha_{c,\pi ld}$ close to 1 would suggest that small changes in monetary policy cause large changes in price expectations; a low value would suggest that inertia and backward-looking expectations cause prices to respond with greater delays to changes in monetary policy. The estimated Philips curve for India is backward looking (the backward-looking component in the core inflation is 0.8), suggesting that inflation is highly inertial and that shocks to inflation are persistent. Patra and Kapur (2010) have found similar estimates for the forward- and backward-looking components.[8]

The $\alpha_{c,ygap}$ parameter depends on the extent to which output responds to price changes and, conversely, how much core inflation is influenced by real demand pressures, and is typically between 0.25 and 0.50. This parameter is estimated to be 0.25 for India. This is in line with the literature estimates of 0.20–0.30 (Patra and Kapur 2010). The $\alpha_{c,zgap}$ parameter represents the short-term pass-through of (real) exchange rate movements into prices, and depends on trade openness, price competition, and monetary policy credibility. The exchange rate pass-through coefficient is estimated to be 0.15 in India. This is in line with the findings of Patra and Kapur (2010) and other cross-country findings that estimate exchange rate pass-through to be about 0.16 for countries with low (less than 10 percent) inflation (Choudhuri and Hakura 2001).

Finally, the parameter $\alpha_{c,\pi}$ represents the pass-through coefficient from headline to core inflation; that is, the extent to which price setters keep their prices rising in step with past movements in headline CPI. If $\alpha_{c,\pi}$ is zero, the gap between past headline and core inflation (namely, inflation of food and energy

[8]This is also consistent with the cross-country evidence that finds the coefficient on expected inflation to be below 0.5 (Berg, Karam, and Laxton 2006a).

prices) will have no effect on core inflation. In other words, there will be no second-round effects in the economy. Our estimation of the second-round effect coefficient indicates that if headline inflation exceeds core inflation by 1 percentage point, it will lead to a 0.3 percentage point increase in core inflation in the next quarter. As expected, the pass-through from headline to core inflation is relatively large. This estimate is consistent with our analysis of year-over-year inflation dynamics in India, as discussed in an earlier section. However, some caution is warranted in interpreting a rather large pass-through coefficient. An alternative interpretation of a strong pass-through coefficient estimate may reflect a faster response of food inflation to aggregate demand, because commodity prices, including food items, tend to be more flexible than nonfood prices. Another reason could be that food inflation may also react faster than nonfood inflation when inflation expectations are not firmly anchored.

Estimated Uncovered Interest Parity Equation

$$z_t = \delta_z z_{t+1} + (1-\delta_z)z_{t-1} - (RR_t - RR_t^{RW} - \rho^*)/4 + \varepsilon_t^z$$

The δ_z parameter in the real exchange rate equation determines the relative importance of forward- and backward-looking real exchange rate expectations. If δ is equal to 1, the equation behaves as in the Dornbusch overshooting model; that is, the real exchange rate is a function of the future sum of all real interest rate differentials. The estimated coefficient of 0.5 makes monetary policy potentially a more effective tool, though the incomplete exchange rate pass-through in India somewhat reduces its efficacy (Table 9.5).

Estimated Open-Economy Taylor-Rule Equation

$$RS_t = \gamma_{RSlag} RS_{t-1} + (1-\gamma_{RSlag}) * [RR_t^* + \pi 4_t + \gamma_\pi(\pi 4_{t+4} - \pi_{t+4}^*) + \gamma_{ygap} ygap_t] + \varepsilon_t^{RS}$$

The γ parameters in the monetary policy rule equation depend on the speed and aggressiveness with which the monetary authorities adjust the nominal interest rate, and the relative importance of the inflation target versus the real activity target (Table 9.6). There is a high degree of interest rate smoothing in India

TABLE 9.5

Uncovered Interest Parity Equation

Parameter	Prior Mean	Estimate (Posterior Mean)
δ_z	0.60	0.40

TABLE 9.6

Taylor-Rule Equation

Parameter	Prior Mean	Estimate (Posterior Mean)
γ_{RSlag}	0.80	0.82
γ_π	1.90	1.88
γ_{ygap}	0.60	0.64

(the coefficient is 0.8), which is in line with the estimates of this parameter by Mohanty and Klau (2004) and Anand, Saxegaard, and Peiris (2010). The value of γ_π is 1.9. The estimate of γ_{ygap} is 0.6, suggesting that the RBI puts weight on stabilizing real activity, which is expected, considering that the central bank followed an approach of multiple objectives during most of the analysis period.

Key Results of the Model

Estimated results of the model suggest the following:

- A temporary increase of 100 basis points in the interest rate leads to a peak widening of the output gap by almost 1 percent in about four quarters, slowing in the core CPI inflation by about ¾ of a percentage point, an almost 1 percentage point decline in headline CPI inflation, and a nearly 2 percent peak real appreciation.
- With a 1.5 percentage point jump in food and fuel price inflation, the output gap widens at peak by about 0.5 percentage point, and headline and core inflation rise by about 0.5 percent. The interest rate increases by about 80 basis points, while the exchange rate appreciates by about 2.5 percent. Inflation shocks lead to widening of the output gap, a rise in inflation and the interest rate, and real appreciation. Furthermore, the headline inflation shock passes through to core inflation, which rises by about 0.2 percentage point.

We can use the estimated model to study the behavior of interest rates in India to examine its monetary policy stance since 2000. Figure 9.3 presents actual and model-predicted nominal interest rates. As is evident, since mid-2008 actual interest rates are consistently below those predicted by the model, suggesting that monetary policy shocks have been negative. The gap between the two rates (actual and predicted) was large during 2008–09. The gap again opened in late 2010 and averaged about 100 basis points during 2011–12. This was highlighted by

Figure 9.3. Interest Rates in India: Predicted versus Actual
(Percent)

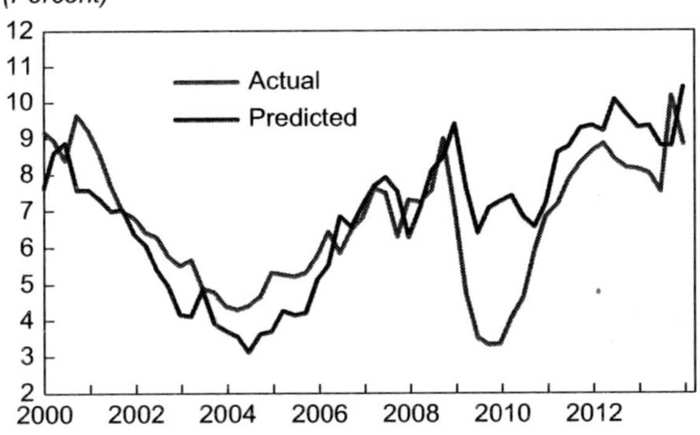

Sources: Anand and Tulin (2014); Haver Analytics; and IMF staff estimates.
Note: Interest rates correspond to three-month Treasury bill yield.

successive IMF India Article IV Staff Reports, which argued for a tighter monetary stance to counter inflation and inflationary pressures (IMF 2011b, 2012, 2013, 2014a, 2014b).

CONCLUSION

India has seen a prolonged period of high inflation, to a large extent driven by persistently high food inflation. This has made the RBI's task more challenging, with many arguing that the central bank has a very limited role in combating food inflation, particularly when growth has slowed considerably and external demand remains subdued. While economists agree that a central bank should look through transitory supply shocks, they also agree that monetary policy should react to second-round effects.

There is growing evidence that second-round effects could be large in emerging market economies for several reasons: the high share of food in households' expenditure, less firmly anchored expectations, and highly persistent supply shocks. India has these characteristics, suggesting that second-round effects are important and play a role in inflation dynamics.

Indeed, recognizing the seminal nature of food inflation and its second-round effects for inflation dynamics in India, the Patel Committee Report (RBI 2014, 20) recommends: "Since food and fuel account for more than 57 percent of the CPI on which the direct influence of monetary policy is limited, the commitment to the nominal anchor would need to be demonstrated by timely monetary policy response to risks from second round effects and inflation expectations in response to shocks to food and fuel."

Our results suggest that monetary policy needs to respond decisively to tackle India's high and persistent inflation. Furthermore, as emphasized in the Patel Committee Report, headline CPI inflation should be the nominal anchor for monetary policy—and because of the persistent and entrenched nature of CPI inflation, it should be the guiding factor for the monetary policy stance.[9] At the current juncture, with food inflation remaining persistently high during 2009–14, monetary policy needs to remain tight to control generalized inflation. This analysis suggests that the RBI may also need to raise rates to tackle inflation durably, particularly if faced with a persistent and sizable supply-side food price shock putting pressure on broad-based inflation. Because inflation is mostly backward looking, monetary policy has to remain tight for a prolonged period. Nevertheless, recent revisions to the RBI's liquidity management framework should improve monetary transmission, thereby requiring lower policy interest rate adjustments to contain inflation and inflationary pressures. Finally, given that India's Phillips curve is relatively flat, progress on structural reforms to raise potential growth is critical to reduce the burden of adjustment on monetary policy.

[9] Says the Patel Committee Report: "The CPI-Combined based headline inflation measure appears to be the most feasible and appropriate measure of inflation—as the closest proxy of a true cost of living index—for the conduct of monetary policy" (RBI 2014, 15).

REFERENCES

Anand, Rahul, and Eswar Prasad. 2010. "Optimal Price Indices for Targeting Inflation under Incomplete Markets." IMF Working Paper 10/200, International Monetary Fund, Washington.

Anand, Rahul, Magnus Saxegaard, and Shanaka J. Peiris. 2010. "An Estimated Model with Macrofinancial Linkages for India." IMF Working Paper 10/21, International Monetary Fund, Washington.

Anand, Rahul, and Volodymyr Tulin. 2014. "Disentangling India's Investment Slowdown." IMF Working Paper 14/47, International Monetary Fund, Washington.

Berg, Andrew, Philippe D. Karam, and Douglas Laxton. 2006a. "A Practical Model-Based Approach to Monetary Policy Analysis, Overview." IMF Working Paper 6/80, International Monetary Fund, Washington.

———. 2006b. "Practical Model-Based Monetary Policy Analysis: A How-To Guide." IMF Working Paper 6/81, International Monetary Fund, Washington.

Calvo, Guillermo A. 1983. "Staggered Prices in a Utility-Maximizing Framework." *Journal of Monetary Economics* 12 (3): 383–98.

Catão, Luis, and Roberto Chang. 2010. "World Food Prices and Monetary Policy." IMF Working Paper 10/161, International Monetary Fund, Washington.

Cecchetti, Stephen C., and Richhild Moessner. 2008. "Commodity Prices and Inflation Dynamics." *BIS Quarterly Review* (December).

Choudhuri, Ehsan, and Dalia Hakura. 2001. "Exchange Rate Pass-Through to Domestic Prices: Does the Inflationary Environment Matter?" IMF Working Paper 01/194, International Monetary Fund, Washington.

Clark, Todd E. 2001. "Comparing Measures of Core Inflation." *Federal Reserve Bank of Kansas City Economic Review* 86 (2): 5–31.

International Monetary Fund (IMF). 2011a. "Slowing Growth, Rising Risks." Chapter 3 of *World Economic Outlook*. Washington, September.

———. 2011b. "India: 2010 Article IV Consultation—Staff Report." IMF Country Report 11/50, Washington.

———. 2012. "India: 2012 Article IV Consultation—Staff Report." IMF Country Report 12/96, Washington.

———. 2013. "India: 2013 Article IV Consultation—Staff Report." IMF Country Report 13/37, Washington.

———. 2014a. "India: 2014 Article IV Consultation—Staff Report." IMF Country Report 14/57, Washington.

———. 2014b. "India: Article IV Consultation—Selected Issues." IMF Country Report 14/58, Washington.

Mohanty, Deepak. 2012. "Price Stability and Financial Stability: An Emerging Market Perspective." Address at the Central Bank of Nigeria Board, Cape Town, June 27.

———. 2014. "Why Is Recent Food Inflation in India So Persistent?" Annual Lalit Doshi Memorial Lecture at St. Xavier's College, Mumbai, January 13.

Mohanty, Madhusudan, and Marc Klau. 2004. "Monetary Policy Rules in Emerging Market Economies: Issues and Evidence." BIS Working Papers 149, Bank for International Settlements, Basel.

Patra, Michael, and Muneesh Kapur. 2010. "A Monetary Policy Model without Money for India." IMF Working Paper 10/183, International Monetary Fund, Washington.

Reserve Bank of India (RBI). 2014. *Report of the Expert Committee to Revise and Strengthen the Monetary Policy Framework*. Mumbai.

Walsh, James P. 2011. "Reconsidering the Role of Food Prices in Inflation." IMF Working Paper 11/71, International Monetary Fund, Washington.

CHAPTER 10

Inflation and Monetary Policy in Small Open Economies

PAUL CASHIN AND AGUSTÍN ROITMAN

Large fluctuations in commodity prices in recent years have renewed interest in optimal monetary policy to contain large and unexpected swings in domestic inflation. Figure 10.1 shows the evolution of world food and fuel price inflation rates, by decade, during the past 50 years. Policymakers and academics are now debating the advantages and disadvantages of alternative monetary policy responses in dealing with commodity price shocks. Unfortunately, neither the academic literature nor practitioners have reached a consensus.

On the one hand, the Federal Reserve—which is not an explicit inflation targeter and declares a dual mandate to stabilize both prices and output fluctuations—and explicit inflation targeters such as the Reserve Bank of Australia, the Czech National Bank, the Reserve Bank of New Zealand, and the Bank of Thailand focus heavily on core inflation when implementing monetary policy actions and deciding whether to modify policy interest rates. On the other hand, some analysts and policymakers (even within the Federal Reserve) suggest paying more attention to overall inflation and not just to a particular subset of prices (see Bullard 2011 for details). Arguments exist to support both views, but it is important to acknowledge that different countries have particular idiosyncratic elements that affect monetary policy and its transmission channels in very different ways. Obviously, the exchange rate regime is a key element affecting not only the available monetary instruments, but also how, and how strongly, central banks should react to inflation shocks.

Often, countries with large shares of food and fuel in their consumption baskets have relatively weak transmission mechanisms; therefore monetary policy is less effective in influencing aggregate demand. Moreover, if exchange rate regimes (that is, currency boards, predetermined exchange rate regimes, and crawling pegs) are relatively rigid, the set of tools available for monetary policy is limited. This chapter seeks to understand whether central banks operating under such regimes should react to exogenous inflation shocks and, if so, how strong that response should be.

The literature on optimal monetary policy and oil price shocks is vast (Bodenstein, Erceg, and Guerrieri 2008; Kilian 2009; Blanchard and Galí 2007),

We thank Elva Bova, Mario Catalan, Pablo Lopez-Murphy, Nicolas Magud, and Carlos Vegh for useful comments and suggestions.

Figure 10.1. World Commodity Prices Inflation, 1960–2011
(Percent, monthly year-over-year average by decade)

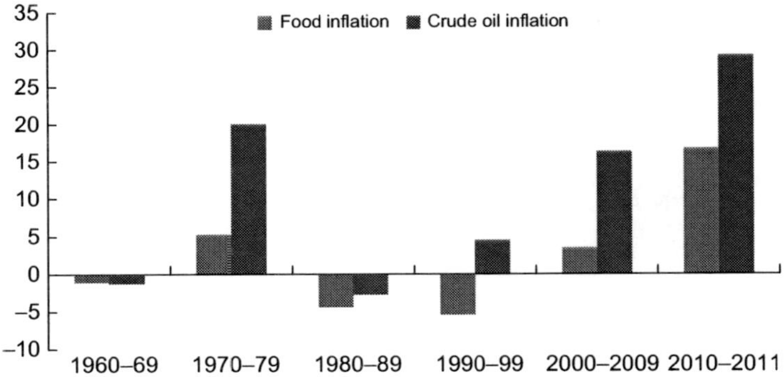

Source: IMF (2011).

Figure 10.2. Volatility in World Commodity Price Inflation, 1960–2011
(Percent, monthly year-over-year, standard deviation by decade)

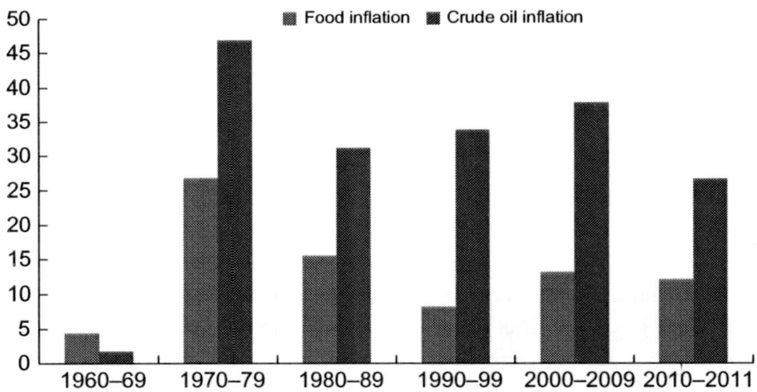

Source: IMF (2011).

but there are not many studies about optimal monetary policy and food price shocks. To the extent that commodity prices tend to comove over time, one could think that food shocks are not substantially different from oil shocks. But it turns out that they are not all the same. It is evident that oil prices can affect many sectors in the economy (and probably more sectors than food prices). Yet, in many countries, food shares in consumption baskets are substantially larger than oil shares, particularly in emerging market and developing economies (IMF 2011).

Interestingly, as Figures 10.2 and 10.3 show, crude-oil inflation is more volatile but less persistent than food inflation. This suggests that the nature and transmission mechanism of oil and food shocks to domestic inflation is not necessarily the same.

Figure 10.3. Persistence in World Commodity Price Inflation, 1960–2011

(Percent, monthly year-over-year, persistence by decade)

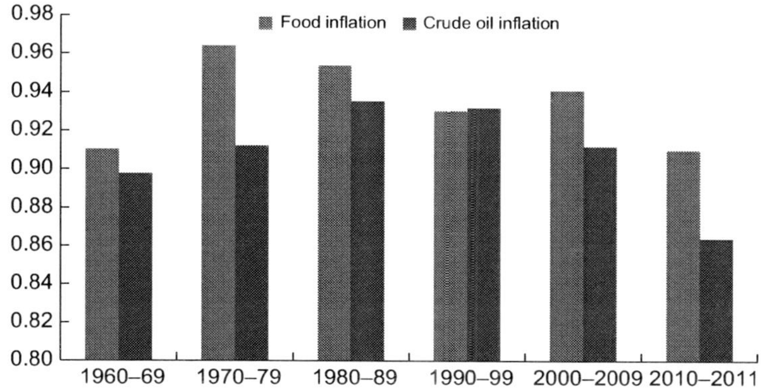

Source: IMF (2011).
Note: Persistence is computed as the first-order autoregressive coefficient.

In this context, Catao and Chang (2011) develop a dynamic stochastic general equilibrium model to study the effects of food shocks in a small open economy. They show that consumer price index targeting (as opposed to producer price index targeting) can be an appropriate monetary regime for food-importing countries facing large exogenous fluctuations in food prices. They consider temporary shocks to food prices, with given and fixed persistence and volatility over time, and they focus their analysis on optimal monetary policy responses to temporary relative price changes (as opposed to inflation shocks). Anand, Prasad, and Zhang (2015) highlight the importance of incomplete markets at the time of choosing different measures of inflation as inflation targets. Using a closed economy model, they show that in the presence of financial frictions and large shares of food in consumption baskets, welfare-maximizing central banks should target a broad measure of inflation with some weight on the output gap.

On the empirical side, Walsh (2011) presents evidence on food and nonfood inflation developments for emerging market and developing economies. He shows that excluding some prices from the overall consumer price index, focusing only on a subset of prices (core inflation, usually excluding food and fuel and other volatile items) can distort the picture of the actual level of inflation. His main focus is on food and nonfood measures of inflation, and he shows that second-round effects from food to nonfood can be important, and should be taken into account for a good understanding of underlying inflation trends and dynamics. The IMF's October 2011 *World Economic Outlook* also presents stylized facts suggesting that food and fuel prices affect emerging market and developing economies more than advanced economies, and one of the reasons explaining those facts could be the larger shares of food and fuel in domestic consumption baskets.

With price stability being the main (and sometimes the only) objective of almost all central banks, it is necessary to understand the behavior and main drivers of headline inflation to implement appropriate monetary policies to achieve that goal. This chapter uses a standard small open economy model to assess whether it is better to conduct monetary policy focusing on core or headline inflation.

In the chapter's first section, we use a simple small open economy model to illustrate the macroeconomic effects and the differences of two alternative monetary policy reactions, and how the economy reacts to a commodity inflation shock under a predetermined exchange rate regime. Focusing on core inflation, the monetary authority reacts only to core inflation shocks; whereas in focusing on headline inflation, it reacts not only to core inflation, but also to foreign (that is, commodities) inflation shocks. We show that responding to headline inflation is welfare superior to responding to core inflation, and is the better response for containing overall inflation and for mitigating consumption and output fluctuations.

The next section presents a small open economy model to illustrate how a commodity price shock will affect the dynamics of key macroeconomic variables in the domestic economy, and studies alternative monetary policy responses to that shock. We then conduct a sensitivity analysis, and discuss some policy implications.

MACROECONOMIC EFFECTS OF ALTERNATIVE MONETARY POLICY RESPONSES TO INFLATION SHOCKS

We use a standard small open economy model with tradable and nontradable goods, and sticky prices, to illustrate the macroeconomic effects and differences of alternative monetary policy responses to inflation shocks. Having a framework with both tradable and nontradable goods is useful in thinking about nontradable goods inflation as core inflation, and foreign inflation as commodity (food or fuel) inflation coming from the rest of the world.

Consumer's Problem

Consumer's lifetime utility is given by:

$$\sum_{0}^{\infty}\beta^{t}\left[\frac{c_{t}^{1-\frac{1}{\sigma}}-1}{1-\frac{1}{\sigma}}\right], \tag{10.1}$$

in which

$$c_{t}=z_{t}^{\frac{\rho}{\rho-1}},$$

and

$$z_t = \gamma (c_t^T)^{\frac{\rho-1}{\rho}} + (1-\gamma)(c_t^N)^{\frac{\rho-1}{\rho}},$$

in which β is the subjective discount factor, and c_t^T and c_t^N denote consumption of tradables and nontradable goods, respectively.

The flow constraint is given by:

$$b_t + \frac{M_t}{P_t^T} = (1+r)b_{t-1} + \frac{M_{t-1}}{P_t^T} + y_t^T + \frac{y_t^N}{e_t} + \tau_t - c_t^T - \frac{c_t^N}{e_t}, \tag{10.2}$$

in which b denotes the stock of net foreign assets held by the private sector, y^T and y^N are the endowments of tradable and nontradable goods, M_t are nominal money balances, τ_t are transfers from the government, e_t is the real exchange rate defined as P_t^T/P_t^N, and r is the real interest rate.

We assume that there is a cash-in-advance constraint, which requires nominal money balances to be acquired one period before consuming, and is given by:

$$M_{t-1} = P_t^T\left(c_t^T + \frac{c_t^N}{e_t}\right) \tag{10.3}$$

Given that the relevant real money balances for period t are acquired one period in advance we define:

$$m_t \equiv \frac{M_{t-1}}{P_t^T} \tag{10.4}$$

And we can rewrite the cash-in-advance constraint as:

$$m_t = c_t^T + \frac{c_t^N}{e_t} \tag{10.5}$$

Using this definition of real money balances we can also rewrite the flow constraint as:

$$b_t + m_{t+1}(1+\pi_t^T) = (1+r)b_{t-1} + m_t + y_t^T + \frac{y_t^N}{e_t} + \tau_t - c_t^T - \frac{c_t^N}{e_t}, \tag{10.6}$$

in which

$$\pi_t^T \equiv \frac{P_{t+1}^T}{P_t^T} - 1$$

is the inflation rate between periods t and $t + 1$.

The maximization problem for this economy consists in choosing $\{c_t^T, c_t^N, m_{t+1}, b_t\}_{t=0}^{\infty}$ to maximize lifetime utility, given by equation 10.1, subject to the sequence of flow constraints in equation 10.6 and the cash-in-advance constraint in equation 10.5.

The first-order conditions are given by:

$$c_t^{-\frac{1}{\sigma}} z_t^{\frac{1}{\rho-1}} \gamma (c_t^T)^{-\frac{1}{\rho}} = \lambda_t + \psi_t, \tag{10.7}$$

$$c_t^{-\frac{1}{\sigma}} z_t^{\frac{1}{\rho-1}} (1-\gamma)(c_t^T)^{-\frac{1}{\rho}} = \frac{\lambda_t + \psi_t}{e_t}, \tag{10.8}$$

$$\beta(\lambda_{t+1} + \psi_{t+1}) = \lambda_t (1 + \pi_t^T), \tag{10.9}$$

$$\beta \lambda_{t+1} (1 + r_t) = \lambda_t, \tag{10.10}$$

in which λ_t is the Lagrange multiplier associated to the flow constraint and ψ_t corresponds to the cash-in-advance constraint.

Since we assume perfect capital mobility, interest parity holds:

$$(1 + i_t) = (1 + r_t)(1 + \pi_t^T), \tag{10.11}$$

in which i_t is the nominal interest rate.

Lagging equation 10.9, substituting it into equation 10.7, and using equation 10.11, we can rewrite equation 10.7:

$$c_t^{-\frac{1}{\sigma}} z_t^{\frac{1}{\rho-1}} \gamma (c_t^T)^{-\frac{1}{\rho}} = \lambda_t (1 + i_{t-1}). \tag{10.12}$$

This equation highlights the relationship between consumption and its effective price $(1 + i_{t-1})$, and will be useful for understanding the main results and transmission channels in this model economy.

Combining equations 10.7 and 10.8 we obtain a standard intratemporal condition between tradables and nontradables:

$$\frac{c_t^T}{c_t^N} = \left[\frac{1}{e_t} \frac{\gamma}{(1-\gamma)} \right]^{\rho}, \tag{10.13}$$

Using this last equation in the cash-in-advance constraint 10.5, we obtain the following expression for money demand:

$$m_t = \left\{ 1 + e_t^{\rho-1} \left[\frac{\gamma}{(1-\gamma)} \right]^{\rho} \right\} c_t^T. \tag{10.14}$$

Supply Side

We assume that the supply of the tradable goods is constant over time and equal to y^T. The nontradable sector is characterized by sticky prices, following Calvo (1983), where there is a staggered price setting and output is demand determined:

$$\pi_{t+1}^N - \pi_t^N = \theta(\overline{y^N} - c_t^N), \tag{10.15}$$

in which π_t^N denotes the inflation rate of nontradable goods, θ is a positive parameter, and $\overline{y^N}$ is the "full employment" level of nontradables output. Equation 10.14 captures the basic dynamics involved in an environment in which firms set prices in an asynchronous manner, taking into account the expected future path of the average price of nontradable goods and the path of excess demand in that market (see Vegh 2013 for details).

Government

The government's flow constraint is given by:

$$h_t = (1+r)h_{t-1} + \frac{M_t - M_{t-1}}{P_t^T} - \tau_t, \tag{10.16}$$

$$h_t = (1+r)h_{t-1} + m_{t+1}(1+\pi_t^T) - m_t - \tau_t, \tag{10.17}$$

in which h_t are government's net foreign assets, m_t are real money balances, and τ_t are transfers.

Equilibrium Conditions

The real exchange rate definition: $e_t = P_t^T / P_t^N$. implies:

$$\frac{e_{t+1}}{e_t} = \frac{(1+\varepsilon_t)(1+\pi^*)}{(1+\pi_t^N)}, \tag{10.18}$$

in which π^* is the foreign inflation rate and ε_t is the devaluation rate.

The output level of nontradable goods is demand determined, hence:

$$y_t^N = c_t^N. \tag{10.19}$$

Combining equations 10.16, 10.6, 10.11, and 10.12, the economy's flow constraint is:

$$k_t = (1+r)k_{t-1} + y_t^T - c_t^T, \tag{10.20}$$

in which $k_t = b_t + h_t$ is the economy's total stock of net foreign assets.

Monetary Policy Rule

Given that this economy operates under a predetermined exchange rate regime, the nominal anchor is the nominal exchange rate, which obviously implies that the monetary policy instrument for the central bank to affect aggregate demand is the devaluation rate.

Let's assume that the central bank chooses the devaluation rate using the following rule:

$$\varepsilon_t = \xi \bar{\varepsilon} + (1-\xi)\left[\eta\left(\pi_t^N - \overline{\pi_{ss}^N}\right) - (1-\eta)\left(\pi_t^* - \widetilde{\pi^*}\right)\right], \tag{10.21}$$

where $\bar{\varepsilon}$ is a "long term" or "structural" devaluation rate chosen by the monetary authority.

Notice that if $\xi = 1$, the model is a completely standard small open economy model under a predetermined exchange rate regime. For any $\xi \in [0,1]$ the devaluation rate becomes an endogenous variable. Now the central bank chooses the devaluation rate as a function of both foreign and nontradable goods inflation rates. Therefore, if $\eta = 1$, the central bank will only react to core inflation, and if $\eta \in [0,1]$, it will respond to headline inflation (core plus foreign).

The intuition for this rule is that the central bank's objective is to stabilize real exchange rate fluctuations. Increases in π_t^* put upward pressure on the real exchange rate (real depreciation), whereas increases in π_t^N exerted downward pressure (real appreciation). Hence, increases in foreign inflation would be offset by reducing the devaluation rate, whereas increases in nontradables inflation would be offset by increasing the devaluation rate.

Solution Method and Parameterization

We employ the numerical linearization methods of King, Plosser, and Rebelo (1988) to solve our model and study dynamic responses of macroeconomic variables to exogenous shocks.[1]

Our baseline parameterization is described in Table 10.1, and each period represents a quarter.

We employ standard values in the literature for key parameters.[2] Sensitivity analysis shows that qualitative results of the model are robust to different parameterizations.

---

[1] This method involves linearizing the model around a nonstochastic steady state. Given that this model has a unit root (because it is possible to borrow and lend at a fixed exogenous interest rate), the accuracy of the numerical approximations might be affected because the linearization is around a steady state to which the economy might never return.

[2] Notice that the intertemporal elasticity of substitution is smaller than the elasticity of substitution between tradables and nontradables, which is the empirically relevant case; see Reinhart and Ostry (1992) and Reinhart and Végh (1995).

TABLE 10.1

Parameter Values for Standard Model

Parameters	Baseline Values
International real interest rate (r)	0.015
Discount factor (β)	0.99
"Long-term" rate of devaluation (ε)	0.001
Elasticity of intertemporal substitution (σ)	0.5
Elasticity parameter, momentary utility (ρ)	0.8
Share of tradables in consumption (γ)	0.5
Share of nontradables in consumption ($1 - \gamma$)	0.5
Level of net foreign assets (k)	−0.6
Sticky prices parameter (θ)	0.1
Full employment level of nontradables	1.0
Endowment of tradables	1.0
Foreign inflation	0.08
Rule/no rule, exchange rate rule parameter (ξ)	**1.0**
Core/headline, exchange rate rule parameter (η)	1.0 (for core only) 0.5 (for headline)

Source: Authors' calculations.

Unanticipated and Temporary Increase in Foreign Inflation under Predetermined Exchange Rates

Suppose that before time $t = 0$, the economy is in a stationary equilibrium where the foreign inflation rate is at its "equilibrium/long term" level. At time $t = 0$, there is an unanticipated and temporary increase in the rate of foreign inflation (Figure 10.4, panel 1). By interest parity, the nominal interest rate also increases at time $t = 0$ and returns to its original level at time $t = T$ (Figure 10.4, panel 2). The effective price of consumption, $(1+i_{t-1})$, is thus high between time $t = 0$ and time $t = T$ and low afterward. As equation 10.12 indicates, this implies that consumption of tradable goods (c_t^T) will be low between time $t = 0$ and time $t = T$ and high afterward. For this time profile to be consistent with the economy's resource constraint, consumption of tradables must jump down at time $t = 0$ and then increase at time $t = T$ above its original level (Figure 10.4, panel 4). The initial reduction in c_t^T leads to an improvement in the trade balance (panel 6) and net foreign assets (panel 12).

Nontradables inflation might go up or down, on impact, depending on the persistence of the shock, and its effect on the nominal interest rate and consumption. Intuitively, two forces determine the impact effect on nontradables inflation. The first, which tends to increase inflation, is the direct effect of the increase in foreign inflation. All else being equal, an increase in foreign inflation will lead to an increase in nontradables inflation. For a given increase in foreign inflation, the increase in nontradables inflation will be larger the more persistent the shock is (the larger is T). Conversely, for very temporary shocks (small T), this effect is very small. The second force, which tends to decrease nontradables inflation, is the consumption bust in nontradables. Other things being equal, a fall in c^N will tend to reduce nontradables inflation. To see this, notice from equation 10.15

Figure 10.4. Standard Model

(Percentage point deviations from steady state, vertical axes; Time period, horizontal axes)

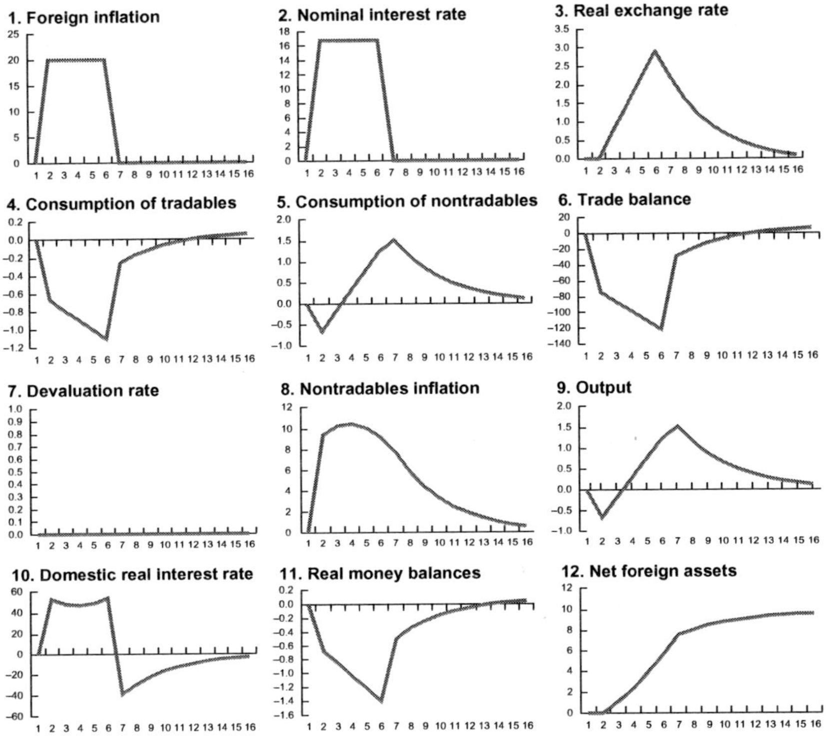

Source: Authors' calculations.

that a fall in c^N will lead to a positive change in nontradables inflation. For this to happen, nontradables inflation must fall so as to increase over time to its steady state.

For the parameterization shown in Table 10.1, given that the shock is relatively persistent, inflation rises on impact because the nominal interest rate effect is stronger than the nontradables consumption effect (Figure 10.4, panel 8).

The path of nontradables consumption (c_t^N) follows from equation 10.13. Consumption of nontradables will rise during the transition, because the real exchange rate rises (depreciates). Furthermore, given that consumption of tradables falls on impact, but the real exchange rate does not change, consumption of nontradables must also fall on impact (Figure 10.4, panel 5).

The domestic real interest rate path follows from the definition $r_t^d = i - \pi_t^N$. On impact, r_t^d increases because inflation of nontradable goods goes up by less (if at all) than the nominal interest rate. Since between time 0 and time T, the nominal interest rate is unchanged, the behavior of r_t^d follows from that of nontradables inflation (π_t^N): the real interest rate increases at $t = 0$, remains high, behaving as a mirror image of nontradables inflation, and jumps down at time T, reflecting the decrease in the nominal interest rate. It then monotonically increases over time, toward its steady state (Figure 10.4, panel 10).

Nontradables output is demand determined; thus its path follows from the behavior of nontradables consumption. Output declines on impact, rises until time T, and starts declining, after foreign inflation is back to its steady-state level, mimicking the path of nontradables consumption (Figure 10.4, panel 9).

As equation 10.14 indicates, real money demand is affected by the real exchange rate and consumption of tradables. All else equal, and given that $\rho < 1$, an increase in the real exchange rate (a depreciation) reduces real money demand. Furthermore, equation 10.14 also shows that real money balances are directly related to consumption of tradable goods. As a result, the path of real money balances reflects the behavior of tradables consumption (Figure 10.4, panel 11).

A Devaluation Rule

We now examine how this economy "absorbs" an unanticipated and temporary increase in foreign inflation under the devaluation rule in equation 10.21. By following this rule, the monetary authority will seek to stabilize any deviations from the equilibrium (that is, steady-state) real exchange rate. Because the external shock introduces an intertemporal distortion, affecting the nominal interest rate and therefore causing consumption of both goods to fall, we are interested in assessing whether the reaction of the central bank would dampen or amplify the intertemporal distortion caused by the shock.

Following the devaluation rule, the central bank has three options. The first is to behave as if it had no devaluation rule and to choose the devaluation rate exogenously. The second is to use the devaluation rate rule with positive weights on both nontradables (core) and foreign inflation (commodities). The third option is to use the devaluation rate rule putting zero weight on foreign inflation and focus only on nontradables inflation.[3] Given that the devaluation rate is the policy instrument, the central bank can choose any combination of weights for core and foreign inflation. This rule is useful to illustrate the differences between reacting only to core inflation and reacting to headline inflation.[4] Our objective is to assess whether focusing only on core inflation is a more appropriate policy response than focusing on headline (core plus foreign) inflation.

[3]The parameterization corresponding to Figure 10.5 is presented in Table 10.2.

[4]Introducing a devaluation rule in an otherwise standard model, making the devaluation rate endogenous, is just for convenience and simplicity. But given that under predetermined exchange rates the devaluation rate is the monetary policy instrument, one could also think about the central bank changing the devaluation rate in a discretionary fashion in response to a particular shock.

Figure 10.5. Models with and without Devaluation Rules
(Percentage point deviations from steady state, vertical axes; Time period, horizontal axes)

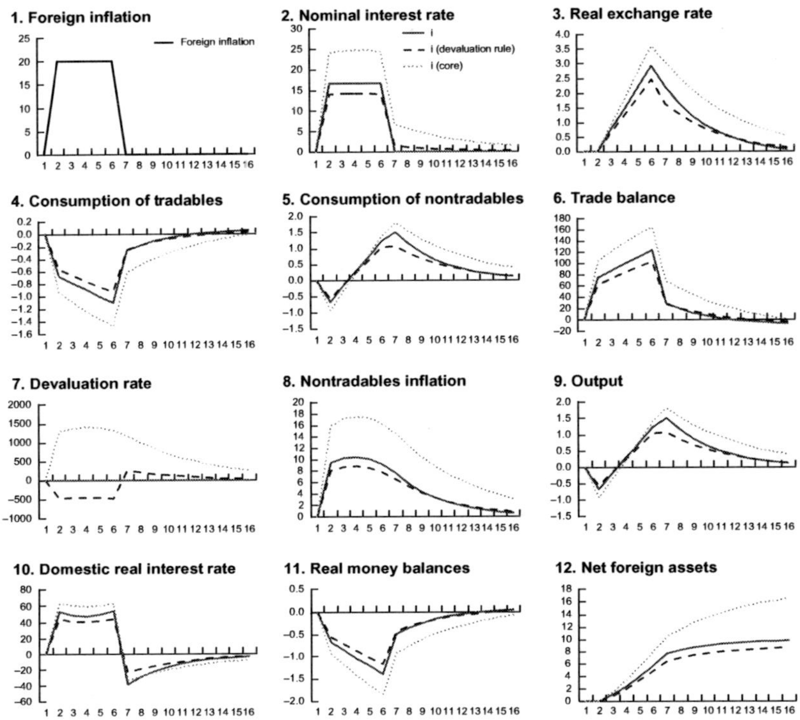

Source: Authors' calculations.
Note: i = standard predetermined exchange rate regime. i (devaluation rule) places half the weight on core inflation; i (core) focuses on core inflation only.

Given that consumers are risk averse, they like to have a smooth consumption path, and any deviations from that flat (optimal) path is welfare reducing. So, analyzing which policy option is more successful in dampening the intertemporal distortion and therefore mitigating consumption fluctuations can give us a good indication about which policy reaction is better in terms of welfare. We also assess which of these policy options is more successful in keeping inflation down and at what cost in terms of output.

Figure 10.5 shows impulse responses to an unanticipated and temporary shock to foreign inflation under three alternative policy responses from the monetary authority. The solid lines show how the economy reacts under a standard predetermined exchange rate regime where the central bank chooses the devaluation rate exogenously. The dashed line shows the response of the economy operating under a devaluation rule that puts half of the weight in core inflation and half in foreign inflation; thus, the devaluation rate is endogenously determined in response to headline (core plus foreign) inflation. The dotted line

TABLE 10.2

Parameter Values for Model with Devaluation Rule

Parameters	Baseline Values
Rule/no rule, exchange rate rule parameter (ξ)	**0.5**
Core/headline, exchange rate rule parameter (η)	1.0 (for core only) 0.5 (for headline)

Source: Authors' calculations.

represents the reaction of the economy under a devaluation rate rule focusing on core inflation only.

As follows from the devaluation rate rule, the central bank would offset depreciation pressures (coming from foreign inflation) by reducing the devaluation rate, and offset appreciation pressures (coming from nontradables inflation) by increasing the devaluation rate. The direction and strength of the central bank policy response, and thus the direction of the change in the devaluation rate, will be determined by the relative weights assigned to both nontradables and foreign inflation.

Table 10.1 presents the parameterization used in the all the experiments, changing relevant parameters depending on the particular issue under study. Table 10.2 shows the key parameters corresponding to Figure 10.5. The devaluation rate reacts in different directions, depending on whether the central bank focuses on headline or core inflation (Figure 10.5, panel 7). In turn, this determines whether the initial impact on the nominal interest rate is dampened or amplified (panel 2).

Consumption falls under the three alternative policy responses, but it falls more under the core-only rule than under the headline rule (Figure 10.5, panels 4 and 5), and the same pattern is observed for output (panel 9) and real money balances (panel 11). Both the trade balance (panel 6) and inflation (panel 8) rise more under the core-only rule than under the headline rule. And a similar behavior is shown for net foreign assets (panel 12) and the domestic real interest rate (panel 10).

The key difference between reacting to core and reacting to headline, under a predetermined exchange rate regime, is whether the initial shock is dampened or amplified. Interestingly, and contrary to what many studies suggest for advanced economies (often operating under inflation targeting), a monetary policy response focused on headline inflation is more appropriate to contain exogenous fluctuations and prevent their being transmitted to domestic fluctuations, rather than a policy response focused on core inflation only (see Tables 10.3 and 10.4).

Core or Headline?

To assess whether a focus on core inflation is better than a focus on headline inflation, it is necessary to understand, first, what is the key transmission channel

TABLE 10.3

Parameter Values for Model with Devaluation Rule and Different Weights

Parameters	Baseline Values
Share of tradables in consumption (γ)	0.9
Share of nontradables in consumption (1 – γ)	0.1
Rule/no rule, exchange rate rule parameter (ξ)	**0.5**
Core/headline, exchange rate rule parameter (η)	1.0 (for core only) 0.1 (for headline)

Source: Authors' calculations.

TABLE 10.4

Parameter Values for Model with Devaluation Rule and Different Weights

Parameters	Baseline Values
Share of tradables in consumption (γ)	0.1
Share of nontradables in consumption (1 – γ)	0.9
Rule/no rule, exchange rate rule parameter (ξ)	**0.5**
Core/headline, exchange rate rule parameter (η)	1.0 (for core only) 0.9 (for headline)

Source: Authors' calculations.

of the shock, and, second, what is the criterion for choosing which policy response is better.

The key transmission channel of a foreign inflation shock in this model is the intertemporal distortion generated by the change in the nominal interest rate affecting the effective price of consumption.

Policy reactions should be ranked according to their ability to dampen intertemporal distortions and therefore smooth consumption intertemporal paths. Policies capable of mitigating intertemporal distortions are welfare superior to others, and, obviously, superior to those that amplify those distortions. In this model, the optimality (dampening/amplification) of the policy reaction depends on the relative weights that the central bank assigns to preventing real exchange rate appreciation (due to domestic inflation pressures) versus preventing real exchange rate depreciation (due to foreign inflation pressures).

Regardless of the relative weights for core and foreign inflation in the devaluation rule of the central bank, the model indicates that reacting to headline (core plus foreign) inflation is always better than reacting only to core (Figures 10.6 and 10.7).[5] Intuitively, reacting to core only implies an overreaction to a foreign inflation shock, simply because the central bank is not taking into account the explicit and direct effect of the exogenous shock on the real exchange rate. It is as if the monetary authority were only concerned with preventing real appreciation without considering depreciation pressures arising from exogenous commodity price shocks.

[5] Figures 10.6 and 10.7 correspond to the parameterizations of Tables 10.3 and 10.4.

Figure 10.6. Devaluation Rule with Large Weight on Foreign Inflation

(Percentage point deviations from steady state, vertical axes; Time period, horizontal axes)

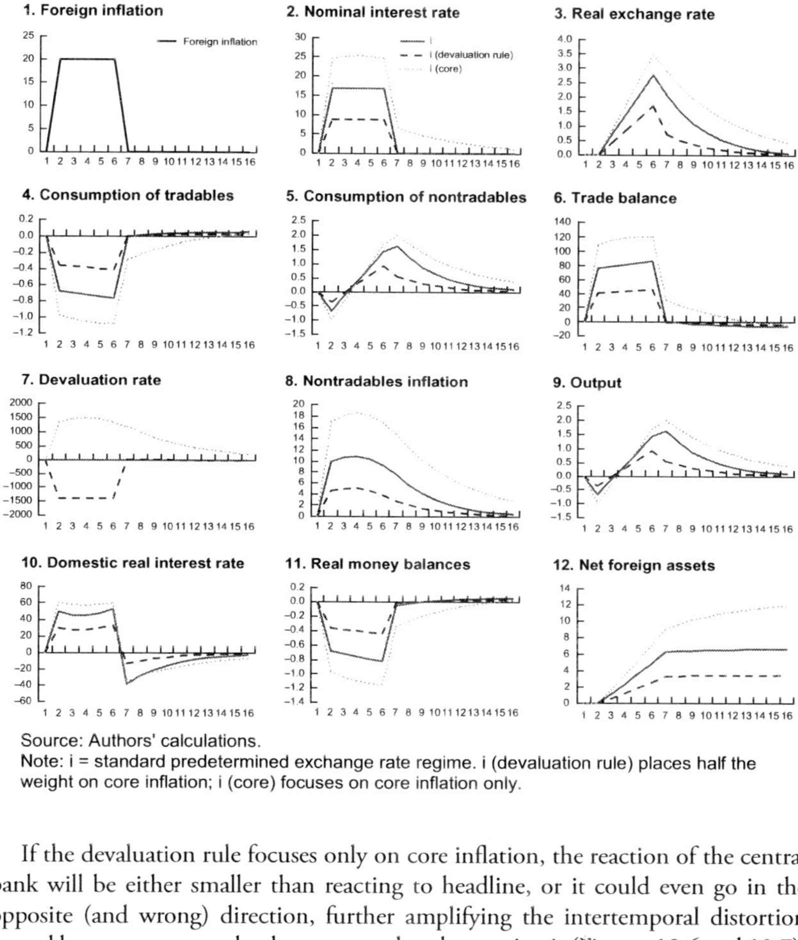

Source: Authors' calculations.
Note: i = standard predetermined exchange rate regime. i (devaluation rule) places half the weight on core inflation; i (core) focuses on core inflation only.

If the devaluation rule focuses only on core inflation, the reaction of the central bank will be either smaller than reacting to headline, or it could even go in the opposite (and wrong) direction, further amplifying the intertemporal distortion caused by an exogenous shock, as opposed to dampening it (Figures 10.6 and 10.7).

Reacting to headline inflation will not only imply a stronger reaction when the shock hits, but also an appropriate reaction, in the sense that monetary policy would be reacting to both appreciation and depreciation pressures on the real exchange rate. As a result, the change in the devaluation rate will offset the intertemporal distortion, thus dampening fluctuations in all variables in the model.

In terms of inflation, the bigger the weight on foreign inflation, the larger the decline in the devaluation rate, and, therefore, the smaller the intertemporal distortion (Figure 10.6). Consequently, the smaller the initial fall in consumption (both tradables and nontradables), the smaller the initial increase in inflation, and, obviously, the smaller the initial decline in output (Figures 10.6 and 10.7).

Figure 10.7. Devaluation Rule with Large Weight on Core Inflation
(Percentage point deviations from steady state, vertical axes; Time period, horizontal axes)

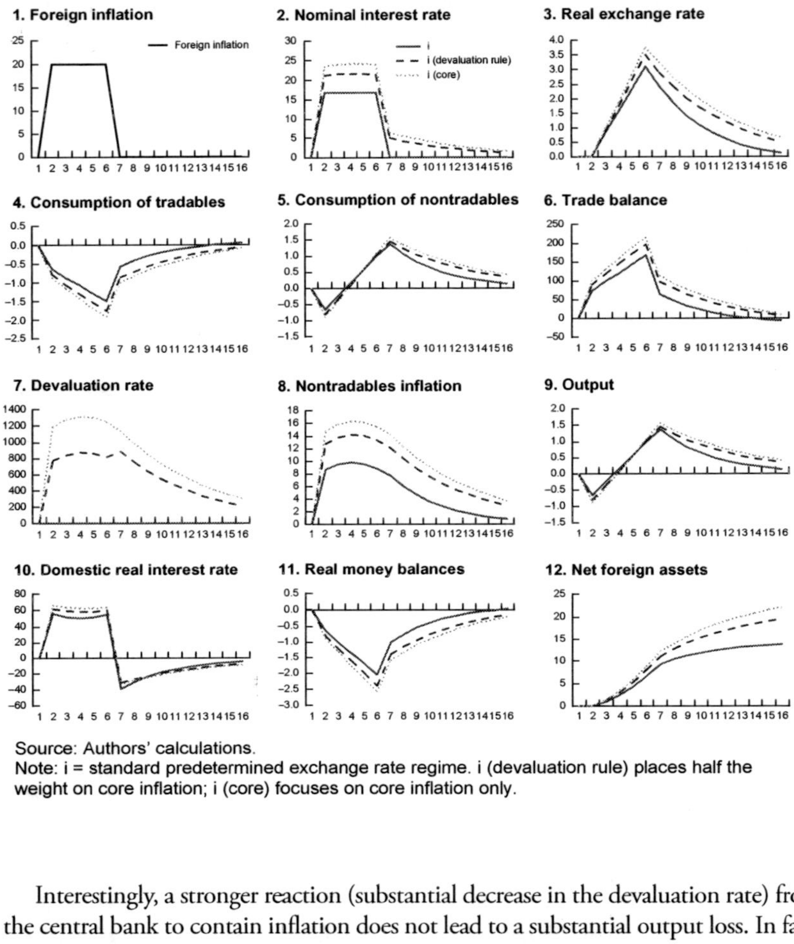

Source: Authors' calculations.
Note: i = standard predetermined exchange rate regime. i (devaluation rule) places half the weight on core inflation; i (core) focuses on core inflation only.

Interestingly, a stronger reaction (substantial decrease in the devaluation rate) from the central bank to contain inflation does not lead to a substantial output loss. In fact, the output loss, on impact, is smaller under the devaluation rule (provided the weight on foreign inflation is sufficiently large) than under no rule (Figure 10.6). Naturally, the higher the weight on core inflation in the devaluation rule, the less the central bank would tend to react, or even react in the wrong direction, amplifying rather than mitigating the initial output loss (Figure 10.7).

SENSITIVITY ANALYSIS

This section analyzes how this economy reacts when hit by the same, but less persistent, foreign inflation shock (this shock lasts only for one quarter). We analyze the same cases studied in the previous section (see Figures 10.5, 10.6, and 10.7). Specifically, we analyze a case in which the devaluation rule assigns

Figure 10.8. Models with and without Devaluation Rules (one period shock)

(Percentage point deviations from steady state, vertical axes; Time period, horizontal axes)

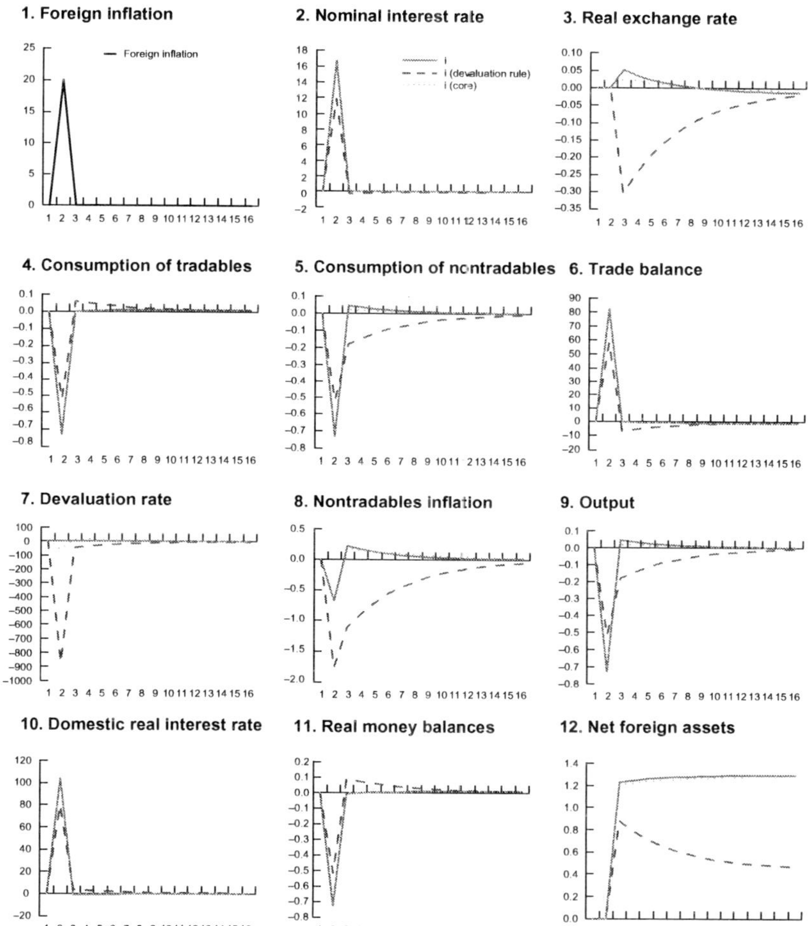

Source: Authors' calculations.
Note: i = standard predetermined exchange rate regime. i (devaluation rule) places half the weight on core inflation; i (core) focuses on core inflation only.

equal weights to core and foreign inflation, a case in which headline receives a large weight, and a case in which core receives a large weight.

Figures 10.8, 10.9, and 10.10 reproduce Figures 10.5, 10.6, and 10.7 for the case of a one-time shock. In it, the transmission channel remains exactly the same. The foreign inflation shock introduces an intertemporal distortion that affects the intertemporal path of the nominal interest rate, and this affects both the tradable and nontradable consumption profile.

Figure 10.9. Devaluation Rule with Large Weight on Foreign Inflation (one period shock)

(Percentage point deviations from steady state, vertical axes; Time period, horizontal axes)

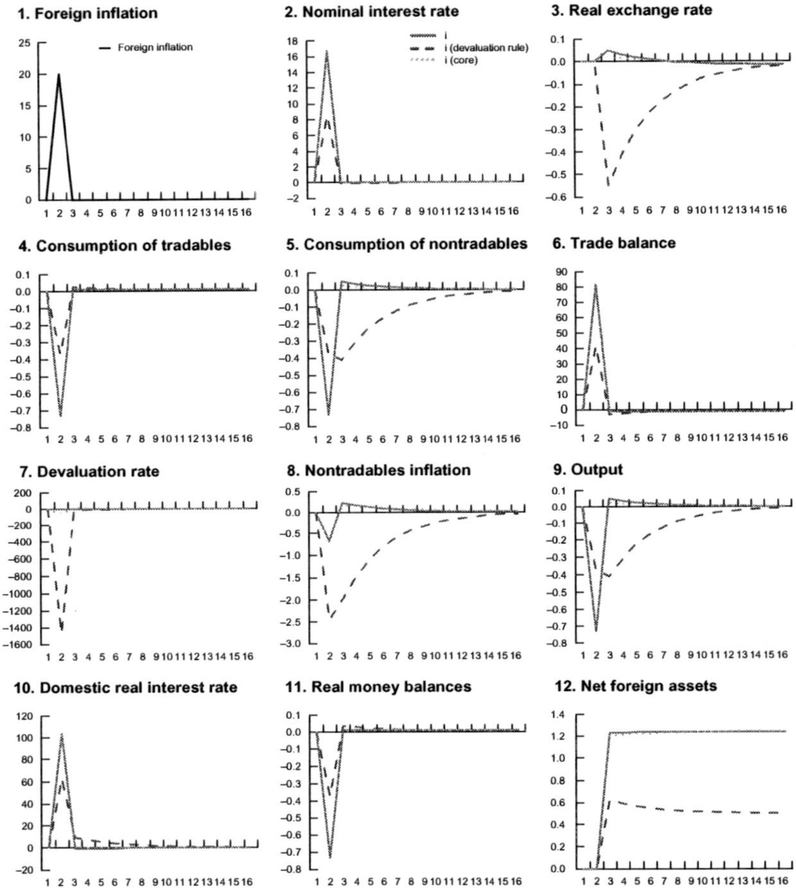

Source: Authors' calculations.
Note: i = standard predetermined exchange rate regime. i (devaluation rule) places half the weight on core inflation; i (core) focuses on core inflation only.

The difference in this case is the impact effect on nontradables inflation. As earlier explained, two forces affect nontradables inflation on impact.[6] The fall in nontradables consumption, which brings inflation down, and the rise in the nominal interest rate, which increases inflation. As Figure 10.8 shows, the reaction of the central bank is substantially bigger when focusing on headline than when focusing on core (panel 7). As a result, there is a real appreciation (panel 3) and a larger reduction, on impact, in nontradables inflation (panel 8).

[6] See Végh (2013) for additional details.

Figure 10.10. Devaluation Rule with Large Weight on Core Inflation (one period shock)

(Percentage point deviations from steady state, vertical axes; Time period, horizontal axes)

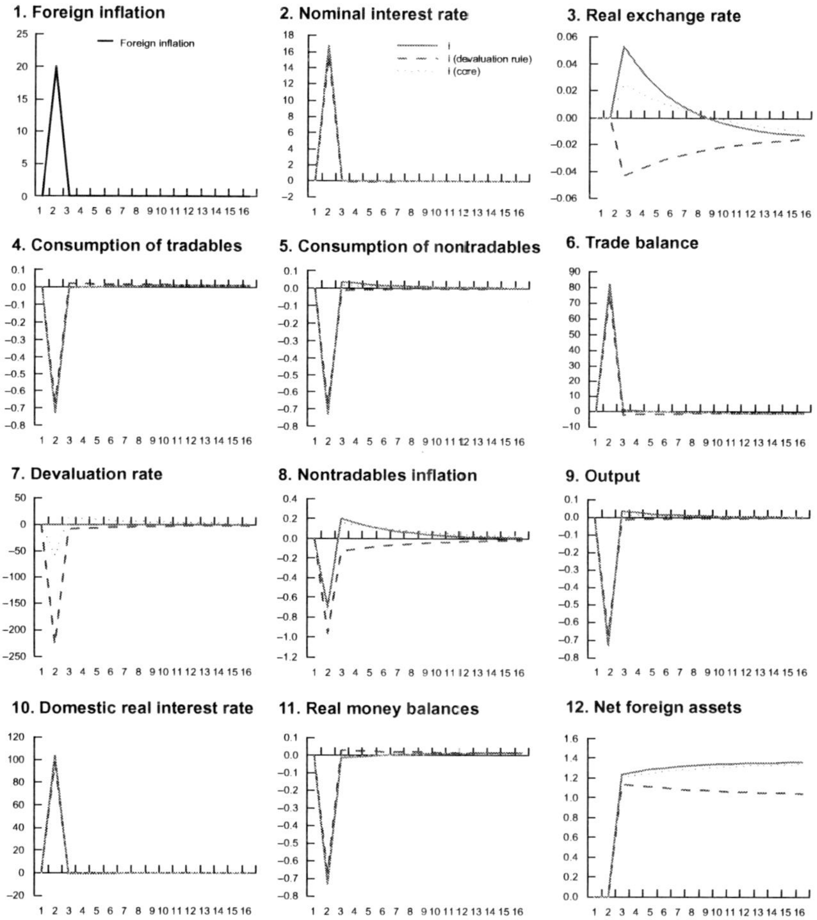

Source: Authors' calculations.

Note: i = standard predetermined exchange rate regime. i (devaluation rule) places half the weight on core inflation; i (core) focuses on core inflation only.

Regardless of the relative weights on core and foreign inflation in the devaluation rule, focusing on headline inflation proves to be superior, because it manages to dampen the intertemporal distortion (that is, nominal interest rate) and therefore mitigates the effect on consumption. But a strong reaction to the shock implies keeping both consumption of nontradables (and obviously output) and nontradables inflation below the steady state for a longer period of time than if the focus is on core only.

Focusing on core inflation only implies a sharp decline in both consumption and output on impact, followed by a rapid recovery compared with the headline inflation rule. The problem is that a faster recovery is accompanied by second-round effects as nontradables inflation increases above its steady state before converging. So even when the shock is not persistent, reacting to headline inflation, as opposed to core inflation only, proves superior, because it prevents second-round effects in nontradables inflation (Figure 10.10).

This section shows that the appropriate relative weights, and therefore the appropriate relative strength of the policy reaction to core or foreign inflation, depend on the persistence of the shock. The central bank may want to put more or less weight on core or foreign inflation, but focusing on core inflation only is always suboptimal.

POLICY IMPLICATIONS

Optimal monetary policy responses focused on core inflation only could not only systematically underestimate the level of overall inflation, but also delay appropriate responses to exogenous price fluctuations.

Given that commodity (food, fuel) inflation is an important driver of overall inflation, as documented in IMF (2011), central banks focusing on core inflation only could send misleading and confusing signals to the public. This is because the public will be forming their expectations on food inflation developments, given the large share of the relevant commodity in consumption baskets. Accordingly, central banks focused on stabilizing core inflation rather than headline inflation could create incorrect and distorted inflation expectations.

Contrary to what many studies in the literature and conventional wisdom indicate (which is mainly based on advanced economies under inflation targeting regimes), small open economies operating under relatively rigid exchange rate arrangements risk amplifying exogenous fluctuations transmitted to the domestic economy if they focus only on core inflation. Regardless of the relative weights on core and foreign inflation in monetary policy responses, and the particular determination of these, central banks should monitor headline, as well as core inflation. This is because first, there is no fundamental reason to focus only on a narrow basket of goods, and second, such a focus could even be misleading.

CONCLUSIONS

Central banks in small open economies, operating under relatively rigid exchange rate regimes, should not only focus on core inflation, but should also be prepared to respond appropriately to headline inflation if needed. Often, monetary authorities adopting predetermined exchange rate regimes claim that being pegged to the U.S. dollar (or another hard currency) is a sufficient condition to mimic U.S. monetary policy by focusing on the same key variables that are obviously relevant for the Federal Reserve. Although it is true that when operating under a nominal exchange rate anchor, domestic monetary policy channels and transmission mechanisms in small open economies might be relatively weaker than under other monetary arrangements, central banks still have some instruments to affect aggregate demand. Even if central banks do not use the devaluation rate as the main monetary policy tool, there is still some room to use reserve requirements, discount window rates, and so on to affect interest rates under predetermined exchange rate regimes. Therefore, even under this kind of rigid monetary arrangement, monetary authorities need to closely monitor both core and headline inflation so that they can react in a timely manner and achieve the main objective of any independent central bank: price stability.

It is crucial to understand that in small open economies, even if their exchange rate is pegged to a strong currency, transmission mechanisms of shocks and propagation channels can be substantially different from those in industrialized countries. Global shocks often have a very different impact in small open economies operating under predetermined exchange rate regimes than in advanced economies operating under inflation-targeting regimes.

Using a standard small open economy model with sticky prices, we show that focusing on headline inflation proves not only welfare superior to focusing only on core inflation, but also more appropriate for containing domestic inflation pressures and mitigating output losses. Moreover, having a clear, easy-to-understand, and transparent rule can help an economy form accurate and realistic inflation expectations, and can serve as an effective nominal anchor in the face of international commodity price fluctuations. Implementing such a rule is also useful to build and enhance credibility in the monetary authority, and therefore increase the effectiveness of monetary policy in maintaining price stability.

REFERENCES

Anand, Rahul, Eswar Prasad, and Boyang Zhang. 2015. "What Measure of Inflation Should a Developing Country Central Bank Target?" *Journal of Monetary Economics* 74 (C): 102–16.

Blanchard, Olivier J., and Jordi Galí. 2007. "The Macroeconomic Effects of Oil Price Shocks: Why Are the 2000s So Different from the 1970s?" MIT Working Papers 0711, Massachusetts Institute of Technology, Center for Energy and Environmental Policy Research, Cambridge.

Bodenstein, Martin, Christopher Erceg, and Luca Guerrieri. 2008. "Optimal Monetary Policy with Distinct Core and Headline Inflation Rates." *Journal of Monetary Economics* 55: 518–33.

Bullard, James. 2011. "Measuring Inflation: The Core Is Rotten." *Federal Reserve Bank of St. Louis Review* 93 (4): 223–33.

Calvo, Guillermo A. 1983. "Staggered Prices in a Utility Maximization Framework." *Journal of Monetary Economics* 12 (4): 383–93.

Catao, Luis, and Roberto Chang. 2011. "World Food Prices and Monetary Policy." IMF Working Paper 10/161, International Monetary Fund, Washington.

International Monetary Fund (IMF). 2011. *World Economic Outlook*. Washington, October.

Kilian, Lutz. 2009. "Not All Price Shocks Are Alike: Disentangling Demand and Supply Shocks in the Crude Oil Market." *American Economic Review* 99 (3): 1053–69.

King, Robert, Charles Plosser, and Sergio Rebelo. 1988. "Production Growth and Business Cycles: I. The Basic Neoclassical Model." *Journal of Monetary Economics* 21 (2–3): 195–232.

Reinhart, Carmen, and Jonathan Ostry. 1992. "Saving and Terms of Trade Shocks: Evidence from Developing Countries." MPRA Paper 6976, Munich Personal PePEc Archive, Munich.

Reinhart, Carmen, and Carlos Végh. 1995. "Nominal Interest Rates, Consumption Booms, and Lack of Credibility: A Quantitative Examination." MPRA Paper 13898, Munich Personal PePEc Archive, Munich.

Végh, Carlos A. 2013. *Open Economy Macroeconomics in Developing Countries*, Cambridge, Massachusetts: MIT Press.

Walsh, James P. 2011. "Reconsidering the Role of Food Prices in Inflation." IMF Working Paper 11/71, International Monetary Fund, Washington.

CONTRIBUTORS

Rahul Anand is Assistant to the Director in the IMF's Institute for Capacity Development. Prior to this, he worked in the African Department and the Asia and Pacific Department, covering South Africa, India, and Sri Lanka. His research spans a range of areas, including general equilibrium modeling to study monetary policy issues in emerging markets, macro-critical structural reforms, subsidy reforms, and growth-enhancing structural transformation. He has published widely, including in the *Journal of Monetary Economics*, and his research has also featured in *The Economist*, the *Financial Times*, and the *Wall Street Journal*. Before joining the IMF in 2010, he held various senior positions in India as a member of the Indian Administrative Service—designing, implementing, and monitoring government economic programs and policies. He has a PhD from Cornell University and a master's degree from Harvard University.

Paul Cashin is Assistant Director in the Asia and Pacific Department and Mission Chief for India. Prior to this, he worked in the IMF's Research Department, on issues related to developing countries; in the IMF's Western Hemisphere Department, where he was Chief of the Caribbean Division and Mission Chief to the Eastern Caribbean Currency Union, St. Lucia, and St. Vincent; and in the Middle East and Central Asia Department, where he was Chief of the Regional Studies Division and Mission Chief to Jordan. Before joining the IMF, Mr. Cashin was Principal Research Economist at the Ministry of Agriculture in Victoria, Australia, and Associate Professor in the Department of Economics at the University of Melbourne, Australia. Mr. Cashin has published widely in several fields of economics, including macroeconomic modeling, commodity prices and exchange rates, international economics, and economic development. He obtained his PhD and an MA in Economics from Yale University, and holds an MAgrSc in Agricultural Economics and a bachelor's degree in Economics from the University of Melbourne in Australia.

Sonali Das is an Economist in the IMF's Asia and Pacific Department, covering India and Nepal. Prior to this, she was in the IMF's Strategy, Policy, and Review Department, where her responsibilities included working on the IMF program with Pakistan. Ms. Das received her PhD in Economics from Cornell University in 2012 and holds an MA from McGill University and a BSc from the University of Toronto. During the course of her doctoral studies she was a visiting fellow at the Federal Reserve Bank of San Francisco, a research associate at the Brookings Institution, and a summer intern at the IMF. Her research interests include banking, financial stability, and financial development.

Roberto Guimarães is a Deputy Division Chief in the Regional Studies Division of the IMF's Asia and Pacific Department. He has worked on a number of countries, including covering financial sector issues in Mexico and Argentina, and on IMF surveillance teams covering India, Malaysia, Singapore, Costa Rica, and Panama. He has also led IMF missions to Bhutan and Fiji. Mr. Guimarães has published in *Economics Letters*, *Economics Bulletin*, *Applied Financial Economics*, *Finance & Development*, as well as IMF working papers and Occasional Papers. He has worked on a range of policy issues in international finance and macroeconomics, including capital flows, foreign exchange intervention, and monetary policy. He holds a PhD in economics and an MSc in Statistics.

Naresh Kumar is currently a Research Analyst in the IMF's African Department. Previously, he worked on India at the IMF office in Delhi and on Latin American countries while in the private sector. He joined the IMF in 2009. He is an Indian national and has a master's and a bachelor's degree in Economics from Delhi University. He has published on growth and inequality, labor market issues, and inflation in India. His research interests are in monetary policy in low-income countries, trade, structural issues, inequality, and labor market issues.

Kamiar Mohaddes is a Senior Lecturer and Fellow in Economics at Girton College, University of Cambridge. He is also a member of the Economic Research Forum (ERF) advisory committee, an ERF Research Fellow, and an associate researcher at the Energy Policy Research Group (EPRG), University of Cambridge. He holds a BSc in Economics from the University of Warwick and an MPhil and a PhD in Economics from the University of Cambridge. His main areas of research are macroeconomics, global and national macroeconometric modeling, and energy economics. His articles have been published in a number of edited volumes (Cambridge University Press and Routledge) as well as in leading journals, including the *Journal of Applied Econometrics* and *Energy Economics*.

Adil Mohommad joined the IMF as an Economist in 2011. He currently works in the Asia and Pacific Department on Australia and New Zealand, and previously also worked on Nepal and Bhutan. His research includes work on trade, institutions, productivity, and growth. He received his BA from Delhi University, MA from Delhi School of Economics, and his PhD from the University of Maryland in 2010.

Prachi Mishra is on leave from the IMF as Specialist Adviser (equivalent to Chief General Manager) in the Department of Economic and Policy Research at the Reserve Bank of India. Prior to that, she was Senior Economist in the Office of Chief Economic Advisor in the Ministry of Finance, and at the Prime Minister's Economic Advisory Council in the Government of India; and Senior Economist at the IMF. At the IMF, she has worked for the Monetary and Capital Markets, Research, Western Hemisphere, and Fiscal Affairs Departments, and in the office of the First Deputy Managing Director. She received a PhD in Economics from Columbia University in 2004, and a master's degree from the Delhi School of Economics in 1999.

Yasuhisa Ojima is a Senior Economist in the Asia and Pacific Department and Mission Chief for Tonga. Prior to joining the IMF, he was a Director in the

Credit Risk Analysis division at the Japan International Cooperation Agency (JICA) and a Resident Representative for the Japan Bank for International Cooperation (JBIC) in Vietnam. He has published several textbooks and articles in the field of international and development economics and taught at Waseda University in Tokyo. Mr. Ojima holds degrees from Yale University and Keio University.

Laura Papi is Assistant Director in the African Department of the International Monetary Fund, heading the Southern 2 Division, and IMF Mission Chief for South Africa. She has worked on a broad range of emerging market countries: immediately before South Africa, she was IMF Mission Chief for India, and before that she covered Brazil, China, Malaysia, and Mexico. Previously she worked as Associate Director at Deutsche Bank, London, in Emerging Market Research concentrating on Turkey and Emerging Europe (1997–2000). She has a PhD from the University of Warwick (UK).

Mehdi Raissi is an economist in the Asia and Pacific Department of the IMF. Mr. Raissi joined the IMF in 2010 and worked in the Middle East and Central Asia Department, as well as in the Strategy, Policy, and Review Department on several multilateral surveillance issues and a range of surveillance and program countries. He holds a PhD in Economics from the University of Cambridge. His main areas of research are global and national macroeconometric modeling, cross-country spillovers of financial stress, and energy economics. His articles have been published in leading journals, including the *Journal of Applied Econometrics* and *Energy Economics*.

Agustín Roitman is an Economist in the IMF's European Department, currently working on Greece. Prior to joining the IMF, he held research positions at the Inter-American Development Bank. In previous positions at the IMF, he has covered a range of economies, including Qatar, Jordan, Malaysia, and Russia, and was involved in several research projects on the Middle East and Central Asia. His main areas of expertise include international finance and open economy macroeconomics, and his research centers on fiscal and monetary issues in emerging market and developing countries. Mr. Roitman holds a PhD in Economics from the University of Maryland, and a BA in Economics from Universidad Nacional de Cordoba (Argentina).

Devesh Roy is a Research Fellow in the Markets, Trade, and Institutions Division of the International Food Policy Research Institute (IFPRI). He is currently based at IFPRI's New Delhi office. His main areas of research are agricultural markets, with a special focus on food safety issues. He is currently involved in analysis of several inflationary commodities in India (such as onions and pulses), and he is completing a book on evolution of the pulses sector in India. Devesh Roy studied Economics at Delhi University for his undergraduate degree and obtained a master's degree in Economics from the Delhi School of Economics. Subsequently, he obtained a PhD in Economics from the University of Maryland.

Volodymyr Tulin is an Economist in the Asia and Pacific Department of the IMF. Previously he worked in the Monetary and Capital Markets Department, focusing on systemically important banks in major emerging market economies. During his IMF career, he has also worked in other departments, covering Mexico and the United States, Central and South America, as well as emerging Europe. His research interests include inflation dynamics, inclusive growth and inequality, and capital flows. Mr. Tulin holds a master's degree in Development Economics from Harvard University.

James P. Walsh is a Deputy Division Chief in the IMF's Monetary and Capital Markets Department, focusing on issues related to macrofinancial linkages and financial stability. He joined the IMF in 2001 and has held a wide range of positions, including in the IMF's Policy Development and Review Department and country surveillance work on emerging markets in all regions of the world. His analytical work has covered capital flows, inflation, infrastructure investment, and systemic financial risks. He has a PhD in economics from the University of Chicago and a BA in Economics from the University of Pennsylvania.

Jiangyan Yu is a Senior Economist in the IMF's Asia and Pacific Department, covering Korea. Prior to this, he worked on Mongolia and Nepal, as well as Tuvalu. Before joining the IMF in 2009, Mr. Yu had more than 10 years' working experience in the Central Bank of China.

Index

[Page numbers followed by *b, f, n,* or *t* refer to boxed text, figures, footnotes, or tables, respectively.]